BEATING
INFLATION
WITH
REAL ESTATE

BEATING INFLATION WITH REAL ESTATE

Kenneth R. Harney

RANDOM HOUSE
New York

Library of Congress Cataloging in Publication Data

Harney, Kenneth R   1944–
  Beating inflation with real estate.

  1. Real estate investment.   I. Title.
HD1375.H347   332.6'342   78-21809
ISBN 0-394-50342-2

Manufactured in the United States of America

9 8 7 6 5 4 3 2

First Edition

Acknowledgments

My special thanks, for their help in important ways, go to Claudia Levy and William B. Dickinson, Jr., of the *Washington Post*, who pushed things along in the early stages; Anne Freedgood and Nancy Inglis of Random House, editors as fine as one could hope ever to encounter; Dr. John Kokus of American University, Walker V. Mannes and John C. H. Lee, Sr., of Lee Financial Services, who reviewed chapters in their areas of expertise. My personal thanks go also to John Sullivan for insights on vacation property rentals, and to Marla Price and Kathleen Adgate, who assisted so well with typing chores.

K.R.II.

*For Andy,
whose love and help
always have made
the difference*

Foreword

This book is an outgrowth of a series of articles I did in the *Washington Post* on options open to the small-scale real estate investor in an inflationary economy. It is intended to be an introductory, plain-language guide to the fundamentals of investing in rental houses, land, second mortgages, vacation rental property and related areas for the many people who've never done it before but would like to try their hand. It is not a textbook, not a substitute for professional legal, accounting or brokerage advice on specific properties. I've tried to keep real estate jargon to a minimum and have intentionally omitted the cash-flow charts and comparative-yield computations that fill more academic and advanced works in the field. I have also omitted or compressed treatment of traditional real estate segments that I believe have decreasing relevance to the newer investor—such as apartment buildings over eight units and commercial properties—and have strongly emphasized growth areas like rental houses.

My book rests upon the thesis that well-chosen, properly financed real estate can protect investors' capital better than, or as well as, *any* alternative available today. Every chapter, however, points out the risks and potential pitfalls that face the small investor. Contrary to what the gee-whiz genre of "how I made a million in two months" books in the field would have you believe, real estate can be harmful to your financial and mental health. It's no sure thing. But if you pursue it sanely, it can be extraordinarily profitable and fun in the bargain.

—Kenneth R. Harney
Washington, D.C.
October 1978

Contents

BEATING
INFLATION
WITH
REAL ESTATE

1

Money

There is a powerful, overriding fact about your money in today's economy: if you are not using it defensively, countering the twin impacts of inflation and federal taxes, you are losing it. And it's happening faster than you realize because in dollar terms your income is going up.

The money you've got safely tucked away in a bank account at 5 percent interest is pushing you into debt. Every $1,000 of it produces $50 a year in dividends, but loses $73.50 to inflation and $20 to federal and local taxes. In other words, if you begin the year with $1,000, you end it with $946.50 in real terms.* The money you've got in stocks and bonds doesn't do much better. One thousand dollars in a corporate note at 9 percent produces $90.00 in taxable gains in a year, but loses $76.30 to inflation and $36.00 to taxes. You go backwards in this economy in almost any taxable investment yielding less than 10 percent on the dollar, in part because your rising income keeps putting you in progressively steeper tax brackets.

* Assuming 7 percent inflation and a 40 percent effective combined federal, state and local tax rate for a married, working couple filing jointly. The losses were even worse in 1978, when the Consumer Price Index rose by 9 percent.

Take a look at the two federal tax tables below. Most of us—whether as an individual or as part of a married, two-worker household—find ourselves being pushed into tax brackets we never dreamed we'd be in. Average incomes have risen at 6 to 7 percent a year in the past decade, but the IRS's bracket definitions have hardly changed since 1965. A $24,200 adjusted annual income for a single person may have seemed a princely sum worthy of 40 percent marginal taxation in 1965, but in today's economy, it's worth what $12,000 was in 1965. It doesn't go a long way in most metropolitan areas. Yet it's taxed at a confiscatory level in real terms. The additional pounds of flesh

FEDERAL TAX BRACKETS

Married Individuals Filing Joint Returns and Surviving Spouses

Taxable Income	Tax +	Percent on Excess	Taxable Income	Tax +	Percent on Excess
$ 3,401	$ 0	14	35,201	8,162	43
5,501	294	16	45,801	12,720	49
7,601	630	18	60,001	19,678	54
11,901	1,404	21	85,601	33,502	59
16,001	2,265	24	109,401	47,544	64
20,201	3,273	28	162,400	81,464	68
24,601	4,505	32	215,401	117,504	70
29,901	6,201	37			

Single Individuals

Taxable Income	Tax +	Percent on Excess	Taxable Income	Tax +	Percent on Excess
$ 2,301	$ 0	14	18,201	3,565	34
3,401	154	16	23,501	5,367	39
4,401	314	18	28,801	7,434	44
6,501	692	19	34,101	9,766	49
8,501	1,072	21	41,501	13,392	55
10,801	1,555	24	55,301	20,982	63
12,901	2,059	26	81,801	37,677	68
15,001	2,605	30	108,301	55,697	70

exacted by Social Security, state and local tax systems based on equally "progressive" scales make things even worse.

Every 10 percent increase in personal income now produces an estimated 16 percent increase in federal tax collections, because the tax system, instead of adjusting to inflation, simply gobbles up the paper income inflation produces. The present tax system is, in fact, a self-fueling, perpetual money machine: it produces windfall revenues that encourage higher federal spending, higher deficits and higher federal borrowing in the capital markets. This in turn keeps interest rates high, induces inflation, pushes up prices of goods, services and wages—and sends more and more taxpayers into the upper brackets. *Ad infinitum.*

This system of taxation is having dramatic and as yet not fully recognized effects on the nature and perception of money in our economy. Money no longer is something to hold on to, conserve, put in a safe place at a safe return. Money is something to borrow, not to hold in the form of cash. Money is something you convert assets into when necessary—if you can manage to accumulate assets in the first place. Above all, money is something very frightening when you consider major financial obligations in the future, such as college education of children, your own retirement, the care of a spouse or relative. If goods and services rise at their average compound rate of increase for the years 1962–1977 (which includes five early years' worth of modest inflation), you can look forward to annual college costs of $13,000 to $14,000 a year *per child* by 1987, $9,000 to $10,000 for a typical family car, $115,000 to $120,000 for a typical new single-family detached house, $1.75 a gallon for gasoline.

True, your income will be significantly higher, perhaps 50 to 60 percent more than it is right now, but take a look at the tax bracket you'll be in if the tax system retains anything near its current shape.

DEFENSIVE INVESTING

When confronted with such an economy, the only tools most of us have are those the economic system permits: ingenuity in the use of our money before it's taxed away, and intelligent defensive investment in areas that capitalize on the system as it exists. Defensive investing means pinpointing those commodities and investment alternatives that grow in value faster than inflation and that offer refuge, through incentives available in the law, from the teeth of taxation.

Real estate, for the manifold reasons spelled out in this book, is the most attractive, practical hedge against inflation for most small investors today. It is by no means the only good investment around: gold, Swiss francs, antiques and other art collectibles, silver, gems, select speculative commodities and a handful of high-flying corporate stocks have all outrun inflation impressively over the past decade. Nor is real estate the safest investment alternative around, the least complex or the sole focus of any sensible investment portfolio.

But real estate, measured against every essential test for wealth building in a depreciating-dollar economy, comes out with extremely high scores.

• Real estate not only has kept up with inflation in the last decade but has jumped well out in front. We've all read about or experienced the 15 to 20 percent year-in, year-out increases in single-family home values in a few metropolitan areas on the West Coast and in Washington, D.C., Chicago, Houston and Dallas. In southern California, the saying goes, most $100,000 homes make more a year than their owners. And in Washington, D.C., in the words of one Midwestern congressman, "They pay $100,000 for houses we'd *condemn* back home." The fact of the matter is, though, that residential property and land value increases over the past ten years have been rapid *nationwide*. According to federal data, the sales value of the average American home went up *113* percent—more than doubled—between 1967 and 1977. The average per-acre price of unimproved land rose by *150* percent in the same period. Meanwhile, inflation in the cost of goods and services in the overall economy was 83 percent. In contrast, one dollar's worth of common stock, as measured by the Dow-Jones industrial average and with dividends reinvested, *lost* 20 percent of real value during the decade— which comes as no surprise to the tens of thousands of small investors who finally abandoned Wall Street in the past several years.

• Capital value appreciation is only one aspect of sound investment in an inflationary economy. Real estate—more than any other taxable investment—also offers abundant ways to defer, decrease or avoid taxation altogether, not only on its own gains, but on your other, ordinary income as well. Most investors who already own a home know the tremendous benefits of the eighteen-month tax-free period IRS allows for reinvestment of the capital proceeds of the sale of their principal residence. But that's the least of the tax incentives open to those who invest in various types of real estate. The chapters that follow examine the incentives as they apply to ownership and sale of rental properties, land, second-home or vacation property, rental condominiums and the rapidly growing number of "historic" or landmark buildings, among other forms of real estate. All these alternatives can transform inflation-fed increases in the market value of one's holdings into *capital gains*, rather than ordinary income, and thus obtain highly favorable tax rates. Most of the alternatives also offer the possibility of substantial tax write-offs—deductions for expenses attributable to the conduct of one's investment "trade or business" and the theoretical *depreciation* of the investment property. Chapter 2 describes the basic contours of depreciation and capital gains treatment. Suffice it to say here that "losses" in real estate terms are very different from the losses in the value of common stocks that you read about glumly in the Dow-Jones industrial averages. Many real estate investors actually cherish their losses, do little to avoid them and even take steps to accelerate them. And a few doctors and lawyers in very high tax brackets will pay hard cash to people who will sell them the right to share in someone's anticipated tax losses.

• Real estate—more than any other option open to small investors—permits the advantageous use of the concept of *leverage*. Leverage has been the subject of scholarly studies in business journals and books, but for our purposes it boils down to this: using borrowed money for your own gain. The more money you borrow to acquire a piece of property, and the less you put into the purchase from your own pocket, the greater return on your dollar you stand to receive.

Let's imagine, for example, that you buy a $100,000, two-unit rental building by putting down $50,000 in cash and obtaining a deed of trust or mortgage for the balance. Say you picked your property extremely well, and a year later, you receive and accept an offer of $150,000 for the building. Your proceeds, exclusive of transfer and sales cost, will be $50,000, or 100 percent on your original $50,000. That's a superb return on your investment by any standard.

But consider this: suppose you borrowed $90,000 of the original $100,000 and put only $10,000 of your own money into the deal. Your return would be $5 for every $1 you invested, for a leverage ratio of 5:1 and a yield (a dollar-for-dollar return expressed as a percentage) of 500 percent. Meanwhile, you could use the $40,000 you didn't invest for other high leverage purchases.

Admittedly, this is a simplified case, but it shows the potential inherent in well-chosen real estate. Investors strive to keep their cash outlays at a minimum and to finance as much of the acquisition costs as lenders will permit. They rent money for their business, just as they rent copying machines or cars. Thanks to the rapidly inflating values of properties that secure the loans lenders make, the opportunities for high leverage financing are increasing in most sectors of real estate.

• A burgeoning source of money for small-scale real estate investment is the personal residence of the investor. In other words, real estate has performed so well in the past that it now supplies the initial capital for a large percentage of new investors in the field. You can take inflated dollars out of your house tax-free by *refinancing* your existing mortgage, or by obtaining a second mortgage or trust.

Refinancing involves paying off an older, generally lower-interest-rate mortgage with part of the proceeds of a new mortgage—and keeping the rest of the proceeds for yourself. For example, assume you have a $43,500 loan balance on a house purchased several years ago for $65,000. Assume also that the house now has an appraised market value of $100,000. You can easily get a new $75,000—or $80,000 or $90,000—mortgage on the house from your present lender or another, thereby freeing some of your accumulated, inflation-fed idle equity. The refinancing transaction might look something like this:

New loan:	$75,000
Old loan:	43,500
Initial proceeds:	$31,500

Less:

Title insurance (mortgagee's policy)	$182
Title examination	125
State taxes	330
Settlement fee	75
Recordation	24
Survey update	10
Title attorney	10
Deed of trust	30
Tax certificate and report	2
Total costs of refinancing transaction:	$788
Net proceeds	$30,712

You'd end up, in short, with nearly $31,000 to invest elsewhere. Not, of course, that you wouldn't also end up with higher monthly payments as the result of your larger mortgage and higher interest rate. In the example above, your principal and interest payments might have been $323 on the thirty-year, 8 percent $43,500 loan you began with. This would jump to $604 on the replacement loan at 9 percent. But the additional $281 a month you'd have to pay would be minor when compared to the potential investment opportunities it would open up.

No other investment offers quite the wide and exciting range of vehicles for getting involved as real estate does. This book explores the pros and cons of the principal methods open to the small investor—from low-risk farmland to high-risk equity syndications. Generally, the perspective is that of a husband-and-wife household or a single individual, rather than that of an organized group. But the basic principles are the same for groups—whether investment clubs, limited partnerships, full partnerships, joint ventures or trusts—and the per-person costs are spread thinner.

The diversity of real estate allows the investor to step back and assess his or her financial capacities and goals before choosing an appropriate entry point. Investment goals vary widely,

REAL ESTATE INVESTMENT GOALS AND ALTERNATIVES

	Net Income*	Tax Shelter	Capital Gains
One- to four-unit residential property	◐	●	●
Second mortgages	●	○	○
Land	◐	◐	●
Vacation property	◐	○	●
Condominiums	◐	●	●
Apartment houses	◐	●	●
Rehabilitation of historic properties	◐	●	●
Syndications Public, commercial. Income property oriented	◐	◐	●
Private placement, low-income housing project	○	●	○

* Pretax, exclusive of depreciation.

KEY
● Good opportunity
◐ Possible under certain conditions
○ Not likely or never

and you ought to be clear about your own before committing yourself to any particular type of real estate. For example, if you're primarily concerned with cutting your immediate taxes, either by deferring them or by dropping to a lower bracket, you almost certainly don't want to buy improved land. Land can increase impressively in capital value and provide attractive leverage on your invested dollar, but it doesn't generate much in the way of tax losses. If you want to generate depreciation and other tax losses, it is far better to buy rental residential property or rehabilitate and rent out a house in an historic district of your community.

On the other hand, say your real need is a high, steady monthly return from your money. As the table opposite suggests, you'll want to avoid rental houses and consider taking a plunge into second trusts or mortgages, or to buy units in a public realty syndication that emphasizes high-quality commercial property acquisitions. It all depends on your objectives and the personal and financial resources you can muster.

There are no guarantees in real estate, of course. No one can warrant that the market value of American houses, land and other forms of real estate will rise indefinitely as fast as it has in the past ten to fifteen years. There is no certainty that inflation in the 7 to 9 percent range will forever be a fixture of our economy. Congress may recognize the insanity of a tax system that institutionalizes inflation and take measures to reform it. Let's hope that the necessary changes are made, but as prudent investors, let's not bank on it.

2

Houses

The fastest-growing and one of the most profitable small-scale real estate investments in the United States today is the single-family rental home. The pattern differs from metropolitan area to metropolitan area, but the basics are the same: tens of thousands of people worried about inflation and taxes are plunking down cash to buy up small residential properties for rental. The investors are two-worker married couples, housewives, salesmen, accountants and professionals. In general they have no formal background in real estate and no desire to become brokers. The properties in which they invest are central city row-houses in some areas, suburban tract houses in others, or duplexes, triple-deckers, quadruplexes and even condominiums.

• In a suburb of Cincinnati, Ohio, Daniel and Esther Kipp raise bees as an avocation; and inside the city they are acquiring a bumper crop of fifty- to eighty-year-old houses for rental, tax shelter and long-term capital appreciation. They look for sturdy turn-of-the-century, two-floor brick or frame units, fix them up if necessary and rent them out to middle-income families. Some of their units cost under $10,000, and some return their initial cash investment in net rental income *within the first twelve*

12

months. The Kipps began buying houses five years ago with no specific long-term goals. Today they own nearly fifty units.

• In Kensington, Maryland, Thomas Belcher searches for suburban ten- to twenty-year-old "colonial brick boxes," as he calls them, for purchase by local families looking for tax shelter and a wise place for their discretionary savings. The houses Belcher finds are all tucked away in prime, solidly middle-income neighborhoods. They rent out for $350 to $450 a month and cost $50,000 to $70,000 apiece. Belcher's several hundred active clients buy one or more single-family houses, lose money on some of them, break even on others, and still come away with regular 25 to 40 percent annual returns after taxes when they sell after a few years. His main challenge, Belcher says, is "finding enough houses to meet the incredible demand."

• In the suburbs of cities like Houston and Dallas, shrewd small-scale investors are gobbling up newly constructed medium-priced tract houses and duplexes for rental and long-term capital growth. Some of the houses have jumped 10 to 15 percent in value before construction is even completed, and buyers look for a minimum 12 to 15 percent appreciation the first year. The same patterns hold true outside of Denver, Phoenix and in many parts of California. And in California, where the housing game is played more intensely than anywhere else, investors were behind 25 to 40 percent of initial sales in some suburban subdivisions during the hectic 1977–78 speculative home-buying boom, according to studies by savings and loan associations.

• In inner-city Washington, D.C., Philadelphia and Baltimore, the focus is on row houses in reviving neighborhoods. Single-family brick units in downtown Washington, on streets that used to be known as "riot corridors," now sell briskly in the $70,000 to $90,000 range. The houses can't command enough in rent to cover investors' out-of-pocket monthly costs—$500 in rent versus $700 or so in outgo—but they've grown in market value by 20 to 25 percent or more a year since 1975. In downtown Chicago, just north of the Loop, small investors concentrate on duplexes, brownstone "three-flats" and four-unit buildings. Dan Kaplan, a real estate broker in Chicago, says he could sell a $125,000 to $130,000 three-flat "every hour of the day, every day of the week" to young, two-worker couples with highly taxed incomes. "The market is wild for small residential properties in the right neighborhood in the city."

WHY HOUSES?

The investment boom in single-family properties is hardly ephemeral. Houses offer the small investor perhaps the most compelling combination of advantages available in the market today. But they also entail significant risks and complications that shouldn't be ignored.

Here are the most important factors on the plus side:

1. *High returns.* Buying a rental house promises a substantial annual yield per dollar invested. At its best, this yield far surpasses what you'd get from most alternative non-real estate *and* most real estate investments. The right house, with the right financing, can return 20 to 40 percent or more per year via tax shelter, capital appreciation and rental income.

2. *Low risk compared with yield.* Compared to the stock market, parcels of land or high-return speculative investments like gold or silver, the market values of single-family housing in the United States have been exceptionally solid over the past forty years. Median-priced houses have been appreciating in value at 8 to 15 percent for the past six years; in the decade prior to that, the increase ranged from 5 to 6 percent. Prices have inflated by 20 to 30 percent or more per year in certain areas in the South and Southwest and on the West Coast, as well as in "reviving" central-city areas of Chicago, Washington, D.C., Philadelphia, St. Louis, Atlanta and others. Demand for single-family housing is seemingly insatiable, particularly as the baby-boom generation of the 1950s moves into the prime home-buying years. This information is important to the investor, since the ultimate value of a rental house is often tied to its potential for use as an owner-occupied home. In the interim, demand for rental accommodations is at post–World War II peaks. Vacancy rates hit the 5 percent "danger" level nationally

in 1978 and are running far below that figure in many of the country's major metropolitan areas.

3. *Ease of investment.* Investing in real estate is relatively simple. Houses are tangible, observable; you can drive by and look at your property and make sure it's all there and in good shape, unlike your investment in, say, a municipal-bond fund. Two out of three American families, three out of four members of unions like the AFL-CIO, and well over nine out of ten households in the $25,000-and-up income bracket buy houses. Buying a second house and renting it out isn't that different from buying and living in the first. Almost anyone with a grasp of basic economics and the ability to handle the risks noted below can do it. Even teenagers in high school—fourteen- and fifteen-year-olds—can buy shrewdly with some encouragement (and cash) from parents.

4. *Small scale.* In buying rental houses, you can start small, sometimes amazingly small. Because most of the money you'll use will be borrowed, $1,000 or $2,000—or $5,000 to $10,000 in higher-priced properties—is often enough to start with. Many investors buy houses with *nothing* down. Many more start by refinancing their present house, buying a new one and renting out the first.

5. *Flexibility.* Houses are more flexible and "liquid" than land, apartment buildings or commercial property. If you need to raise cash and you own several houses but don't want to borrow against them, you can sell one relatively quickly; your other properties are undisturbed and keep working for you. Contrast this with ownership of a multi-unit apartment building or land. The latter is extremely "illiquid"; to sell it in a rush you may be forced both to take a much lower price than the property would normally command and to help your buyer by providing part of his financing. An apartment building presents a similar do-or-die situation; if you can't or don't want to borrow against it, you've got to sell the whole thing. You can't sell off the top two floors of a four-story building. Once you sell the project, you're out of the rental real estate business, at least temporarily.

THE TROUBLE WITH RENTAL HOUSES

Rental homes can be excellent investments, but they're not cakewalks by any standard. You don't get 20 to 30 percent returns without complication and risk. Here are the main drawbacks, each of which will be dealt with in more detail later in this chapter:

1. You can lose money—lots of it—on rental houses. And you can have terrible yields, even in comparison with such conservative investments as passbook bank accounts. However impressive the national percentages are, your own returns will reflect the quality of your decisions concerning how much to put into a property, how to finance it, how and whether to rehabilitate it, how to market it for rental and keep it filled with tenants, how to handle it for taxes, and how and when to sell it. You can do better by keeping your money under the bed than by overpaying for a house, putting too much into it, and then selling too early —procedures by which you can lose your shirt.

2. Rental houses, by definition, entail tenants, leases, rent deposits, calls in the night about leaky toilets and nonfunctioning air conditioners—and the myriad problems that can flow out of any of these. Even if you hire a rental agent to serve as the landlord, legally you're still responsible for everything.

3. Relative to alternative investments, rental houses can involve large amounts of time. To buy wisely, you must be in touch with the market. Time and personal effort are necessary to become familiar with what's available, at what price and where. Once you own one or more properties, you'll have to invest time in keeping records (even if you have an accountant), inspections and related chores.

4. Compared with many other non-real estate investments, the value of rental houses depends upon the ability of the owner to hold on to them for extended periods. You can sell houses with greater ease than a fifty-unit apartment building, but rarely can you take money out of them as readily as out of a savings account or a bond fund.

5. Rental houses can have high transfer costs, which in turn can drastically reduce your investment yield. Transfer costs include financing charges ("points," and commitment fees imposed by lenders, for example), brokerage commissions, local and state real property transfer taxes and settlement fees, among others. Rental properties can also have significant carrying costs—including negative cash flows every month—that you should consider before going ahead with an investment purchase.

RENTAL HOUSE INVESTMENT PATTERNS

Although the variety of properties, market situations and individual investment approaches are virtually limitless, there are a few basic patterns and strategies that you can identify from coast to coast. Most investors fit into at least one category; many pursue different strategies for different properties and locations within the same geographical market area.

Rental Houses for Income. Back in the golden years when mortgage interest rates ranged from 5 to 7 percent, virtually everyone who purchased single-family homes did so with the idea of making a monthly net cash profit. The very thought of buying real estate knowing that it wouldn't support itself with income from rent was—and is—considered ludicrous by many experienced investors. Dan Kipp of Cincinnati is one of these. "I would never—and I repeat, never—buy a place that couldn't bring in enough to more than pay for itself. It doesn't make sense to me. You're banking totally on appreciation in the value of the house—and who knows, the house just might not go up as fast as you assumed, or the economy might fall apart. Then where are you?"

Many investors choose not to depend on inflation alone to make sense out of their property choices. They insist on the internal financial logic of net income for every house. In Kipp's view, a rental house ought to produce something like this in terms of typical return:

House No. 1: Midwest location; acquisition cost four years ago: $32,000. Current estimated appraisal: $60,000. Initial investment four years ago: $3,500.

Monthly Expenses:

Mortgage (principal + interest)	$284
Property taxes	70
Maintenance and insurance	60
Utilities (paid by tenants)	—
Outgo	$414
Rental Income	$500
Net Income per Month	$ 86
Net Income per Year	$1,032

All you need is a couple of such houses—each turning out $1,000 per year net and growing in market value at 6 to 10 percent a year—and you've got a nice source of additional income. Put together a dozen of them, as Kipp and hundreds of others have done around the United States, and you can quit whatever else you were doing and run your rental house business full-time.

Here's another example—this one taken from the author's porfolio—of how a rental can produce income, even in a high-cost metropolitan area. The property had been used as a single-family home prior to acquisition, but was turned into a three-unit rental property, with alterations costing less than $2,000.

House No. 2: East Coast location; acquistion cost 1978: $68,000. Estimated appraisal 1979: $90,000. Initial investment: $6,800.

Monthly Expenses:

Mortgage No. 1	$490
Mortgage No. 2	100
Property taxes	80
Utilities	50
Maintenance and insurance	50
Outgo	$680

Rental Income:	
Unit No. 1	$135
Unit No. 2	300
Unit No. 3	375
	$810
Net Rental Income per Month	$130
Net Rental Income per Year	$1,560

What's special about this house, of course, is that it's located in a high-growth area. Its market value has skyrocketed, in part because of the neighborhood, in part because of the transformation from a single-family dwelling into an income-producing property (with the potential of being returned to single-family ownership status at any time). In fact, the appraised market value of this building went up more than the initial equity investment within three months of purchase and conversion. This investment was truly a diamond in the rough.

Rental Houses for Capital Growth and Tax Shelter. Unfortunately, making newly acquired rental houses turn a monthly profit is becoming increasingly difficult in most areas of the country. The components of an investor's costs—mortgage money, the price of the dwelling itself, property taxes, and utilities—have grown so rapidly in the past eight to ten years that they've outpaced tenants' incomes (see the charts on pp. 20 and 21). Prevailing rent levels in many communities simply do not support the full cost of houses any longer, and landlords face a monthly cash drain for at least the first year or two following purchase. The loss ranges from a few dollars to several hundred dollars—every four weeks.

As a result, many investors opt not to scour the market for houses that will yield monthly income. Instead, they seek properties that promise long-term appreciation in market value and provide immediate tax shelter. The latter, as we saw in Chapter 1, can translate into significant returns, thanks to the tax deductions allowed for depreciation, mortgage interest, taxes, maintenance and the other costs that offset an investor's income.

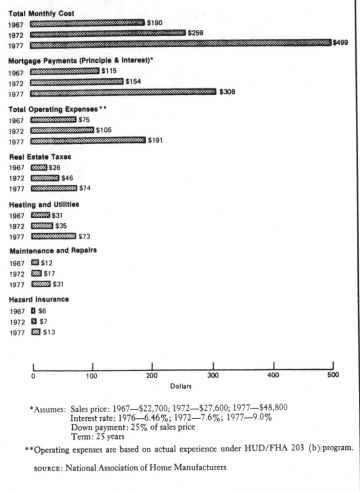

TRENDS IN TYPICAL MONTHLY HOUSING COSTS TO THE BUYER OF A MEDIAN-PRICED NEW HOUSE, 1967–1977

Total Monthly Cost
1967 — $190
1972 — $259
1977 — $499

Mortgage Payments (Principle & Interest)*
1967 — $115
1972 — $154
1977 — $308

Total Operating Expenses**
1967 — $75
1972 — $105
1977 — $191

Real Estate Taxes
1967 — $26
1972 — $46
1977 — $74

Heating and Utilities
1967 — $31
1972 — $35
1977 — $73

Maintenance and Repairs
1967 — $12
1972 — $17
1977 — $31

Hazard Insurance
1967 — $6
1972 — $7
1977 — $13

0   100   200   300   400   500
Dollars

*Assumes: Sales price: 1967—$22,700; 1972—$27,600; 1977—$48,800
    Interest rate: 1976—6.46%; 1972—7.6%; 1977—9.0%
    Down payment: 25% of sales price
    Term: 25 years

**Operating expenses are based on actual experience under HUD/FHA 203 (b) program.

SOURCE: National Association of Home Manufacturers

TRENDS IN INCOME, PRICES AND HOUSING COSTS
(Annual Rate of Increase, 1963–1972 and 1972–1976)

Median Family Income
'63 – '72   6.6%
'72 – '76   7.0%

Consumer Price Index (All Items)
'63 – '72   3.5%
'72 – '76   8.0%

Median Price of New, Single-Family Home
'63 – '72   4.9%
'72 – '76   12.5%

Median Price of Existing, Single-Family Home
'66 – '72   5.3%
'72 – '76   9.3%

Mortgage Payments for Median Priced New House**
'63 – '72   6.7%
'72 – '76   15.9%

Operating Expenses for Median Priced House*
'63 – '72   7.2%
'72 – '76   11.8%

Rents
'63 – '72   2.6%
'72 – '76   5.0%

0   1   2   3   4   5   6   7   8   9   10   11   12   13   14   15   16
Annual Percentage Increase (Compound)

*Operating expenses are based on actual experience under HUD/FHA 203 (b)
program.

**Based on the following assumptions:
   Sales price: 1963—$18,000; 1967—$22,700; 1972—$27,600; 1976—$44,200
   Interest rate: 1963—5.89%; 1967—6.46%; 1972—7.6%; 1976—9.0%
   Down payment: 25% of sales price
   Term: 25 years

SOURCE: National Association of Home Manufacturers

"Long-term" appreciation can mean anything from twelve months—the Internal Revenue Service's minimum holding period for an asset to be eligible for capital gains tax treatment—to five, ten or more years. It depends on the needs and goals of the investor and the type and location of the property.

In many areas, inflation in housing prices keeps adding 15 percent a year to the market values of single-family rental houses. So, as one Chicago investor pointed out, "Who cares if I lose $50 a month on a $60,000 house? I lose $600 over the course of a year, save several times that in taxes, and can turn around and sell the house myself at the end of the year for $9,000 more than I paid (before taxes). I'm crying about my monthly loss all the way to the bank, believe me."

Put another way, in the words of Dave Glubetich, a rental home realty adviser in San Francisco, "Cash flow is a nice thing to have. It can go toward needed repairs on the home or it can take you and your wife out to dinner once a month. But cash flow is unimportant. . . . It has kept many a would-be investor out of the rental business."

Nine out of ten new rental houses today, by Glubetich's estimate, produce negative cash flows at the outset. "If this scares you off," he says, "then you really can't afford to invest in rental property." Most of these houses, however, steadily improve their cash position over a period of several years, as the owner raises rents and costs remain relatively controllable.

Although thousands of real estate investors around the country own houses with negative cash flows, most people have a limit on how many such units they can handle at once. The out-of-pocket care and "feeding" of houses that lose $100 a month becomes a burden if you lack offsetting cash resources; multiply that monthly drain by five- or tenfold a month and you begin to see why investors cherish properties that stand squarely on their own rents.

Rental House Upstairs (or Next Door). A third category of rental-home investment involves purchase of a duplex, or a triplex or quadruplex, and use of the extra rental units to defray or pay completely for the cost of the owner's unit. This is most popular and effective among new, and often younger, investors as a way to live rent-free and beat inflation in the process. Two- to four-unit buildings are readily available for purchase in metropolitan areas throughout the country. In Boston, the three- to four-unit building is the predominant residential structure. In Chicago, three-flats and six-flats are prized investments. In California, suburban quadruplexes are growing foci for small investors. And with the advent of a new, federally assisted financing vehicle for two- to four-unit buildings via the Federal National Mortgage Association, this type of housing investment should become even more widespread in coming years (see p. 50 for a detailed discussion).

The economics of small multi-unit buildings can be very attractive. Take the units marketed in 1978 at Scotch Run, a townhouse-type development in northeastern Philadelphia. Double-decker duplexes (one unit on top of another) sold quickly for $47,990 apiece. Each duplex sits on a lot 115 feet deep and contains two two-bedroom apartments, identical in layout except for their entrances. Roughly 60 percent of the units were bought by first-time owner-occupant-investors who planned to live in one apartment and rent the other. According to brokers, the balance was sold to nonresident investors. The typical occupant-owner-investor put down $7,940, including closing costs, and incurred mortgage, tax and related expenses of $471 a month for the first year. Of the latter, rent from the second apartment covered well over half—$245 or more. After tax benefits from depreciation, interest and other costs are figured in, it should have been possible for an owner to live rent-free or better.

Nonresident owners did just as well. In the first year, their gross rentals generally exceeded their monthly expenses. They can look for 5 to 8 percent annual gains in market value in the future, regular rent increases to handle property-tax increases, and a healthy long-term yield on the dollar.

Houses for Rehab, Rental or Resale. A fourth common approach involves finding single-family properties that require substantial rehabilitation to bring out their investment potentials, and then either selling them immediately in their improved state or holding on to them for income or capital gains. Most suitable to central-city neighborhoods where rundown units can be purchased at relatively low cost, this technique adds some interesting opportunities and risks to the investment process.

• "Rehabbing" can, if you know what you're doing, add far more dollar value to the property than the cost of materials and labor you put in. Investors in many areas—including one U.S. congressman, Republican Stewart McKinney of Connecticut— find that they can get two, three, four or more dollars back for every dollar spent on rehabilitation. A shabby row house costing $12,000 can be turned into an $80,000 townhouse in a matter of months, if it is the right house in the right "growth" neighborhood.

• On the other hand, rehabbing and reselling, or renting, can be disastrous if you don't understand the local market or the structural characteristics of your property. If you don't have at least a basic knowledge of construction techniques, you ought to seriously question taking this investment approach; if you have to depend on a slew of outside contractors and sub-contractors, you're probably getting in over your head.

• Rehabilitating and reselling properties can involve you in federal tax situations you may not want to be in—especially being treated as a real estate "dealer" (see the discussion on p. 87). This can affect other, nonrehabilitated properties you own and can force you to pay tax on proceeds of sales at regular income-tax rates, not at preferential capital gains rates.

Homes for Cosmetic Repair. A common variation of the previous approach, and one favored by numerous advisers to rental-home purchasers, is to look for properties that *appear* to require substantial repair but actually need only light cosmetic changes to jump sharply in marketability. A coat of paint, minor electrical work, inexpensive plaster boarding over cracked walls and ceilings, and a little work that brings out the oak floors hidden under coats of wax can add thousands of dollars to the selling price of a house and hundreds to the yearly rent roll. This minor improvement can mean the difference between long periods of vacancy, which amount to heavy out-of-pocket losses for you, and a full house providing a steady investment income.

A Maryland home that wouldn't rent for $200 a month in its unrehabilitated state rented immediately for $475 with a fresh exterior coat of paint and clever cosmetic work inside. Investors across the country can describe dozens of such examples; they take pains to search for houses that offer "Cinderella" possibilities.

GETTING STARTED

Let's assume you've decided to try one or more of these basic rental investment approaches and that you've made an accurate appraisal of the finances, time and talent that you can bring to your investment efforts. You've decided, for example, that you've got $_____ in cash you're willing and able to put into a piece of property and $_____ dollars a month you can afford for related expenses for a year or more. You've answered the key question: whether fixing up houses is or isn't one of your talents. And you've come to grips with your real objectives for getting into this business in the first place: you're after either immediate income or a nice long-term, two-to-five-year gain; or you're interested in turning over your properties frequently; or you're interested in pyramiding your properties into an eventual fortune.

Now you're ready to take a hard look at the *area* or *areas* where you're most likely to achieve your objectives.

ANALYZING YOUR MARKET

Where and how do you find houses that are good investments? Ask any successful real estate investor and he'll give you roughly the same clues: you study local economic trends; keep on top of transactions in the specific neighborhoods that contain the type of housing you're really after; put the word out about your objectives, as precisely defined as possible, to realty brokers and others; and then be prepared to act.

Here are some guidelines on these points, based on the collective experience of investors around the country:

1. Real estate is a highly localized type of investment game, and the best part-time players concentrate on their own immediate areas. The better you know a market area—its economy, its residential patterns, zoning, laws, population composition and trends—the better equipped you are to make an intelligent investment decision on a property. This can pay dividends not only at the time of purchase but later on in the property's management and resale as well.

2. Use the information resources that professionals in the field use. If you want to know what neighborhoods are gaining in resale values faster or slower than others, take time to visit your community's property tax assessment office. (Assessors in the era of property-tax revolt are so accustomed to being the targets of complaint that they're often more than willing to share their knowledge and statistics about realty valuation patterns with sympathetic, interested buyers and investors.) Study the property transaction data available in many areas through specialized services that publish all recorded real estate sales prices *and* mortgage data. You can isolate streets or neighborhoods and follow price movements with great precision. By checking the prior acquisition prices of properties currently for sale before visiting them for inspection, you have a leg up on other prospective buyers. These services are often found in public libraries and realty brokers' offices; you can also subscribe as an individual, but the annual costs are high. On the East Coast, one major service available in over half a dozen cities is the *Lusk Real Estate Guides*, published by the Rufus Lusk Company. In New Orleans, a comparable service is known as Deed Fax. In Philadelphia, a large realty resource is Philadelphia Directories, Inc.

Realty boards' multiple listing services also provide valuable information on current sales-price levels, length of typical selling periods (a good clue to the vigor of the market) and housing characteristics.

A review of basic economic data for the region or community as a whole, even if you've lived there all your life, can add depth to your understanding of what's really going on. This is especially important in communities where the local economy is stagnant, or where there are early signs of coming rapid economic growth. Is the area losing or gaining jobs? Is a major employer about to relocate here? Is the local tax base shrinking or expanding? Are there rent controls that affect one- to four-family rental property? Are there local usury, land-use or historic-preservation taxes or profit-recapture regulations that could affect your ability to buy and sell? You can get answers to these and related questions from city, state and county departments of economic or community development, from city departments of housing, and from local chambers of commerce or similar business groups (such as metropolitan councils of trade and realty boards).

3. Identify the specific subareas within neighborhoods that appear to have the overall price and potential return characteristics you're after. Then spend time in them. Drive or walk around the neighborhoods, both in the day and at night. Get to know the locations of important shopping, employment and recreation facilities. Look at the area with the eyes of a tenant. Watch the real estate classifieds—the listings for sale as well as for rent—for current price levels and descriptions; visit as many properties as you can and follow up on their actual selling prices and terms. You'll need a good idea not only of what constitutes a $40,000 or $50,000 or $90,000 asking price but of what kind of house in the area is *worth* $40,000 or $50,000 or $90,000.

4. Contact real estate brokers who appear to specialize in the areas you've identified—for starters, several different brokers if possible. Let them know in as much detail as possible what type of property you're after, what you can realistically afford, how fast you're prepared to move on a property, and what your investment objectives are. Brokers and sales personnel will probably be your most important tie to the market; it is therefore essential that they understand you are *seriously* in the market. In your initial contacts, ask for a realty firm's residential investment property specialist. Many realty salespeople have little experience in dealing with investors, the financing of investment property, and local investment opportunities. Go around with

the specialists to properties they recommend to you and don't hesitate to challenge agents on their estimates of projected rents, appreciation rates or carrying costs for properties; they are instinctive optimists unless they know that you know better.

5. Aim for properties in the lower-to-middle range of the local price structure. Higher-cost single-unit houses often return less in rent, proportionate to the outlays they require, than lower-priced houses do. A $45,000 unit, for example, may produce $375 a month, or 1/120 of its market value, in rent, but a $90,000 house in the same town may bring in $500, or 1/180 of its sales price. Dwellings at the high end of the market appeal to a far smaller segment of the renting public. Families who can afford to shell out $600 or more a month usually prefer to buy.

Houses priced below the average in predominantly high cost neighborhoods—the ugly ducklings of the area—are worth special attention because of their potential to appreciate rapidly with cosmetic repairs or additions. The highest-priced houses in a neighborhood, on the other hand, inevitably are held back by the majority.

6. Look for houses that will appeal to the widest range of tastes in your market area. Avoid highly unusual properties unless the unusual features will appeal to an underserved segment of the market. For example, although conservative brick colonials dominate the housing market in many central Atlantic states, a well-priced California contemporary can command premium rents from younger professionals.

7. New houses, particularly those purchased from a subdivision builder at preconstruction discounts with mortgage financing, can offer superb financial returns. The drawback here, one not relevant to houses that are ten to fifteen years old, is the unknown physical quality of new construction. Get warranties up front on such units. Be careful, too, that the subdivision is not going heavily rental at the start, as that will depress market values and rent levels indefinitely.

8. Pursue your objectives and properties aggressively. If it means scouring the daily and weekend classifieds and visiting a large number of properties, take the time to do it. If it means watching for notices of tax or foreclosure sales, do it. If it means staying in touch with a dozen different realty firms, do it. If it

means responding to a 10:30 P.M. call on a Friday night from a breathless agent who has just listed what he thinks is the greatest investment house in history, and if the property description fits some of your needs, move fast—go through the place early the next day.

EVALUATING PROPERTIES

The only way to come up with consistently good investment decisions in real estate is to use a logical framework for analyzing properties—either something written down on paper, such as the accompanying checklist, or something very like it in your head. You can buy the wrong investment house by falling in love with its looks, its spacious lot, its $20,000 kitchen, and forgetting what all this is worth on a monthly basis to tenants and what the bottom line per month and per year will be for you. You can also pass up excellent investment opportunities by reacting emotionally to properties and failing to judge their potential objectively in detached, market-savvy terms.

"I wouldn't buy anything I wouldn't want to live in myself" is a common, and mistaken, view among beginning buyers of rental houses. You are not going to live in your rental house or houses. The odds are strong that your economic position and standard of living are very different from those of your future tenants, even in well-to-do suburban locations. The key is the market—what tenants currently get for their rent money—and not your personal preferences. This is not a matter of being callous, and it certainly doesn't mean offering poor-quality rental properties; quite simply, it means approaching every prospective acquisition with your investor's head screwed on right.

The checklist on pages 30–35 gives a better idea of what the investor's attitude should be. The sections are designed to bring out in a formal way the important factors for consideration in a one- to four-unit investment property. On its own, the checklist doesn't make the decision whether or not to buy, but it can help you get an approximate idea of the bottom line. Analyze several properties using the same procedure and you've got comparative data that *will* lead you to a decision.

EVALUATION CHECKLIST FOR A ONE- TO FOUR-UNIT RENTAL HOUSE

Address of Property————————————————————

Asking Price———————— Age (approximate)—————

Structural Type———————— Number of Units————————

Unit Mix: Basement——— 1st Floor——— 2nd Floor——— 3rd Floor———

I. LOCATION	Excellent	Average	Poor

I. LOCATION

A. Is it in a neighborhood or community with a good to excellent economic future?

    1. Property values are increasing or projected to increase.

    2. Demand for rental housing is strong, and vacancy low.

    3. Demand for owner-occupied housing is strong.

    4. Public plans for the area will foster or permit strong residential market for foreseeable future.

B. Does its location offer advantages to tenants as well as future owners?

    1. Is public transportation convenient?

    2. Are there adequate schools in the vicinity?

    3. Are shopping facilities convenient?

    4. Are employment facilities convenient?

    5. Are police and fire services adequate?

    6. Does the area offer special attractions to tenants/

	Excellent	Average	Poor

owners, such as cultural
facilities, recreational
facilities, etc.?

   7. Are public utilities adequate?

C. Is the property adequately
situated away from such adverse
influences as excessive traffic,
noise, pollution, freeways, an
airport, flood-hazard areas, etc.?

D. Are any adjacent lots or structures subject to development or
redevelopment under present
zoning that would have an
adverse (or positive) effect on
the value or use of your investment property?

E. Does the property offer inherent
locational advantages for its
price range, such as special
views or siting; end unit in
group of row houses, etc.?

II. STRUCTURE

A. Does the overall condition of
the house fit your investment
strategy? That is to say, if the
house is in less than adequate
condition, are the necessary
repairs achievable within your
resources?

		Costs of Repair/
B. *Structural Checklist and Rating*	Rating	Improvement

   1. *Basement:*
     Walls/foundation
     Floor
     Visible flooding/dampness
     Structural supports/jacks
       necessary?
     Visible termite damage?

	Rating	Costs of Repair/ Improvement

2. *Plumbing:*
   Pipes (condition/type)
   Hot-water heater (capacity,
      type/age)

3. *Electrical system:*
   Service amperage: number
      of amps
   Needed for rental usage:
      number of amps
   Circuit breakers or fuses?
   Condition/type of wiring
   Separate metering for units?

4. *Heating/air conditioning:*
   Furnace condition/age/
      type
   Radiators/vents—age/type
   Air conditioner (central)—
      condition/age/type
   Insulation

5. *Kitchen:*
   Overall size and layout
   Condition/quality of
      appliances
   Cabinets—condition/
      capacity/quality
   Electrical outlets
   Ventilation
   Special amenities

6. *Walls and ceilings:*
   Condition/painted surface

7. *Floors:*
   Type and condition

8. *Windows:*
   Condition and type

9. *Doors:*
   Condition and type
   Locks and hardware

10. *Overall room sizes and
    layout:*

	Rating	Costs of Repair/ Improvement

Bedrooms and storage
   adequacy
Bathrooms
Living and dining
Additional

11. *Roof:*
Condition/age
Guarantee in effect?
Attic ventilation

12. *Fireplace/chimney:*
Condition/type

13. *Gutters/downspouts:*
Condition and type

14. *Exterior:*
Condition and type
Adequacy of current finish

15. *Landscaping:*
Overall quality and
   condition

16. *Parking:*
Garage/carport/space:
   condition and adequacy

17. *Special amenities or
problems:*

_____
_____
_____

                     TOTALS $_____

III. MAXIMUM SELLING PRICE
TO YOU
(discounted, if appropriate, for
projected repairs or improvements) $_____

IV. PROJECTED RECURRING
COSTS OF OWNERSHIP   Per Month   Per Year

   A. *Mortgage Principal and Interest*
   Mortgage No. 1 (estimated
       principal + interest)
   (Mortgage No. 2   )
   (Additional:)

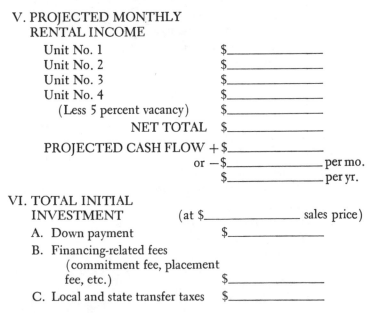

                                        Per Month   Per Year

B. *Property Taxes*
   Current
   Estimated after next reassess-
   ment

C. *Utilities*
   Current utility costs (per
   month)
   Gas_____ Electricity_____
   Oil_____ Water_____
   Estimated utility costs to be
   paid by owner following rental
   Gas_____ Electricity_____
   Oil_____ Water_____

D. *Insurance*

E. *Management and Maintenance*

F. *Other:*

   _____
   _____
   _____

         ESTIMATED OUTLAYS $_____ $_____

V. PROJECTED MONTHLY
   RENTAL INCOME
      Unit No. 1 $_____
      Unit No. 2 $_____
      Unit No. 3 $_____
      Unit No. 4 $_____
         (Less 5 percent vacancy) $_____
                      NET TOTAL $_____

   PROJECTED CASH FLOW + $_____
                      or − $_____ per mo.
                           $_____ per yr.

VI. TOTAL INITIAL
    INVESTMENT   (at $_____ sales price)
    A. Down payment $_____
    B. Financing-related fees
       (commitment fee, placement
       fee, etc.) $_____
    C. Local and state transfer taxes $_____

D. Settlement and miscellaneous
   expenses $_____
E. Improvements prior to rental $_____
F. Other $_____
                         TOTAL $_____

VII. ESTIMATED TAX IMPACTS
     DURING OWNERSHIP   Per Month   Per Year
     _____

A. Depreciation (based on estimate of _____ years of
   economic life of building,
   _____ percent of property
   value assigned to building
   itself; and _____ depreciation method) $ $

B. Deductible costs
   1. Interest $ $
   2. Taxes $ $
   3. Insurance $ $
   4. Management/maintenance $ $
   5. Capitalized improvements $ $
   6. Other $ $

   _____

   _____

C. Estimated Tax Savings (For
   _____ percent tax bracket) $ $

VIII. PROJECTED APPRECIATION OF PROPERTY*

Market Value At _____% At _____% At _____%
End of year 1   _____   _____   _____
End of year 2   _____   _____   _____
End of year 3   _____   _____   _____
End of year 4   _____   _____   _____

IX. How does this property compare overall with others in terms
    of price, overall monthly costs versus projected income, tax
    benefits and projected appreciation?

    * Note that to calculate your later returns you must subtract
    disposition costs (broker's fees, if any; taxes and settlement
    fees, if any), as well as taxation of the gain by federal and
    state taxing authorities.

Section I deals with the basic economic characteristics of the property's neighborhood and community, now and in the future. Some of this is necessarily subjective. A "marginal" central-city area in a community such as Cincinnati or Baltimore may have a relatively poor economic profile at present but be in the path of substantial future redevelopment. Don't reject such neighborhoods out of hand, because historically they have been among the most spectacular for investment opportunity. Subpart B poses questions that define the property's present appeal as a rental investment, its attractiveness to tenants, and its promise to subsequent owners. Rental houses in areas that are predominantly owner-occupied often pull in higher rents, but don't neglect single-family rental opportunities in neighborhoods with large numbers of apartment projects.

Section II isolates the key structural components of a one- to four-unit property that should be carefully evaluated before purchase. The general rule on projected repairs and improvements is that whatever you estimate they're going to cost, you can be certain they'll cost more. So tote up your figures in this section conservatively; you can overdose on repairs and ruin your return on the investment.

Some other tips:

• Room sizes, numbers and layouts are important determinants of what a house can earn in rent. Look at the existing layout as a prospective tenant would. Is there adequate room for a family? A single? A couple with kids? A group that you can charge with higher rent per person? Does the existing room layout offer any possibilities for more intensive use—that is, can you carve out another bedroom by converting a porch or dividing a large room? Remember the "single-family" house that with a modest initial expenditure produced three separate units yielding $810 in monthly gross rent? The sellers of the house didn't see those possibilities, but the buyer did. Sometimes the reverse is true; less intensive use can mean more rent. Converting a row house from three one-bedroom units into two more spacious units can attract tenants who will pay higher rents but who would otherwise consider the space inadequate.

• Pay close attention to the structural features that can cost you the most money and cause you the worst headaches as a landlord. The house's electrical system, for example, must be adequate to handle the load when the property is fully rented. That sounds elementary, but it's often overlooked. What is the electrical capacity now coming into the house? If it's an older dwelling with 100 amps or below, it will probably cost a couple of hundred dollars to get it raised to the local minimum standard (150 amps in many areas). Raising the service level to 200 amps probably makes the most sense in the long run, as this will handle just about any normal combination of appliances and heating equipment that you'd find in a small residential building.

• Check the type and quality of wiring in the property as well; if the house was built between 1960 and 1970, it may contain aluminum wiring, which requires repair or replacement for safety reasons. Don't neglect the number and position of outlets per room; bad outlet arrangement not only will violate updated building codes, but can also lead to nasty lawsuits if tenants stretch long extension cords all over your unit and then trip over them. The house may need a large number of new outlets, and that can involve breaking into walls and ceilings, installing new lines—and eye opening costs.

• The plumbing system is also in the high-expense, migraine-headache category for landlords. In walking through a property, check to see whether the water-pipe system is copper—a distinct plus—or galvanized iron or lead. Over time, galvanized pipes tend to rust; the insides narrow and cut water pressure significantly. Turn on every faucet and flush every toilet as you walk from floor to floor; if you notice big decreases in pressure with, say, the kitchen faucet running and a toilet flushing, the house may have pipe problems. Under most local building codes, leadwaste piping found in older houses generally requires replacement whenever remodeling is done.

And while you're poking around, scrutinize the house's hot-water heater. Does it have sufficient capacity to handle the anticipated tenant load? Forty to fifty gallons are recommended for single-family dwellings. And if the heater is over five years old, it may have to be replaced in just a few years.

• If there is a basement, look for the telltale signs of leakage or flooding—rippling of tiles, salt or precipitate stain marks on foundation walls, rotted wood—which may have been concealed by the seller. You may want to consider requiring the seller to provide a warranty clause in the contract against unusual moisture or leaks for the first year. The mere suggestion of such a clause will often bring out the facts—"Well, yes, I guess there *is* a little leak that we've painted over, and . . ." And while in the basement, also look for cracks or signs of unusual settling in the floor; such signs may portend serious structural problems. Watch as well for jacks, steel beams, and other unusual supports that might be tucked away innocuously; find out when and why they were installed.

• Check the condition, age and type of the house's heating plant. Forced-air units—gas, electric or oil—are typical of newer structures. Oil hot-water units with radiator systems are more common in older houses and sometimes have been converted from coal burning. Ask to see the past twelve months' bills for oil, gas and electricity to get a precise idea of heating costs and efficiency. Central air conditioning units are becoming standard equipment for new houses in many parts of the country. If your prospective investment doesn't have one, should it have one to compete in the rental market? Forced-air heating systems with ducts are the least costly and most readily convertible into central air conditioning.

• Beware of houses with poorly designed and equipped kitchens. It can cost you a mint to bring such a kitchen up to a level that will attract the segment of the rental market you're after. Cabinets and counter space alone can run into the thousands, major appliances into the hundreds or thousands, refinishing a floor into the hundreds, and so on.

• Look very carefully at the roof—not only for leaks and damage but for insulation. Putting in a new roof costs $1,500 or more, reinsulating will be in the hundreds.

Hire professional help, such as an engineering or inspection service, if you're not confident of your own ability to analyze structural problems. A typical report on a property covers detailed points not mentioned here, costs from $75 to $125, and can save a prospective buyer thousands. For example, in the case of a small property currently operating as a two-family dwelling, you might ask how much it would cost to convert it to single family, or vice versa.

Avoid properties that are overequipped, and therefore overpriced, for their immediate areas. Look instead for houses with no more amenities, features and equipment than your prospective renters require. You can always add amenities and raise the rent, but it's hard to tear them out.

Given what you now know about the property in terms of location and structure, is it worth the seller's asking price? If significant rehabilitation is necessary, how much of this cost, if any, should you take off the selling price? The answers depend finally on how the property stacks up against others in the market and on the overall pace of the market. If it's a seller's market, and people are scrambling for properties like this one, you may not want to consider making an offer below the asking price. The reverse would be true in a buyer's market; you'd want to set your maximum price as low as possible. The point in Section III is to come up with a figure you can use as your "working maximum." This will enable you to calculate the mortgage-related costs and complete the remainder of the checklist. A word of caution: don't set your maximum price by the old rule of thumb that a house should sell for 100 times the maximum monthly rent. In the inflationary 1970s you will often do very well to agree to a price that is 150 or 160 times the rent—because you're really aiming for rapid capital appreciation, not monthly income.

Section IV looks at the recurring costs the property is likely to saddle you with. Investors are often in such a rush to buy that they don't project a year in advance to calculate how much it will drain them every four weeks.

Mortgage- and finance-related costs come first. These include principal and interest (and mortgage insurance, if used) applicable on the first mortgage or trust. Then the principal and interest on the second or additional mortgages. If you're a stickler, you'll also want to figure in any financing costs that are indirectly linked to the purchase of the property; for example, if you refinanced your home to obtain some of your down payment on the investment unit, your additional monthly principal and interest might be included here.

Next are property taxes reduced to a monthly basis, with a look ahead at the likely revised figure following reassessment. After this, as listed, are: cost of utilities to be paid by you as owner, before rental occupancy and after; insurance, including not only fire and hazard insurance for the property but personal liability protection for you (a $1 million "umbrella" liability policy can be added to your existing insurance at relatively low cost and makes sense if you plan on having more than one property); routine maintenance costs; fees for professional management of the property; and any other recurring costs, such as owners' association fees and special assessments.

Section V, rental income, is the plus side of the equation. Remember that you're looking for rents competitive with the going market. Don't plan on the highest figure possible; it may take you four months to land the one tenant who'll pay your top price. It's far better, in all but income-producing properties, to plan on charging the highest rent consistent with a quick rent-up. When in doubt, err on the side of reducing vacancy even at the risk of being low man in the market. Empty houses or units bring in no money and more than their share of trouble. They attract vandals. They foster poor maintenance and upkeep. Proportionally, they cost far more than you might imagine. Happiness is no vacancies—and the rents to ensure you stay full. Once you've estimated total income and adjusted for likely periods of vacancy (5 percent is a reasonable assumption), you're ready to calculate the net cash flow you can expect from this property. Simply compare the numbers in sections IV and V, and you'll have a rough idea.

Section VI asks you to project your anticipated out-of-pocket costs up to the time of rental. This can be sobering. Include as part of your down payment the deposit you'll put in escrow upon signing the contract. Then estimate your commitment fees, service charges and points; your realty agent can give you an approximate idea of the fees current in the market. You must also include any appraisal, survey and inspection costs; tax costs of buying the property, such as transfer levies, local or state tax stamps, and recording fees; other settlement-related charges, such as the lawyer's fee, title search and insurance; the projected costs of alterations you've anticipated; and the probable cost of marketing the property, with newspaper ads, signs, transportation and the like.

Section VII looks ahead to some of the tax aspects of the property. Depreciation and allowable deductions are discussed later on in this chapter. Here the bottom line begins to look promising and you find out how much you're going to save on taxes because of your acquisition. Comparing one house with another in the terms of this section will be helpful in deciding which property makes the shrewdest inflation hedge.

Section VIII is the capital appreciation factor in your investment. How quickly will this house jump in market value, given what you plan to do with it? The rates can vary within the same community by 400 to 500 percent. Base your guess on the past performance of similar dwellings in the neighborhood, national and regional inflation trends, and local factors you think may prove important. See how well the house does under three scenarios: an exceptionally low rate of appreciation, a moderate rate and a rate that would meet your fondest dream.

FINANCING OPTIONS

You can find the perfect rental house and ruin it *as an investment* by ignoring the importance of its financing terms. Financing should be as important to you as price, if not more so, and at least as high on your list of priorities as any other element of the entire transaction. (An old maxim, revised for real estate, goes: "I'll pay your price if you'll meet my mortgage terms.")

What you arrange in the way of financing will determine:

• How much hard cash you'll have to put into the deal immediately.

• How much you'll have to put out on a monthly and annual basis, and how large your positive or negative cash flow will be.

• How much leverage you'll receive throughout the life of the investment.

• The bottom line on the purchase, the return for your risk, money and time.

You need to think about financing *before* you start negotiating with the seller, before you write out an offer or sign a contract. As you walk from floor to floor checking out the plumbing and the electrical system, think money. What are your options for financing the place? Does the owner have an assumable mortgage? What are the pros and cons of one financing method versus another? How and where do you obtain the loan or loans tailored to fit your needs?

The answers to these questions are based on your overall investment objectives and opportunities. If your aim is rapid growth and property acquisition with as little outlay as possible, you'll concentrate on one group of financing options. If you are looking for net operating income and moderate growth and are ready to put significant amounts of money into a purchase, you'll want to concentrate on other options. Since your objectives may change from property to property or from month to month, it's worthwhile to get a grasp of the full range of choices open to you.

THE BASICS AND BEYOND

You can buy an investment house with essentially the same financing tools you used when you purchased your own home. Chances are that you obtained a conventional (non-government-backed) loan from a savings and loan association, a savings bank, or a commercial bank; or that you bought with the help of a loan guaranteed by the Veterans Administration (VA) or the Federal Housing Administration (FHA). With some noteworthy differences, as discussed below, most rental-home investors use one or both of these options in the financing of their purchases. The basic process is therefore familiar to you and most homeowners.

You can apply for a long-term loan secured by the property you plan to purchase. You put down a prearranged amount, agree to an interest rate for the life of the loan, and go to settlement. In cases of mortgage or trust assumptions, you take over the equity position of the current owner, make whatever adjustments in interest rate or terms may be required by the lender, and go to closing.

If you're like the overwhelming majority of owner-occupant home buyers, this just about exhausts the range of financing you will need or care to get involved in. Noninvestor buyers tend not to be *primarily* concerned with leverage and return. Down payments of 25 to 30 percent are common; secondary mortgages and use of alternative financing sources are relatively rare.

As an investor, however, you wear a different hat. You take the basic financing vehicles as a given and look to a wide range of potential sources to supplement or replace the basics whenever appropriate. You are concerned with financing devices that will minimize your up-front outlays without overburdening you with large monthly debt-service payments. The table on pp. 44–45 summarizes the six basic sources you should consider whenever an assumption of an existing mortgage and is not feasible.

Savings and Loan Associations. Savings and loan associations (S&Ls) are the single most specialized lenders for small residential properties in most areas of the United States. They are primarily interested in owner-occupant housing and in times of credit shortages tend to withhold mortgage money for investor loans. But they are worth consulting whenever you anticipate a purchase or need to help a prospective buyer obtain financing. Loans for investors go no higher than 80 percent of appraised value, but many S&Ls have no objection to seller take-backs (deferred purchase money loans) of another 10 percent (see secondary financing discussion below). However, S&Ls doing investor loans in high demand areas are apt to tack on heavy "placement fees," service charges, nonrefundable commitment fees and other expenses that raise both their profits and your out-of-pocket costs appreciably. These points and fees sometimes run to 3 or 4 percent of the loan amount—$1,350, for instance, on a $45,000 loan in a three-point market.

S&Ls' interest rates also tend to be ¼ to ½ percent higher on investor than on homeowner loans and their restrictive terms and clauses can be burdensome. For example, prepayment penalties may run to several months' interest or higher; or your deed of trust or mortgage may contain prohibitions against subsequent loans being placed on the property—a precondition you should definitely try to avoid. Be aware of other "accelera-

BASIC SOURCES AND TYPES OF FIRST MORTGAGES/TRUSTS FOR ONE- TO FOUR-UNIT INVESTORS

Source	Types of Loans	Terms	Advantages/Disadvantages
Savings and loan associations	Conventional 80 percent loan-to-value ratio; seller's second trust up to 10 percent may be permitted. Mortgage can go above $75,000, but S&Ls prefer loans under that amount. FHA and VA also available.	Twenty to thirty years; investors can expect ¼ to ½ percent higher interest rates than prime owner-occupant mortgagors. Points, placement and commitment fees likely, dependent on market conditions. Prepayment penalties negotiable; typically call for several months' interest payment.	Most readily available source of funds in many areas; terms are apt to be advantageous compared with banks. Service charge and points tend to be high. Most new loans non-assumable. State-chartered S&Ls may have greater flexibility on terms than federally chartered.
Commercial banks	Conventional 75 to 80 percent loan-to-value ratio as high as most will go. FHA, VA available from some. Loans generally under $100,000, but will go higher on income-producing property.	Twenty to thirty years; market interest rates.	More interested in short-term construction loans than long-term investor loans on non-owner-occupied properties. Regulations permit them to make loans, however; large depositors have better chance than nondepositors.
Mortgage bankers, mortgage brokers	Conventional 80 percent loan-to-value ratio, but sometimes have funds to go to 90 percent, with mortgage	Twenty to thirty years; investor rates and points higher than homeowner applicants.	Readily available in many areas but interest rate likely to be higher than S&Ls, banks. May be more flexible

	insurance. Active in FHA, VA; best source for FNMA two- to four-unit program.		on terms than regulated institutional lenders.
Sellers	Conventional only, but loans and amounts entirely arranged by negotiation.	Can range from a two-year installment loan to a thirty- or forty-year payback. Interest rates vary from several points below market to the local usury ceiling. Interest-only terms possible; balloon payments common.	Can be an investor's most flexible, convenient source of finance. But most sellers are unable or unwilling to provide first mortgage or trust in anything but a distress situation.
Insurance companies, REITs	Conventional 75 percent loan-to-value ratio or less.	Twenty to thirty years, market rates, low fees.	Only occasionally willing to make loans for one- to four-unit investment property; may deal through mortgage banker.
Credit unions	Conventional 80 percent loan-to-value ratio.	To thirty years, if buyer to reside in one of the units, and property cost does not exceed 150 percent of market area median. Second category of shorter-term loans carry twelve-year maximums.	Growing source for one- to four-unit family loans. Credit unions can't put over 25 percent of assets into mortgages, however, and restrict loans to members.

tion" provisions that S&Ls often like to hit their borrowers with; they're in the fine print and allow the S&L to call in the loan in full if you violate any of the rules—for example, by falling behind a couple of months or so in your payments. When comparison-shopping S&Ls by phone, be sure to ask about pre-payment penalties, assumption clauses and other kickers. Ask your realty agent or attorney which S&Ls offer the best total packages of investor terms. In any given metropolitan area, there will be larger variations in S&L terms to investors than to regular home buyers, simply because investor loans are dis-cretionary for S&Ls and not all of them care to get involved.

Sellers. It may strike you as odd to consider sellers a prime source of first mortgages or trusts. But sellers are already sources, and can be turned into larger ones by you. In many trans-actions, sellers can be the ideal primary lender. They have no regulations, except usury laws, to worry about and aren't en-cumbered with traditional loan-to-value ratios, loan pay-back terms or interest rates. Sellers tend to know their property in-side out and usually want to help you acquire it. If one of your needs, for example, is a down payment of 5 or 10 percent, or no down payment at all, the seller is the first source to think about. If you need special terms, like interest-only payments or a below-market interest rate, also consider approaching the seller.

Owners of the property you want to buy may be sophisticated and appreciate the benefits of seller-financing. Providing you a 5 percent down loan—at his asking price for the house and at a 10 percent rate over a ten-year term—should qualify as an install-ment transaction for the seller and result in favorable capital gains treatment (see Chapter 10 for a discussion of installment sales). It will also bring him the full price he wanted plus a marketable investment secured by his property yielding 10 percent a year.

Sellers who aren't informed of the advantages of direct finan-cing may need to be educated by you or your agent. This is worth every minute you put into it. Be certain, however, to engage competent legal help when it comes time to draw up the note and trust deed. Both you and the seller should direct counsel to examine the documents carefully so as to avoid later misunderstandings.

Mortgage Bankers. Known in some areas as mortgage companies or mortgage brokers, these are the middlemen of the housing and real estate finance business. They rarely if ever loan money out of their own resources, but rather convert other people's funds into mortgage investments and then service the loans for a continuing fee. Sometimes their funds are from their own city or states; at other times, from 3,000 miles across the country. Except for property owners, mortgage bankers are the most flexible lenders around; they are your primary source of funds when you want to use FHA, VA or the Federal National Mortgage Association's two- to four-unit program described below. And they are worth calling, particularly during credit squeezes, for comparison of terms against S&Ls on conventional 80 percent first trusts.

Commercial Banks. In general, commercial banks prefer short-term to long-term lending and thus are not best bets for first mortgages or trusts. They usually will go no higher than 75 percent of appraised value on a residential investment property and may offer loans only to large depositors. Don't write them off, but don't think of them first.

Insurance Companies and Real Estate Investment Trusts. If you haven't come up with a loan from any of the other four sources, you're probably in trouble. But it's worth asking your banker, real estate broker or a mortgage banker about the availability of first-mortgage money from large national insurance companies or a local real estate investment trust (REIT). They will occasionally consider a small-scale investor loan. And of course it helps to know someone who knows someone inside the company.

Federally Chartered Credit Unions. These are rapidly growing sources of mortgages, due to a 1977 law improving the terms they can offer. Although chiefly interested in serving members' needs for primary-residence finance, credit unions have the authority to make thirty-year loans on one- to four-unit dwellings when the borrower plans to reside in one unit, as with duplexes, triplexes and quads. The sales price cannot exceed 150 percent of the median sales price of residential real property in the area. Credit unions can finance home improvement loans of up to fifteen years as well as make business loans, including those for real estate purposes, of up to twelve years. Join several credit unions; you may find them surprisingly flexible sources.

Assumptions: VA, FHA and Conventional. Some of the properties you evaluate may have *assumable* loans—mortgages or trusts permitting new buyers to step into the current owner's position at advantageous terms. Such loans can be worth dollars to you as an investor. They may allow you to retain the owner's interest rate, which will be far below current rates, and to take over the loan with low fees and closing costs. All FHA and VA home loans are potentially assumable by investor-buyers; the key question is how much cash you'll need at the outset to do it. VA loans of recent vintage make especially good assumptions because the owner may have little equity in the house. VA loans often allow veterans to buy a $70,000 home with nothing down; therefore the buyer of a VA-guaranteed new $50,000 house may have only a few thousand dollars of equity (inflation-produced equity plus principal payoff) after twelve to eighteen months. As an investor, you could pick up such a loan, with or without veterans' entitlement status, via assumption with a down payment of less than 5 percent of the house's appraised value.

There is, however, a dark side to VA assumptions. Until a veteran's first VA mortgage or trust is fully paid off, he or she cannot use his or her full GI loan entitlement to purchase another house on no-down-payment terms. The veteran also remains technically responsible, if the VA chooses to press the matter, for any losses incurred by the government through a foreclosure. In practice, this rarely happens, and in practice, veterans are often quite willing to give up part or all of their entitlements. They may be retiring, or they may be buying a house with a conventional mortgage so they don't need GI bill assistance any more.

FHA loans carry no such complications for investors but often have larger equity positions as a result of higher initial down payments.

Assumable conventional loans are more and more difficult to find, as S&Ls and banks have effectively discouraged them on level-interest-rate loans since the 1973–74 credit crunch. Most lenders permit assumptions only after renegotiation of the interest rate and payment of an assumption fee—the net effect of which can be to render assumptions more costly than new loans.

However, when you come upon an assumable modest-interest-rate on a good property, don't be discouraged by the large down payment that may be required. You can either ask the seller to take back a deferred-purchase-money second mortgage or get a "hard-money" second loan elsewhere and cut your cash requirement dramatically.

First Mortgages via FHA and VA. The FHA and the VA are primarily in the business of backing private lenders' loans to home buyers who plan to occupy the property as their principal residence. Both agencies, however, will help finance new loans or trusts on two-, three-, or four-family properties where the buyer plans to live in one unit. In VA's case, the buyer must have GI entitlement but can even go beyond the four-unit limit if he can get an entitled veteran to cosign the mortgage for each additional unit and to live in the unit.

The problem with new loans via FHA and VA is that they can be agonizingly time-consuming and cumbersome and require a higher down payment than alternative sources. In FHA's case, for example, a nonoccupant loan on a four-unit property can go to only 72 percent of the appraised value and cannot exceed specified dollar limits in each geographical market area. Often the dollar limits are not high enough to include even modest-priced properties.

Ask a mortgage banker how FHA or VA programs apply to a particular property you have in mind. In your community, the numbers just might work. But be prepared for red tape, ranging from minimum property standards to affirmative marketing standards in your rental activities.

FNMA Two-to-Four Unit Program. An important addition to investors' stock of financing tools is the Federal National Mortgage Association's "two-to-four unit" commitment and purchase program. FNMA (or Fannie Mae) is a congressionally chartered private corporation based in Washington, D.C., whose overall function is to invest in and assist the U.S. mortgage market. The corporation buys FHA, VA and conventional mortgages under a variety of terms and programs; it is the largest single owner of American mortgages, with about $35 billion in its portfolio.

FNMA's two-to-four unit program, begun in 1978, offers the following:

• Mortgages well over $100,000, with down payments as low as 5 percent, for people who want to buy houses with two to four units in urban areas. The buyers must live in one unit while using the rental income from the others to help meet monthly mortgage payments. This fits the needs of many couples or small households who want to live in a city but can't swing the high down payments and purchase prices of the large, multi-unit row houses they find so attractive.

• Mortgages for investors who want to purchase mini-apartment buildings for remodeling or rental in central cities but who don't plan to live in the properties. For such purchasers the down payment terms are slightly higher but allow an investor to put in as little as 20 percent and still come away with a three- or four-unit brownstone or row house costing $150,000 or more. With secondary financing, the down payment can be cut to just 10 percent—with no mortgage insurance.

• A virtually guaranteed source of mortgage money, albeit at the going market rates, for buyers in these two categories who can use it. Investors who found S&L windows closed tight in some parts of the country during the 1978 credit squeeze made substantial use of the program. One Virginia mortgage banker who specializes in the two-to-four unit program considers it "phenomenal because it responds so well to the urban investment market as it is today."

FNMA had this in mind when it designed the program. Such cities as Boston, New York, Philadelphia, Chicago and San Francisco have needed a fresh financing source for years. Large-city neighborhoods contain tens of thousands of buildings that combine excellent ownership and rental opportunities. The problem is that these structures are often expensive, and mortgage lenders like S&Ls won't count the projected rental income in qualifying applicants who plan to be occupant-owners. FNMA's program permits lenders to count that income, but imposes tough appraisal standards, code compliance rules and financial checks on borrowers. FNMA will buy loans on two- to four-unit urban properties but insists that they be high-grade investments. If, for example, you contend that two of the three units in a row house can be rented out for a total of $700 a month, FNMA won't take your estimate on faith. Before your mortgage banker or S&L gets the go-ahead on the loan, an intensive study must be made of the property by an independent appraiser, using rent levels and purchase prices from several comparable properties in the area.

The precise mortgage amounts available under the FNMA program vary city by city, according to the corporation's market minimums, which are available at the offices of participating mortgage bankers and S&Ls.

SECONDARY FINANCING

The dividing line between financial approaches in the regular home-buying market and the investment field is secondary financing. Only 6 to 7 percent of owner-occupied homes have secondary mortgages on them, according to a study by the Federal Reserve Board. On the other hand, two-thirds or more of all investment properties do, by some real estate industry estimates. If you seriously want to invest in one- to four-unit properties, seriously want to beat inflation with real estate, you've got to understand secondary mortgages and how and when to use them.

Secondary finance stands for a wide variety of loans that are related by two common features: they are flexible financing stopgaps, providing the difference between what a borrower chooses or can afford to invest in a property and what is actually required; and they are all junior liens against properties, subordinate in status and precedence to another. The senior lien may be a first, second or third mortgage. Whatever it happens to be, it must be satisfied before the junior lien can be paid off. If the proceeds of a foreclosure did not cover the full combined amount of the first mortgage and the second mortgage, the first mortgage holder would be completely paid off, the second mortgage holder only partially. Precedence among secondary loans is determined strictly chronologically, as registered in local public records. When one mortgage is retired, the next mortgage in line moves up the chain. There is no limit to how many junior mortgages can be secured by a piece of property, but in the residential field it would be unusual to find anything above three. The farther down on the chain of precedence a lien is, the higher the risk to its holder and the higher the expected rate of return.

Purchase-Money Seconds. The form of secondary finance most commonly used by rental-home investors is the deferred-purchase-money second trust or mortgage. This is a very effective tool for cutting initial outlays, and thereby increasing yield on the dollar.

Here's how it works. Say you are the seller of a $90,000 house and have a $60,000, 8 percent mortgage with twenty-four years remaining. An investor sees great potential for the property as a two-unit rental dwelling, covets your 8 percent mortgage, but doesn't have $30,000 in cash to assume your loan. Since the investor happens to be the first person in weeks interested in paying anything near the inflated price you're asking, and since he does have $20,000 in cash, you propose a stopgap solution. You "take back" a second trust of $10,000. The loan will provide the investor with his $10,000—a paper transfer out of the proceeds of your sale—and the debt will be secured by the house itself.

You can arrange the pay-back terms in just about any way that suits you: the debt could be for a five-year period at 9.25 percent interest, to be paid in equal monthly principal and interest installments of $208.80. Or you could provide an interest-only loan at 10 percent—$1,000 per year for five years, $83.33 per month—with a lump-sum balloon payment of the $10,000 principal due at the end of the period.

The advantages of deferred-purchase-money loans are numerous. They are often the necessary catalysts for stalled transactions; in their absence, the buyer can't buy and the seller can't sell. And they are reasonably good investments in their own right. Second trusts almost always yield higher interest rates (a lot higher than certificates of deposit at an S&L or bank, for example), have short terms and are readily salable. Any major real estate broker or real estate lawyer can probably sell a well-secured trust of this sort within hours or days. (Chapter 3 of this book is devoted to the art and science of the secondary mortgage as an income-producing investment vehicle.)

Since purchase-money trusts or mortgages are junior liens, they involve a significant risk of loss. But such cases are rare when the transaction was preceded by a prudent appraisal of the property and thorough credit checks. According to brokers and lenders active in this field, the general rule is that the combined principal amounts of first and second trusts on a residential property shouldn't exceed 80 percent. In the case of the $90,000 house above, the combined figures equal $70,000—$60,000 first and a $10,000 second trust—or about $2,000 shy of 80 percent.

Purchase-money seconds often go hand in hand with 80 percent investor loans from S&Ls to reduce the effective pay-out by the purchaser to 10 percent of the property's selling price. Take the case of a $50,000 single-family owner-occupied house being bought for conversion to rental by a young working couple. The local S&L will provide a $40,000 first mortgage or trust on the property, but the couple doesn't want to sink $10,000 into it. They persuade the seller to take back a five-year $5,000 second at an agreeable interest rate and terms; the S&L has no objection. The buyers have acquired their $50,000 property with just 10 percent down, exclusive of closing costs; the seller has gotten rid of his house at the price he wanted, and gets a short-term

$5,000 note. He can sell the note at a discount to someone else, thus converting it to immediate cash, or hold on to it and take in the periodic payments.

"Hard-Money" Seconds. Another common type of loan is known as a "hard-money" second. Unlike a deferred-purchase-money loan, which involves only a paper transfer, hard-money seconds require dollars on the table. Hard-money seconds are subordinate loans secured by real estate that one already owns— a primary residence, for example, or an investment property. You walk into a bank, credit union, mortgage company, or investment brokerage firm, pledge your property as security for a loan, and come away a week or two later with cash. Real estate investors often use this cash to finance additional property purchases; other individuals use such loans for debt consolidation, business ventures, vacations and so on.

In the case of the $50,000 house purchase above, the young couple could have reduced their $5,000 out-of-pocket to zero by borrowing the 10 percent down payment via a hard money loan against their principal residence. If they owned a house valued at $95,000, with an outstanding principal balance on their first mortgage of $50,000, they would have no difficulty whatsoever getting a second mortgage of $5,000 or $10,000 against their residence. The interest rate on the loan might range from 11 to 16 percent, and the term from three to twelve years, depending upon the lender.

Like the "soft" purchase money loans, hard-money seconds are also readily marketable investments in most parts of the country.

Other Secondary Loans. There are other noteworthy forms of secondary finance, and wraparound mortgages, land leases and blanket mortgages are the three most important. None of these, however, is likely to figure into your financing repertoire until you have a large number of transactions under your belt. If you're curious and need to know the details right now, refer to Chapter 10, which covers these and other creative techniques.

BASIC SOURCES AND TYPES OF SECONDARY FINANCE

Type	Source	Terms	Advantages/Disadvantages
Seller take-back (deferred purchase money mortgage or trust)	Seller of property	Tend to be short-term, three to ten years; carry interest rates higher than first mortgage, although rate is always negotiable. Can be structured to permit interest-only payments, with principal due at end of term. Can be structured to amortize principal and interest monthly.	Known as the deal-maker because the willingness of the seller to take back a second so often clinches the sale to an investor. Buyer can seek a large second in exchange for full price (or higher) offer to seller. Net effect is to increase leverage and cut outlay up front.
"Hard-money" seconds	Institutional lenders, mortgage companies, individual investors, occasionally realty brokers	Generally similar to purchase-money seconds, although institutional rates tend to be higher.	Can be used instead of, or in combination with, purchase money second for acquisition of property. Terms overall may be less favorable than what can be negotiated from a seller, however.
Other secondary loans (wraparounds, land leases, etc.)	Institutional lenders, sellers; varies with type of loan	Highly variable. See Chapter 10 for discussion of several techniques.	"Creative finance"—but solutions that small-scale residential investors rarely need or can use.

No-Money-Down Financing. Down payments of 5 to 10 percent offer leverage enough for most rental-home investors, but
some like more razzle-dazzle in their financing. They prefer to
get as close as feasible to the magic level of zero outlays in
their purchases—look, Ma, no down payment, no closing costs!
These investors can employ a variety of approaches, each one
carrying with it both advantages and drawbacks.

Probably the most common entails the use of two levels of
take-back second trusts. Here is an example, provided by A. M.
Barr, a real estate entrepreneur in Arlington, Virginia.* You have
located an excellent $40,000 rental house with an existing assum-
able first trust of $30,000. The seller is looking for a minimum
of $6,000 in cash and expresses a willingness to take back a
$4,000 second. Rather than providing him with $6,000 out of
your own pocket, you offer to guarantee him $6,000 at settle-
ment, or shortly thereafter, through a discounted sale of another
second trust. The $4,000 trust he offered to take back would
then become a third trust against the property.

Let's take that slowly.

1. $40,000 is the price the seller wants.
2. $30,000 is the first trust you'll assume.
3. You guarantee him $6,000 in cash via sale of a second trust.
   To achieve this, he would provide you a mortgage in an
   amount calculated to bring in $6,000 under prevailing
   market conditions. If trusts are selling at discounts of 25
   percent, thus bringing in 75 cents per dollar of face
   amount, you would sell an $8,000 trust for $6,000 cash.
   Since demand for such "paper" is intense in many areas,
   you could guarantee this sale with confidence.
4. The $4,000 the seller offered to take back in the form of
   a second would now have a third-rung status on the lien
   ladder. The seller presumably would hold it for income.
5. The net effects of these transactions would be to raise

* The example, in somewhat different format, is included in Barr's privately printed seminar book, *How to Buy Real Estate with Other People's
Money*, 1978.

the sale price of the house by $2,000 (in order to handle the $8,000 second trust) and to cut your down payment to nothing, which is your goal. This financing method therefore transforms transaction A into B:

Example A: $40,000 price
                  30,000 first trust assumption by you
                ─────────
                $10,000
      minus   4,000 second trust offered by seller
                ─────────
                $ 6,000 down payment required

Example B: $42,000 sales price
                  30,000 first trust assumption by you
                ─────────
                $12,000
      minus   8,000 second trust sold to outside investor
                            yielding $6,000 cash to house seller
      minus   4,000 third trust taken back by seller
                ─────────
                $ 0 down payment required

Barr suggests financing away the anticipated closing costs on such a transaction by including them in the second trust, which will be sold to an outside investor. In other words, the $8,000 trust might, with closing costs, actually amount to $9,000. The revised trust amount is arrived at by adding approximately 25 percent to the expected closing charges—that is, by taking the market discount into account. Still, only $6,000 cash would go to the seller; you would take the balance to pay your costs.

Presto—no acquisition expense and infinite leverage, not to mention an investment house. But you've also burrowed into debt on this property, with three mortgages, no equity and a higher acquisition cost than with any other available method. You have mortgaged out everything—but are you ready for the big negative cash drains every month? If you're already walking a financial tightrope and lack the personal income or assets to protect yourself if the property proves to be a rental bomb, be careful with this technique.

Other Strategies. Keep in mind:

• The possibility, in a seller-financing deal where the property is in bad physical shape, of your providing *sweat equity* as down payment. Charles W. Dorsey, a broker in Corpus Christi, Texas, says he has arranged such financing on a number of occasions. Normally this involves a contract for deed sale, in which title is held by the seller until specified conditions are met by the buyer. The purchasers agree to rehabilitate the property and make periodic financial payments; if they default, the owner still has the property—and now it's fixed up.

• The possibility, in some situations, of persuading your realty broker to take back, out of his expected commissions from the sale, a trust on the property you're buying. As you might guess, it helps to have a broker who is a very close friend, an unusually large-hearted sport or a shrewd judge of your potential as a long-term client.

OFFERS, NEGOTIATIONS, CONTRACTS

A how-to explanation of real estate negotiation is like a how-to book on sex. You can talk in graphic detail about bargaining positions and techniques until you're blue in the face, but because of the different personalities involved in each case, abstract discussion is of limited value. There are a number of weighty books written on this subject for real estate brokers and sales professionals, yet most people end up doing it their own way.

One well-known author and lecturer advises investors to bring a three-foot level and a stack of index cards (a rival property listed on each card) to bargaining sessions with a property owner. In between snippets of conversation you shuffle through your stack of cards and casually demonstrate with your level that the floor in his house slopes badly. The cards and the level should, according to the author, knock most owners off balance.

Another expert recommends the use of under-the-table accomplices to help lower the selling price. Send your friends, relatives and colleagues to look over the house as interested prospective buyers. Then have them make bids far lower than your own. The seller will be sufficiently miffed at their insulting offers to consider yours rather more sympathetically.

A third authority counsels buyers to shoot for their target price by always offering 25 percent less. Not 30 and not 10 percent lower, but 25 percent—because that's what works.

Various other negotiating theories abound. Some professionals approach the sale of a small single-family house like tacticians in a complex war game, with parries and counterparries figured out far in advance. Others claim to make big money using Indian bazaar techniques. Bombay merchants never begin serious negotiation until the buyer has walked out of the shop in a huff at least three times, called back in each instance by ritualized sweeps of the hand and minor price concessions.

Well, who knows? Try whatever seems to work as long as it's legal and ethical. Let a thousand flowers bloom in the negotiating room. There are, however, some fundamentals that any prudent investor in small residential properties ought to consider before heading into serious bargaining or signing a contract of sale.

The Seller. If you've researched the market and analyzed the house and your financing opportunities along the lines discussed in earlier sections, you're three-quarters of the way to your objective. You know what the property is worth in the market, give or take 5 percent. You know the approximate cost of repairs. And you know what sort of cash flow it's likely to generate.

What you need to know next is the seller's situation, why and how badly he wants to get rid of his property. You're looking for concessions that the seller might agree to. These may be on price, equipment or extras that go with the property, mortgage finance terms, contract contingencies, settlement costs or timing of the transaction.

Potentially everything is negotiable, and everything *is* connected. You're buying a package of terms—price is only one of them, and often not worth losing the deal over. When a $60,000 house will be worth $66,000 to $68,000 in twelve months, is it smart to break negotiations over $500 or $1,000? If the owner of the house is unwilling to give an inch on price, move nimbly to other areas—like his taking back a second, or paying for a specified number of points you may get hit with by your lender—and you might come away with more.

Begin your search for information and insights with the seller's agent or broker. Agents will spill a shocking number of beans about their clients out of the simple desire to sell the property. They can tell you roughly what the seller needs to net out of the sale, after commissions and other costs are subtracted. They can and will tell you the number and size of other offers, and when and why previous contracts fell through. Agents often have a good idea of the owner's personal and financial situation, as well as his quirks, strengths and overall bargaining strategy. They can tell you with brutal frankness why a property has been on the market longer than expected, thus opening the door to a successful offer from you.

After barely ten minutes with a serious investor, agents will frequently divulge what is often regarded as privileged information. They aren't supposed to, but they do it all the time. A seller may be difficult to work with—refusing reasonable offers and making an agent sit for two months of weekend showings because a contract was $1,000 too low. In circumstances like these, agents might turn into *your* representatives, not the seller's, by doing whatever is necessary to complete the sale.

The reverse, of course, may also be true. If strictly protective of the seller, the agent may do no more than to warn you that a large number of bids have been received and that you'd better act fast. Nevertheless, with artful questioning, the agent still will tell you much of what you need to know.

The Property. Never fall in love with a prospective rental house until it's yours. The same market savvy you need at the inspection stage is even more crucial when it comes time to negotiate. There's no better way to blow your chances than to parade your enthusiasm in front of the owner. Better to be a crab. Point out every crack, lament the lack of insulation, bemoan the bathroom tiling. Don't be afraid to walk out—à la Bombay. If you know what you're doing and have one eye cocked on the seller, the other on the market, you'll get called back.

CONTRACTS

The vehicle you'll be using—or hammering out—in your negotiations is a sales contract form. Customs and phraseology differ from state to state, but the essentials are the same. It is legally binding when signed by buyer and seller, so don't regard it simply as a bid or offer. It is both of these things, but it can also be the whole ball game. If you plan to engage legal help for property acquisition, do it before signing and not after.

Your skill in bargaining will determine how the contract is filled out and how it divvies up the costs and responsibilities of the transaction. Skill isn't gauged by how many nifty contingencies or stiff, wordy clauses you can stick in with addenda sheets. Too many contingencies will gum up the works and discourage a seller from signing. Go for the simplest contract possible, while still protecting your essential interests. At the minimum, your draft contracts should address the following:

Definition of the Property. The contract should have a precise definition of the property and all nonrealty included in the sale. If you're counting on such things as kitchen equipment, wall-to-wall carpeting, curtains and drapery rods, and shrubs and plants, make sure that they are specified, and their condition guaranteed, in your contract. The contract should also state that any significant changes to the property between date of agreement and date of conveyance will render the agreement null and void, in which case the buyer's deposit will be returned. Additionally, the contract should note that you, the buyer, are entitled to inspect the entire property immediately prior to settlement.

Deposit. The size of your earnest-money deposit will vary according to the situation. As an investor you want to conserve your cash, and keep it interest-bearing, as long as possible. So you probably prefer to offer a promissory note, due at settlement, for a relatively small dollar amount. The seller, however, is likely to want more assurance that your offer is genuine and that you are financially solid, and thus would be more impressed by a display of hard cash—for example, a $5,000 check on a

$75,000 property. And it is better to err on the high side, even at the loss of a little interest, than to lose the seller to a "stronger" contract from a competing buyer. Whatever you do, never hand earnest money to the seller. Put any deposits in escrow, with the realty agent, a title company or your lawyer.

Financing. This is an "eject button" you should not give up under any circumstances. Your contract should be contingent upon your ability to obtain the financing you want within a reasonable time period, such as forty-five days. If your financing is coming from the seller, no problem. But in most cases it doesn't, so don't risk your deposit through inability to come up with mortgage money. You may, in order to make a concession to the seller, phrase your financing needs in general terms. For instance, rather than making the transaction contingent upon your getting an 80 percent conventional first trust at 10 percent or lower, you may specify simply "10 percent or best obtainable." The existence of rigid contingencies on financing can also work against you in a competitive situation; if you anticipate competitive offers, consider toning down your financing clause at the start. Your offer should be highly specific as to the financing vehicle you intend to employ— whether you're *assuming* the seller's existing mortgage or mortgages, taking title to his property *subject to* his existing mortgages, which forces the seller to retain a contingent liability, or *obtaining* or *placing* a new first or second mortgage.

In your negotiations regarding finance, you should also determine whether the seller is to take care of none, some or all of the discount points or fees that lenders may assess. In a tight-money situation, this concession can save you hundreds or thousands of dollars. And in cases of assumptions, make certain that you also assume the tax and insurance escrows of the seller.

Title. Double-check to make sure your contract guarantees you a title free of encumbrances. It should also specify that any cloud on the title prior to settlement must be removed at the seller's expense.

Inspection and Termites. Many standard residential contract forms state that the seller should deliver a certificate that declares the property free of active infestation by termites and other wood-boring insects. Standard contract boilerplate does not, however, require that the seller repair any structural damage already caused by prior infestations. Both protective clauses can be important; don't give either away without extracting equal concessions from the seller.

Unless you've decided for tactical reasons to accept the property "as is," protect yourself with an inspection clause. You want not only an inspection of the property by a qualified engineer or firm of your choice but also a report that is acceptable to *you*. In fairness, a time limit of three to five working days should be imposed for completing the inspection.

Right to Show. If it seems possible to line up tenants for the property before settlement, persuade the seller to accept a clause to that effect in an addendum.

Life of the Offer. Don't allow a seller to sit on your offer, or an agent to play you off against other buyers. Set a definite time limit on your contract, whether of seventy-two hours or a week. "If not accepted by _____ A.M./P.M. July 17, 19___, this offer shall be null and void."

Seller's Acquisition of Other Property. Some sellers insist on a contingency clause that allows for cancellation of the sale if the seller is unable to purchase a new dwelling within a specified period of time. If the property is borderline in your estimation, the risk of wasting several months of your time waiting for the seller to find an acceptable new home may not be worth it. On the other hand, if the place is a steal, you may decide to risk it. An alternative is to set a contractual "date certain" for transfer of the property, granting rental privileges to the seller at a concessionary rate for a mutually convenient period following settlement.

LANDLORDS, TENANTS AND PROFITABLE COEXISTENCE

Taking title to an investment house can be a superb way to shelter your dollars and nurture big capital gains. But it can also drive you batty if you're not prepared to assume a new and unavoidable role: to make your investment work, you've got to be the landlord. And that means finding tenants who'll pay money to you regularly and the subsequent host of obligations. Some of your responsibilities can be delegated to a professional agent, but only some of them. Not every investor has an easy time of it, particularly in the initial year or two.

Take Bruce Morrow of Bethesda, Maryland. As his first investment, he bought a newly constructed townhouse in a middle-income suburban subdivision and hired a local realty agent to screen and select the first tenants. The agent's screening techniques had some gaping holes, however, because Morrow's first tenants were a group of four teenagers, who brought:

• Live-in boyfriends.

• Pet rabbits who ran wild throughout the second floor. "If you want to see the darndest thing," says Morrow, "you ought to see what a bunch of rabbits can do to nice, new wall-to-wall shag carpeting. . . . It took me weeks just to get the smell out of there."

• Seeds for a soon-flourishing cash crop of marijuana, which was planted in the backyard.

On Thanksgiving Day the county police called him at home with news that the townhouse had just been raided and the occupants arrested on drug and other charges. He'd better get up there right away, holiday dinner or no holiday dinner.

"You've got to have a certain temperament to do well in this field," says Morrow, who has gone on to invest successfully in several other rental properties. "It can be a real test of your whole psychosomatic system." If you can't cope calmly and rationally with frozen pipes, overflowing toilets, malfunctioning heating systems and nonpaying tenants, "you really shouldn't put your money into it in the first place."

Another housing investor, Bill Barnhart of Annapolis, Maryland, recalls several rental nightmares in well-to-do neighborhoods. "I'd get phone calls at midnight from tenants making $30,000 to $40,000 a year—I mean intelligent, professional people—demanding that I come over and fix a light bulb that had burned out or fix a faucet that had been dripping for three weeks. Or I'd get a call at two A.M. telling me that my tenants in one property had just moved out. I'd rush over to the place and find it a wreck. One family broke every pane of glass in the house and pounded the plaster walls to hell with Coke bottles." Barnhart's advice to prospective newcomers: "Anybody who's taken a tranquilizer any time in the past ten years should not become a landlord. Psychologically you're probably not up to it."

But Barnhart overstates the case by a long shot. Certainly you need a cool head, but there is really no reason why you can't avoid such horror stories if you follow the basic rules of this business. Here are some practical guidelines gleaned from discussions with dozens of investors, brokers, tenants and building managers, plus the author's own experience. They're primarily aimed at do-it-yourselfers, but even those investors who plan to hire professional leasing and management help would do well to be familiar with them.

Know the law. Know what you're getting into. Before advertising or renting your investment house, get acquainted with the state and local laws that will govern your relationship with tenants. Local ordinances increasingly determine what you as a landlord can charge as security deposit and if you must place it in escrow or an interest-bearing account; whether your tenants can withhold rent under any circumstances; what type of eviction notice you must give; how long it takes for you to recover a property; how valid all or any of the provisions of your lease will be in court; whether and when you're required to provide special equipment, such as smoke detectors, in your units.

The list of controls is very long in some communities; such cities as New York, San Francisco, Chicago, Philadelphia and Boston tend to have the most extensive regulations. The list is short in places where localities may have scant provisions for tenants and rely heavily on state or common law.

You need not be a lawyer to succeed as a landlord. Just make a little file for every jurisdiction in which you rent property; if you can get copies of relevant ordinances, statutes and regulations, keep them handy for possible reference. Cut out newspaper clippings of court cases, new regulations and rent-control policies in order to stay as informed as some of your tenants are sure to be.

Set competitive rents by offering as good or better an overall product as the guy around the block. Identify your target market —young marrieds, elderly singles or families, for example—and tailor your property to them. If you're offering an unfurnished unit to a middle-income market, put in the amenities that may turn the trick—neutral wall-to-wall carpeting, extra counter space in the kitchen or a bar in the den. Don't strive for mind-stretching rents; you'll have an easier time keeping appreciative long-term tenants if you don't gouge. By reading ads, visiting competing houses in the neighborhood and even having rental agents give you quotes for possible listings, you will get an idea where to set your overall rent level. Establish one monthly figure for singles, families and unmarried couples who are taking long-term (at least one year) leases, and charge 10 to 20 percent more for short-term tenants and for groups of unrelated individuals—if you choose to go after them at all.

Announce creatively that you've got an excellent house to rent. For that matter, put the word out as far in advance of taking title as possible. Contact any large private employers or government agencies in the area and ask to put up notices on their employee bulletin boards. Every year, thousands of units are rented out this way, *without cost*, in cities and suburban areas with major federal or state installations, company headquarters, office complexes and factories. Put up mimeographed notices wherever your market might be found—in shops, churches or social organizations. And as soon as you can, put up an easy-to-read sign in front of your property that lists your name and phone number. You should at least consider the alternative communication networks open to you before spending money on newspaper ads. However, when you finally place an ad in the paper, don't skimp; highly abbreviated ads attract fewer calls word for word than ads that fully describe what you've got.

Rather than

> HILLDALE—2 BR, LR, DR $310/mo.
> TS kit., call 330-6513.

make it

> HILLDALE—Townhouse, large fenced yard, 2 BR, sun porch, separate living and dining rooms, washer/dryer, mountain view, Benton school district, $310 incl. util. Avail. Aug. 1. Call 330-6513.

The cost is a few dollars more, but you're likely to rent that townhouse far quicker.

Discriminate, but never on account of race, religion, sex, age or national origin. Discriminate on every other basis necessary in order to get the sort of tenants *you* want. You don't have to accept a lawyer as a tenant, for example, if you suspect he or she will be a litigious troublemaker. The New York Supreme Court ruled to that effect in 1977, so don't be afraid to say no on reasonable grounds.

Always use *application* forms before proceeding to the lease itself. And don't accept anybody on the spot, however accurate your intuition has been in the past. An application form you might care to use or adapt is on pages 68–69.

The form commits the tenant to sign a lease if you accept the tenant after credit and employment checks. The tenant should provide a good-faith deposit—say, $100—with the application, understanding that $10 of it may be used for a commercial credit check. If an applicant balks at this, don't compromise. Anyone afraid of credit or employer checks probably has a credit or employer problem that one day will become your problem.

Once the application form is completed, check out everything, especially current and prior landlord references. You might even consider dropping by the present address to talk with the landlord or visiting the applicant on short notice to see how the current rental has been treated. At least telephone the landlords listed, and be sensitive to the possibility that the present landlord might want to get rid of the tenant, even at the price of a white lie or two.

RENTAL/LEASE APPLICATION   (side 1 of card)

Property _____	Date _____ Deposit _____ Security Deposit ____
Proposed Lease Date—From ____ to____	Other _____
Maximum Number of Occupants _____	Total Due at Application _____

Applicant's Name _____ Age _____
Social Security Number _____ Marital Status _____
Driver's License Number _____ State _____
Spouse/Co-Applicant's Name _____
Social Security Number _____ Age _____
Driver's License Number _____ State _____
Children _____ Age _____
_____ Age _____
_____ Age _____
Current Address _____ State _____
Dates of Residence
at This Address _____ Phone Number _____
Name/Address of Landlord/Agent _____
_____ Phone Number _____
Current Rent $_____ Date of Lease Expiration _____
Address Prior to Current _____ State _____
Dates of Residence at This Address _____
Name/Address of Landlord/Agent _____
_____ Phone Number _____

EMPLOYMENT: (side 2 of card)
Name of Firm/Organization _____
Address _____ State _____
Position _____ Date of Employment _____
Current Salary _____ Overtime _____ Bonuses _____
Name and Title of Supervisor/Employer _____
_____ Phone Number _____
Spouse's/Co-Applicant's Employer _____
Address _____ State _____
Position _____ Date of Employment _____
Current Salary _____ Overtime _____ Bonuses _____
Other Income and Source _____
_____
Gross Monthly Income Total $_____

PERSONAL/CREDIT REFERENCES
Bank(s) _____ Type of Account _____
_____ Type of Account _____
Installment Obligations/Credit References _____
Name _____ Type _____ Per Month _____
Highest Amount Owed _____ Term Date _____
Name _____ Type _____ Per Month _____
Highest Amount Owed _____ Term Date _____
Have you ever filed for bankruptcy? _____ Been evicted? _____
Personal Reference _____ Phone _____
Nearest Relative _____ Address _____

I (we) hereby agree to sign a lease/month-to-month rental agreement to reside in the property above for a period of _____.
A deposit of $_____ is made herewith, to be subtracted from
the first month's rent of $_____. Deposit to be held by land-
lord or his agent with the understanding that it will be returned,
minus $10 for a credit check, if this application is not accepted. If
application is accepted by landlord, applicant will execute a rental
agreement/lease within _____ days of acceptance, or the deposit
will be forfeited in full as liquidated damages. The undersigned
swears all the above information is accurate and agrees that landlord may terminate any agreement entered into on reliance of the
accuracy of the above.
_____Applicant   Date _____
_____Applicant
Received by _____

Credit and income checks are essential. You should insist that a tenant have a gross monthly income no less than three and a half times the rent you're charging. Stretch it to three times the rent and you're in a danger zone, unless you're paying utilities. Watch out, too, that the other monthly installment debt borne by the tenant isn't beyond what's realistic. As a general rule, rent plus installment debt shouldn't take more than 40 percent of a tenant's income. After all, there's got to be something for food, clothes, transportation, and other necessities.

Calls to employers tend to be straightforward; credit checks tend not to be. You may need help using private credit bureaus who deal only with their dues-paying members. Ask your realty agent for a hand—for the $10 fee, of course.

If your applicant comes through your series of checks with flying colors, contact him within the specified period and have him fill out the lease. If you turn up anything negative about him—false statements on income or a particularly bad review by a prior landlord—simply inform him that you have decided not to rent to him and are returning his deposit herewith.

Leases come in an infinite variety of standard and nonstandard formats, and depend heavily on local laws and custom. Use whatever fits your local situation best; try contacting your local apartment owners' association or realty brokers' board to see whether they have sets of recommended forms for their members. Or ask realty firms that handle single-family rentals for their versions, and tailor your supply of standard legal store forms with their protective clauses.

Your lease should make all the charges to the tenant clear. These include:

• Treatment of the applicant's *deposit*. It's often credited to the security deposit, or becomes the security deposit in full, or is credited to the first month's rent. The size of the typical security deposit varies from area to area, but it should be no less than a half, and preferably a whole, month's rent. Remember, this not only protects you against risk of unpaid repair bills for the unit but can also compensate you in the case of skip-outs or late rent payments.

• First month's rent in advance.

• Last month's rent in advance. Although it's desirable to get this up front, you'll sometimes find good tenants who simply don't have all the cash on hand. Compromise by insisting on at least half at signing, and the balance the following month.

• Key and other deposits, if appropriate.

The lease should also define the precise *period and type of tenancy*. Is the lease on a month-to-month basis, or is it for six months, one year, or two years? If there is to be one month's free rent, as in the case of a two-year lease, this should be clearly stated in the body of the lease or in an addendum. Let the tenant know that the one-year lease he has signed is a *contract* for payment of twelve times the monthly rent, and that it is not subject to cancellation at any time without your express consent.

Operating rules should be spelled out in the lease. These include:

• Maximum number of occupants allowed, an item you should keep under strict control. Eight people in a house intended for two can have unbelievable effects on both the house and your annual balance sheet.

• Late-payment fee, often $10.00, rising to $5.00 a day for every day after five. Let the tenant know at signing that you take rent deadlines very seriously because your mortgage lender takes his due dates very seriously. Follow up any delinquencies immediately in person or by phone. Take the late charge out of the security-deposit escrow as necessary, and send a note to the tenant letting him know that you have. Be aware that in many states effective due dates must be banking days. If the due date happens to be a Sunday and the following Monday is a holiday, don't start your five-day clock ticking until Tuesday.

• Provisions involving pets. Landlords around the United States have split opinions on the subject of pets. For apartments and small units with no yards, prohibitions against pets are reasonable; permitting tenants to keep small pets in such units may even allow you to charge slight rent premiums. In single-family detached houses with yards and a lot of interior space, you may simply require that you approve of any pets in advance. Or you can list the *one* pet that you'll allow by name in the lease: for example, "Fifi, black miniature poodle," or "Sam, five-year-old cat." But bear this blunt advice in mind: the smell of dog and cat urine is among the most indelible odors known to modern carpeting. If you're absolutely confident of your tenant's ability to control his pet husky or Siamese, rent away.

• Subletting. Allow subletting under most circumstances, provided you retain the right to approve subtenants in advance. Subletting is infinitely preferable to empty units because of skip-outs.

• Responsibilities for yard maintenance, proper care of property, exterior and interior. The lease ought to make clear also that excessive noise or other nuisances to the neighborhood will not be permitted and may lead to eviction.

• Minor maintenance. Let tenants know that you are holding them responsible for minor maintenance and repairs in connection with appliances and other house equipment. You can spell this out to mean all routine maintenance costing $25 to $50, or leave it flexible for case-by-case decisions.

Property Check-In/Check-Out Form. Your lease should contain a sentence indicating that the tenant acknowledges that the premises have been delivered in good repair and working order, unless otherwise specified in the attached checklist. You should reinforce this by personally walking around the property with the new tenants just prior to their moving in, filling out a form comparable to the one on pp. 74–75. Give one copy of it, plus a copy of the signed lease, to the new tenants for ready reference. (Incidentally, in signing leases and all other forms, make certain that both husband and wife sign, or in cases of unrelated adults, that everybody in the group signs.)

When a tenant is vacating the property, again walk through with the checklist in hand. This will eliminate poor memories—either yours or the tenant's—and avoid unnecessary friction. The check-out list determines what portion of the security deposit is returned. (Local law determines how quickly it must be returned.) Assign fair repair values to each bit of damage to the property. Talk it over with the tenant reasonably, and you'll part amicably.

Tenants are your customers—and that's the most profitable way to handle the relationship. Tenants aren't doing you any favors by living in your house; you aren't doing them any favors by providing them a place for lease. You're involved in a business relationship, one where it's in your long-term interest to ensure that your tenants are personally satisfied with the product you're giving them. Tenants will stay with you longer and will take better care of your property—even make capital improvements on it—if they feel they're getting a fair shake from you. If that means bending a little now and then to accommodate a particular need—installing a little extra counter space at a tenant's request, or putting in a little more shrubbery, or repainting interiors ahead of schedule—don't hesitate to do it.

On the other hand, don't be a patsy. If tenants are damaging your property, failing to pay the rent on time, breaking your house rules, warn them. If they don't improve, start eviction proceedings against them immediately.

Hiring Rental/Management Agents. Many small-scale investors don't want all the potential hassles of being an active landlord for their properties. This is particularly true of investors who own more than four or five separate dwellings. At that level, you've got to expect to spend an hour or more every day on one aspect of your properties or another—leasing one unit, checking tenants into another, doing the books, arranging for repairs, and so forth.

If you've already got a full-time job and have no time to spare for such chores, by all means hire professional rental and/or management help. Your realty broker may be in the management business or able to suggest whom to call. For a fee that will run around 9 to 13 percent of the gross monthly rent, you can (theoretically) forget routine worries about tenants, proper maintenance of the property, and calls in the night. If the house has special landscaping needs, the management agent should arrange for it and deduct for it. If the house has a pool, the agent should arrange for its maintenance—or should instruct the tenant how to take care of it. Part of the fee should cover keeping your accounts on the property—how much rent came

CHECK-IN/CHECK-OUT

Date _____ (Check-in)
Date _____ (Check-out)

Property Address _____

Tenants' Names _____

_____

	Check-In	Additional Comments	Check-Out	Additional Comments
Kitchen				
Stove	_____	_____	_____	_____
Refrigerator	_____	_____	_____	_____
Cabinets	_____	_____	_____	_____
Counters	_____	_____	_____	_____
Walls	_____	_____	_____	_____
Lights	_____	_____	_____	_____
Sink	_____	_____	_____	_____
Disposal	_____	_____	_____	_____
Windows	_____	_____	_____	_____
Floor	_____	_____	_____	_____
Doors	_____	_____	_____	_____
Overall	_____	_____	_____	_____
cleanliness	_____	_____	_____	_____
Other:	_____	_____	_____	_____
_____	_____	_____	_____	_____
_____	_____	_____	_____	_____
_____	_____	_____	_____	_____
_____	_____	_____	_____	_____
Dining/Living	_____	_____	_____	_____
Floors	_____	_____	_____	_____
Lights	_____	_____	_____	_____
Walls	_____	_____	_____	_____
Bathroom(s)	_____	_____	_____	_____
First	_____	_____	_____	_____
Sink	_____	_____	_____	_____
Shower	_____	_____	_____	_____
Mirrors	_____	_____	_____	_____
Lights	_____	_____	_____	_____
Walls	_____	_____	_____	_____
Toilet	_____	_____	_____	_____
Windows	_____	_____	_____	_____
Other	_____	_____	_____	_____

Second				
Bedrooms				
First				
Walls				
Floor				
Closets				
Lights				
Windows				
Other				
Second				
Walls				
Floor				
Closets				
Lights				
Windows				
Other				
Third				
Walls				
Floor				
Closets				
Lights				
Windows				
Other				
Other				
Porch				
Garage				
Basement				
Exterior walls				
Yard/ landscaping				

I (we) have inspected the above facilities and agree they are in good working condition except as noted.

_____ (Tenant)

_____ (Tenant)   ——————— (Landlord/Agent)

in, what went out in expenses. For additional fees, some agents will provide overall tax preparation and accounting assistance for you and your family.

The service packages property-management firms offer vary from area to area, so shop around before signing up with any one organization. Make sure the lease the firm uses covers at the very least all the areas discussed above. Ask for references and phone numbers of current investor/clients who own houses like yours, and talk to them about the performance of the firm.

If your cash flow can take the additional monthly drain, sign up.

NITTY-GRITTY: ACCOUNTING AND TAXES

Whether you hire professional help or not, you ought to have more than a passing familiarity with two essential elements in any successful rental-house investment plan. You've got to keep accurate, complete *accounting of* every transaction concerning your property. And you need to be conscious of the *tax implications* of your rental houses—and your tax-related options—or you'll find your anticipated gains are being whittled away.

Records. Buying an investment house means going into the residential rental business. As you would in any business venture, you should document every cent you spend—and look for ways to count cents you hadn't even thought about. For example, there may be travel (17¢ a mile for the first 15,000 miles), parking, meals, lodging and entertainment costs associated with acquiring, rehabilitating, renting out or operating a property, and they're all deductible if you've kept records. Many investors forget to keep track of the little expenses that can add up dramatically—the signs you bought for rental display, the portion of your telephone bill attributable to your rental business, market-research costs, subscriptions, books, dues, duplicating fees, licenses, and so forth. You can't deduct the value of your time, but there are scads of seemingly insignificant items you shouldn't ignore.

The biggest cost items—loan-commitment fees, appraisals,

mortgage payments, taxes, property inspections—are hard to miss, but still need to be carefully documented.

Accounting. You can be your own in-house professional accountant (not recommended for nonaccountants), or you can engage a CPA for periodic or year-end duty. If you do the latter —and most investors prefer this course—your responsibility becomes one of maintaining relatively simple ledgers and receipts of rental income versus expenditures.

Methods vary, but the easiest resembles a checkbook record-keeping system. You note dates of receipts (rents) or expenditures and the check number involved, and maintain a file for the actual documents, bills, paid checks, and so forth. Once a month—or once a quarter, if you've got just one or two houses to worry about—go over the books and make sure you're not missing anything. At the end of the tax year you hand over your books and files to your accountant, who'll figure how it all stacks up for the IRS. Large accounting firms will enter all the key data on each of your properties into a computer program, with such items as depreciation schedules, capital improvements and noncapital maintenance and repairs toted up individually year by year.

Taxes: Financing. Your concern with taxes should begin back at the time you select your financing method for acquisition of the property. The amount of *interest* you pay your lender is of obvious importance because every cent of it will be deductible against other income on your federal tax return. The higher the proportion on interest payments in your overall monthly debt service, the greater the deductions, since principal payments aren't deductible. Hence your debt service on a five-year interest-only loan is 100 percent deductible; the balloon payment of principal at the end, of course, isn't. Your lender or your accountant should provide you with a statement of the interest, principal and tax components of your mortgage payments at the end of the year.

Your ancillary financing costs at the time of obtaining your loan will generally be treated by the IRS as *capital costs* attribu-

table to the acquisition of the property. Items such as placement
fees, points, appraisal charges, legal fees, property inspection fees,
title examination and insurance premiums are in effect tacked
on the overall *tax basis* of the house, to be amortized year by
year as discussed below. One notable exception to this involves
legitimate *standby fees* charged by lenders for the service of
reserving funds for your loan at the time of commitment. The
IRS views such fees as business expenses, fully deductible in the
year they occurred, as long as you can demonstrate that the fees
do not constitute advance interest payments, like points.

Taxes: Depreciation. In tax terms, your investment in real
estate is an acquisition of a capital asset. That asset is viewed
as having a limited life span for its economic use. Like a machine in a factory that gradually wears out in efficiency and has
to be replaced, your investment house (unlike your personal
residence*) is assumed to be deteriorating economically year
by year. That may strike you as bizarre in a market where prices
for existing dwellings keep spiraling year after year, but there
is sense to it. Many real estate properties do in fact deteriorate
significantly over time; many become obsolescent—unsupport-
able economically in their original use, too costly to maintain
or to convert to another use—and are knocked down. Demoli-
tions and other losses, as annual housing surveys of the Census
Bureau and the Department of Housing and Urban Development indicate, remove 1 percent of the national building stock
in some years.

In any event, for federal tax purposes, buildings and the
capital improvements inside them depreciate annually; land
doesn't. This recognition of depreciation, even in a structure
that is gaining sharply in actual market value, provides one of
the prime attractions of rental houses to you as an investor. It
offers a way to shelter your regular income from taxation at

---

* Duplexes and other multi-unit properties where the owner uses one
unit as principal residence require proportional treatment for depreciation
purposes. If you live in one unit of your three-unit rental building, you can
depreciate only two-thirds of the property, and deduct only two-thirds of
the operating costs of the building as attributable to your rental business.

your usual high rates, and to recoup part of what you've sunk into a building by taking a paper loss on the property's assumed trek toward obsolescence. It is the true alchemy of real estate investing: it enables you to turn ordinary income into capital gains, taxable at two-fifths of your normal rate at some point in the future.

"Basis." You can't begin to figure out your depreciation losses with a building until you determine how much in capital costs you've actually got tied up in the structure exposed to loss— or what IRS calls your tax "basis." Here are the four steps to calculating this extremely important number:

First, take the *sales price* (the cash you paid plus the principal debt you incurred).

Second, add all associated *acquisition costs* (for example, title, attorney's fees, broker's fees, appraisal, property inspection, survey, any option costs, taxes, placement fees, points, etc.).

Third, add all *capital improvements* made by you to the property following acquisition.

Finally, subtract any depreciation that you've already claimed (in the case of a building you've owned more than one tax year).

The net figure you arrive at will be your basis for tax purposes. Take the following case. Say you purchase an investment duplex for $61,000, pay $10,000 cash and obtain a $51,000 first mortgage. You also pay $1,350 in closing, points, tax and other acquisition costs. And you add a new first-floor bathroom prior to rental at a cost of $2,500. Your basis at that point in the tax year would be as follows:

$10,000 cash
51,000 first trust
1,350 acquisition costs
2,500 improvements
─────────
$64,850 basis

Basis is a key number for not only annual depreciation, but later for calculations of capital gains or losses.

Expenses versus Capital Improvements. When is an expense merely an expense, and when is it a capital improvement? You're likely to find yourself—and your accountant—pondering this question at least once a year, however experienced a real estate investor you may be. Expenses can be *deducted* 100 percent in the year they occur; capital improvements must be depreciated over their life. Anyone owning rental property is naturally tempted to see the world as a succession of deductible expenditures essential to the conduct of one's business, but tax auditors tend to see everything you as an owner do as a capital improvement to your property.

You must therefore keep up, through your accountant or other professional help, with current case law and IRS rulings on this subject. In general, anything you do to or for your property that materially or substantially prolongs its useful economic life, permanently adds to its value, requires a building permit or cannot be considered by any stretch of the imagination as routine maintenance is a capital improvement. Everything else in the way of operating, marketing, maintaining or repairing the property is a business expense—and 100 percent deductible.

How does that work out in practice? Let's take some typical expenditures.

• Repairing a small light fixture or patching a few wall cracks after a tenant's lease expires are clearly routine operating expenses. Deduct them. Rewiring a substantial portion of a house's electric system or replacing entire walls are definitely capital improvements. They get added to your tax basis and amortized.

• Filling holes in the asphalt driveway or the concrete sidewalk, repairing termite damage, plugging leaks, removing dead trees, and doing ordinary repainting or redecorating can all be construed as routine maintenance. Laying an entire new driveway or installing a new sidewalk cannot.

• Utility charges not paid by tenants, property taxes, transfer taxes imposed by states or localities, insurance, replacement of windowpanes, advertising costs, travel, stationery and forms, cleaning, hauling, rental management charges, pool fees, and maintenance are all in the deductible category. Major repairs on the roof, installation of central air conditioning, a new hot-water heater, new kitchen counters or cabinets, a bathroom addition, conversion of a basement to a recreation or family room, and installation of new piping or a heat pump are not.

• There are still a lot of gray areas here. How big a crack in the wall does it have to be to become a capital item and not a routine repair? Where is the dividing line between a major roof job and a minor one? To some extent these and many other items you face are judgment calls. To some extent they're dependent on how prepared you are to stick your neck out and defend your position in the event of an audit. If you want excitement in your life, expense everything away. The worst that can happen is that the IRS will ask for its taxes plus a little interest. If you prefer not to be bothered with frequent audits, capitalize and depreciate.

Useful Life. Before you can depreciate, you also have to decide how fast your property is actually or theoretically falling apart. What is its useful or economic life to you as an investor? How long will it fulfill the function for which you bought it? What will the net salvage value be—if any—after it reaches the end of its economic life?

Under the IRS's "asset depreciation range" rules, most new residential properties are assumed to have a forty- to forty-five-year life span, but arguments can be successfully made for a shorter life. Used, resale houses are assumed to have shorter economic lives, but you will find it difficult to convince the IRS that your building has less than twenty years' life, or a shorter life than your mortgage term. After all, why are you buying it if it's that far gone?

On resale units, figure the economic life to be twenty to thirty years; on new units, ten to fifteen years more. Obviously, you have an incentive to show a lower life span because you'll be able to deduct a higher percentage of its value per year. If you reckon that your $70,000 farm ranch house has a remaining life of twenty years, you'll be taking off 5 percent of its value (minus land and salvage) a year. Depending on how you calculate land and salvage, that could be as high as $3,000 a year—assuming a $10,000 lot and no salvage. That $3,000, applied as an offset against your regular income, could mean $1,500 in direct savings.

Land and Salvage. What is the worth of the lot under the building you buy? For depreciation purposes it's better to have less value attributable to the land and more to the structure. Townhouses and condominiums usually maximize this advantage; tiny houses on large lots in expensive neighborhoods minimize it. The IRS will go along with reasonable estimates, consistent with local market appraisal data they may consult. (One bit of data they may look at is the local property tax bill for the year in which you purchased your rental property. The appraisal sheet will assign specific percentages of value to the land and to the improvement.) If you want to be absolutely safe, check with an appraiser or your accountant. In some areas, allocating 20 percent of the cost to the land may be as low as you can stretch it. In other areas, 5 to 10 percent may be acceptable. In still others, 35 percent or higher may be required.

Salvage value is subject to even wider variation. Many accountants and investors admit they simply have no idea what a property will be worth in the next century and assign no salvage value at all. Others assume there will always be some residual value to the bricks or lumber and assign a token figure, like $2,000 or $3,000. What the figure does, of course, is to set a floor under which you can't depreciate further and cut the annual deductions proportionately. If your $70,000 home is given a $4,000 salvage estimate and $10,000 land value, the base from which you depreciate will be $46,000, rather than $60,000. Generally speaking, the IRS won't challenge your omission of a salvage value if you've chosen a reasonable economic life for the property for depreciation purposes.

Depreciation Methods. There are three principal ways you can calculate the rate of depreciation on your property. One way, known appropriately as "straight line," is simple and logical. The other two are more complicated, but via accelerated depreciation, provide you with larger deductions in the early years of ownership.

Straight Line. If you decide that twenty years is a reasonable estimate for your building's remaining life, the most obvious way to figure annual depreciation is on a fixed percentage basis. Every year the property depreciates one-twentieth, or 5 percent.

A quadruplex with a forty-year life depreciates one-fortieth per year, or 2½ percent. You multiply the percentage against the initial dollar value or tax basis (less land and salvage) and arrive at an annual deduction. In the case of a $60,000 building ($10,000 land, $50,000 structure, no salvage, twenty-five-year life), you deduct $2,000 (.04 × $50,000) in depreciation the first year and every year thereafter through the final year.

Declining Balance. Since it can be argued that such assets as real estate, automobiles and other machinery tend to wear out faster during the early years of their service and more slowly later on, IRS permits taxpayers to use depreciation methods reflecting this. Probably the most commonly used in the rental one- to four-unit dwelling field are variations of the declining-balance (DB) approach. The three DB options permitted by IRS involve multiplication of straight-line deductions by a factor—125 percent, 150 percent, or 200 percent—to accelerate depreciation in the initial years. They require subtraction of each annual deduction from the depreciation base, with no adjustment for salvage value. And unlike straight line, they always result in some remaining balance—built-in salvage value—at the end of the depreciation schedule.

Here's how it works. Take the case of the $60,000 house with $10,000 in land value and no salvage value.

First- and Second-Year Deductions

Useful Life	Straight Line	125 Percent DB	150 Percent DB	200 Percent DB
25 years	4 percent ($2,000)	5 percent ($2,500)	6 percent ($3,000)	8 percent ($4,000)
	4 percent ($2,000)	5 percent ($2,375)	6 percent ($2,820)	8 percent ($3,680)

To calculate the second-year depreciation under the declining balance approaches, you must subtract the previous depreciation from the value base. So in the case of 125 percent declining balance, you would now be depreciating a $47,500 property ($50,000 minus $2,500 taken); multiply that base by the 5 percent factor, and you get a second-year depreciation deduction of $2,375. This is still more than the $2,000 you'd have deducted under straight line. Using the 150 percent approach, the second-year deduction would be $2,820 ($47,000 × .06); and using 200 percent it would be $3,680 ($46,000 × .08).

Tables can be worked up showing the relative deduction sizes you can get via these alternative computations. For simplicity's sake, let's say that it may be to your advantage to take as much depreciation early on as you can. Although some of it may be "recaptured" later by IRS when you dispose of the property (as will be discussed below), you may be able to minimize it. In the meantime, you achieve tax shelter for your present income, deferring any reckoning with Uncle Sam. At some later date, all sorts of other options may be open to you—tax-free exchanges, refinancing or installment sales, to name just three. Better to hold on to your money now and plan your later strategies than pay it out today.

Now the bad news. The 200 percent declining-balance method is available only on new residential rental property where you are the first user. A resale rental house would qualify only for 125 percent declining balance treatment, and then only if its economic life is at least twenty years.

Sum-of-the-Years'-Digits. This, the most complicated of the three basic approaches, is also limited by the IRS to use solely in connection with new rental residential properties. Under this method, the building value base remains the same during the depreciation schedule (e.g., $60,000 every year as in the straight-line computation above), but the depreciation rate is substantially higher in the early years compared with the later years. The rate is arrived at by adding up the digits in a depreciation period. For a ten-year economic life that would mean $1 + 2 + 3 + 4 + 5 + 6 + 7 + 8 + 9 + 10 = 55$. Then you take the final digit (10) and make it the numerator (top figure) of a fraction: 10/55 or 2/11 (18.8 percent). You multiply your base value by that fraction ($60,000 × 18.18 = $10,908) to get your first-year deduction. The next year the fraction is 9/55, the following year 8/55, and so forth.

This approach spins out depreciation and tax shelter very fast during the first five to six years, but then slows down rapidly after that. Since IRS allows you to switch your depreciation method once during a holding period (and only from an accelerated method to straight line), you could change from sum-of-the-years'-digits to straight line some time after the fifth year, according to your tax-shelter needs.

Component versus Composite Depreciation. An effective method of stepping up depreciation is to put your building on one depreciation schedule—say, twenty-five to thirty years—but its major components on shorter, more realistic schedules. The walls, floor and basic shell structure of your rental house, for example, may have a life expectancy of at least thirty years. But what about the $3,000 central air conditioner you installed? And that new heat pump? Or the electrical rewiring you did last year? Or the new roof you installed at a cost of $1,500? They're not likely to last thirty years. In fact, some of them may need replacement within ten years. Rather than lumping them in with the life expectancy of the building shell—bricks and mortar—break them into components.

First, consult IRS Guide No. 534, "Tax Information on Depreciation," and talk to your accountant. Then consider assigning each an estimated economic life—for example, ten years to the roof, eight to ten years to the air conditioning system, fifteen years to the plumbing, ten years to the heating system, fifteen years to the wiring (or whatever is realistic that you can defend). In the case of new components with an economic life of at least three years, you can use accelerated depreciation methods, like 200 percent declining balance. If you choose to be more conservative, you can assign all your improvements an average economic life span (say, ten to twelve years), and depreciate them at 125 percent declining balance. That will still produce significantly larger depreciation deductions up front, but will be less likely to raise eyebrows and trigger an audit from IRS.

Depreciation Recapture. You can't take thousands of dollars in tax-sheltering depreciation "losses" against your income year after year and then turn around and sell your building at double its original cost and think the IRS is going to smile benignly at your financial wizardry. All depreciation you take that turns out, upon disposition of the property, to have been unwarranted or excessive must be considered taxable profit. If you depreciated your $75,000 duplex to a point where your basis was $50,000 and you sold it for $90,000, obviously you misjudged how fast the building was deteriorating. You made a profit of $40,000 in the IRS's eyes. If your depreciation was on a straight-line schedule, the IRS will treat your profit as a capital gain; that means you can have 60 percent of the profit tax-free, and be taxed on the other 40 percent at your regular income-tax rate. Not bad at all.

If, however, your depreciation was on an accelerated basis and it turns out to be excessive, the IRS gets a bit stickier. It allows you capital gains treatment of profits derived from depreciation on a straight-line approach; anything *beyond* that gets taxed at your ordinary income-tax rate. Say the $75,000 duplex above had been depreciated to a $40,000 basis, using an accelerated method, and was sold for $90,000. In the IRS's view, your deductions, to the extent they were excessive, should have been confined to straight-line depreciation, leaving you with a $50,000 basis and a $40,000 profit. Instead, you've ended up with a $40,000 basis and a $50,000 profit. IRS will allow the favorable capital gains treatment (discussed above) on the $40,000. But the extra $10,000 will get hit with your ordinary tax rate. In other words, if your rate is 50 percent, IRS will take $5,000 of the $10,000; if you're in the 40 percent bracket, $4,000.

This doesn't mean you shouldn't use accelerated depreciation techniques. On the contrary, use them to shelter your income according to your needs and objectives, but prepare ahead for the time you dispose of the property. Consider the options open to you to reduce or indefinitely postpone taxation on your gains. Take a look at Chapter 10 for a discussion of the most important techniques.

Tax Classification of Your Investments. Be aware that the IRS will not automatically consider your rental investment activities worthy of capital gains treatment. If you normally hold your properties for over a year and use them as part of what can be shown to be an ongoing rental business, don't worry. You fall within the definition of Section 1231 of the Internal Revenue Code and will be accorded capital gains treatment on the profits you derive from sales of your capital assets, your properties. You will be taxed at ordinary rates only on your net rental profits, and you can deduct all operating and business expenses.

If, however, you buy and resell a number of houses in quick succession—even while holding others for a year or more—watch out. You may be construed as being a dealer, a person whose primary business is selling property to customers. In that capacity, the gains you make on sales will be viewed as ordinary income from sales of your business stock and will not qualify as capital gains. This is one of the touchiest areas in real estate tax law, and constantly causes conflict between investors and the IRS. As an active investor, you may come upon opportunities for purchase and quick turnaround—such as in central-city properties in a suddenly booming neighborhood—where you buy and sell several houses in a matter of months at high profits. IRS may not only seek to tax those profits at ordinary rates but begin questioning other transactions you have underway.

Consult tax or legal counsel before getting too deeply into a potential dealer situation—unless, of course, you're doing so well at dealing you can stand the high tax rates.

WHEN TO SELL, WHEN TO HOLD

How long should you hang on to your rental houses? How many should you buy? When should you unload them? The answers depend entirely on your investment objectives and on what you're trying to get out of particular properties.

If you are very concerned about precise percentage returns on your dollar, you can construct cash flow and yield progressions that will tell you the most favorable year to sell a particular house, when its investment yield to you peaks and begins to drop. Generally, rental houses should be held for at least three to five years to enable them to generate maximum returns. Five to seven years is a common holding period. Selling before that point entails high transfer costs—broker's fees, taxes, settlement charges—that tend to offset whatever the house may have gained in market value.

Of course if you can control any of the big costs, such as selling the property yourself without a broker, or passing on some of the closing expenses to the buyer, selling early won't hurt you as much. Or if you've got a property that has appreciated extremely rapidly, you may want to cash out regardless of the short-term cost, since the net will be so large.

Many rental-home investors build up *portfolios* of properties unit by unit, retaining most of them and selling off old ones when advantageous. A common strategy is to *pyramid* holdings by refinancings of sales when equity positions grow large. If, for example, you bought a property several years ago for $38,000 with a $30,000 first trust that is now paid down to $26,000, take a hard look at what you've got. The house may now have a market value of $50,000 to $60,000, and your equity position may be in the neighborhood of $24,000 to $34,000. Why not refinance your mortgage—say, to $50,000 to $54,000 if your lender will agree to it—and use the net proceeds to buy two more rental houses? Two or three years later these houses in turn become potential sources of still more capital, via refinancing or second mortgage, for still more purchases. The pyramid can also work using proceeds of sales to purchase multiple new units.

Once your equity buildup, via inflation and principal amortization, goes beyond 20 to 25 percent, you should begin thinking of getting your money out and investing further. After all, it's tax-free, and it can be turned into new shelters to beat inflation and build capital. And that is the whole ball game.

3

Second Trusts and Mortgages

America's boom in rental homes is paralleled by only one other real estate phenomenon of the late 1970s: residential second-trust deeds and mortgages bought, sold and held by sharp investors for annual yields of 10 to 24 percent. Although relatively unknown to the general public, hundreds of millions of dollars' worth of second-trust notes—"paper real estate"—change hands across the United States annually. The *Wall Street Journal* cited one estimate that in California alone $500 million worth of seconds were originated or traded in 1977 by professional brokers, up from $200 million in 1973. That doesn't count the millions generated by individual investors and other unregulated lenders. California is undoubtedly the single largest market for these investments, but dozens of other states and metropolitan areas have flourishing markets. In the tristate Washington, D.C., area, for example, trust and mortgage brokers estimate that one category of notes alone—hard money seconds—account for over $5 million a month in average underwriting volume. A second category, known as deferred purchase money trusts, commonly used by rental-home investors and some home buyers, may account for another $2 million a month.

Spurred by the nation's steady high appreciation rates on single-family houses—plus favorable state laws relating to foreclosure and usury—tens of thousands of investors are buying notes secured by residential real estate in their locales. The notes range from $5,000 on up and offer pretax returns that begin in the 10 percent range. Buyers include white-collar employees who have savings or extra funds to invest; professional speculators who borrow money from commercial banks at regular rates and buy mortgages that return nearly twice the bank rate; real estate brokers; high-income professionals; and investment clubs. Some of the investors are large pension funds and other financial institutions who use such notes to improve the overall yield of their portfolios. Many in California are individuals with Keogh tax-deferred retirement plans, and corporations fed up with low 5 to 5½ percent bank and S&L rates on their idle cash. Many buyers in California and elsewhere invest in other real estate and know the tremendous advantages of high-yield loans secured by prime housing.

Sellers of notes are also diverse. In California, there is a well-developed industry, complete with its own trade association, to produce trust deed notes for sale to investors. You walk into a branch office such as Allstate Equity Investment Corporation of America in San José, or Bonded Home Loans Company in Los Angeles, and choose from among the firms' current stock of notes, all bearing 10 percent face rates, the highest permissible under state usury laws. In Miami, Washington, D.C., and other cities, the trading network is less formal. Real estate brokers often sell second trusts as a sideline venture incidental to closing home transactions. Most cities have a few highly specialized loan brokers—generally listed in the yellow pages and classifieds under "mortgages" or "second trusts"—who originate loans for large investors and buy seconds for their own accounts.

In such states as New Jersey, Arizona, Kansas and Massachusetts, the largest second-loan originators retain virtually all loans for their own portfolios. New Jersey's multi-branch Money Store, for example, has lent out over $120 million in seconds and has continued to service and own most of these notes, as would a bank.

What *are* second trusts and mortgages? How does one begin to invest in them? What are their advantages and what are their risks?

A second trust or mortgage* is a loan secured by real estate that is junior to a first trust or mortgage. Should the owner of the mortgaged property default in his payments to the primary (first-trust) lender—typically a savings and loan association or a bank—the first lender (or the trustee) can foreclose and auction off the property. In dividing the proceeds of the sale, the debt to the first lender must be paid off before the claim of the holder of the second trust can be paid. If the sale produces only enough cash to pay the first (or senior) lender, it's tough luck for the holder of the second-trust note. He may have to seek a legal judgment against the borrower to force payment of the loan from the borrower's other assets, if any.

Most of the popularly traded second loans fall into one of two categories. In one type, an owner of mortgaged property needs additional cash for business or personal use—say, $20,000 to rehabilitate a row house in the city or to start a small store. The owner approaches a lender and requests a second mortgage, using his home as security. Say the home's estimated market value is $80,000 and the owner has an unpaid principal balance of $40,000 on the first mortgage. If his credit is otherwise good, he should be able to get a second mortgage of $20,000, secured by the equity in the house. This is known as a "hard-money" loan or a "business-purpose" second. Such mortgages and trusts are not considered in the consumer category and sidestep usury limits in some states. Rates can range from 10 to 18 percent on up, depending upon the length of the repayment schedule, loan-to-value exposure, the purpose of the loan, and local statutory restrictions.

A second category is the deferred-purchase-money trust or mortgage. Most often, these are employed in home-purchase transactions when the buyer doesn't have enough money to cover the cash requirements between his purchase price and the

---

* For the sake of simplicity, the terms "mortgage" and "deed of trust" are used interchangeably here. One or both are in common use in every state. However, there are important distinctions between mortgages and deeds of trust, which will be outlined later in the chapter.

maximum first mortgage he can get from a lender. Take the case of a $50,000 house sale in your community. A local S&L agrees to make a $35,000 loan on the property, but the prospective purchaser has only $10,000 available for his down payment. Where does the missing $5,000 come from? Often the seller of the house will agree to "take back" a second trust—in this case, one for $5,000.

The seller in effect lends the buyer a portion of the sale price at terms and interest rates that may be more favorable than those called for by the first mortgage, or steeper, depending upon the negotiations between the two parties. The seller can hold on to the second mortgage for the five years or so of its term, or can, as is very common, immediately turn around and sell it at a discount through a broker or realty agent.

Discounting is the fuel that powers the second-mortgage business. It produces those high yields attractive to the ultimate investor. To continue with the $5,000 note example: the original terms may have called for flat payments of $50 a month ($10 per $1,000 of face value) for five years at 8 percent interest, with a balloon payment of the remainder at the end of five years. In dollar terms, this $5,000 note would be worth $6,825 after all payments were made ($50 times 60 months is $3,000; balloon payment including interest is $3,825). As an investment for the seller, this isn't bad, but he may want to dispose of it to raise immediate cash. So he sells it to another investor.

Here is where discounting comes in. The going market for such a loan may be a price of anywhere from 75¢ to 85¢ per $1 of face value. So a $5,000 note might sell for 79¢ on the dollar, or $3,950. The new owner of the note—the individual investor—would stand to earn $6,825 on his purchase for the next five years, $2,875 of it gross profit. The average annual yield over the course of the five years to this investor would be 14.7 percent: $570 per year average profit divided by $3,950 cost.*

* *This yield does not include consideration of the time value of the money involved. The "present value" of financial return computations, used in more advanced texts but beyond the scope of this book, would lower this yield. Readers who wish to explore this further may consult Leonard Klee-man's* Handbook of Real Estate Mathematics *(Prentice-Hall, 1978).*

Yields go much higher in second trusts, rising steadily as the risks climb. In the case of business-purpose loans, the original interest rate and terms to the borrower are steep, and therefore the discounted returns can be towering. Deep-discounted yields of 25 to 28 percent are not uncommon. Prepayments of loans before their contract term is up may increase yields still further.

PROS AND CONS

The benefits of investing in second trusts are substantial. So are the potential risks. Let's look at the plus side first.

Yields. Annual, reliable returns on the dollar of 10 percent, 12 percent, 15 percent and more are feasible in seconds, putting them far beyond most competing paper investments, such as corporate bonds, certificates of deposit, and stocks. Investors can double their money every four or five years if they reinvest their earnings along with principal, and triple it in six to eight years via this continual compounding. The $20,000 you put into second trusts in 1979 could be $40,000 in 1983 and $60,000 in 1986. It's a top-notch inflation hedge. Some investors with good bank credit lines can even turn seconds into veritable money machines. They borrow cash at prime bank rates—say, 10 to 11 percent—and lend it out to yield 15 to 16 percent. Their five- to six-point "spread" is virtually all profit with no actual cash outlay on their part.

Relative Safety. Although there are distinct risks in seconds, their overall safety record in recent years has been impressive. In California's mass secondary market, for example, there were only 127 foreclosures of second trusts in 1977, equivalent to about .04 percent of the total number of seconds outstanding, by the reckoning of the state department of real estate. Some dealers in seconds guarantee purchasers of trusts that they will buy them back if they get into serious default trouble—in effect, insuring them against loss. Broker-dealers in metropolitan Washington, D.C., and other cities report that losses to investors in the past have been virtually nil, thanks in part to strong month-by-month inflation in housing values.

Liquidity. Second trusts are in such demand in many areas that selling your note can be accomplished in a couple of minutes on the phone. Some professional brokers guarantee full redemption with no discount or penalty after three years, even if the note has a term of five years. You can also use your portfolio of notes as security for borrowings on your own from banks and other lenders—or to buy real estate.

Convenience. In contrast to the time, red tape and transfer costs associated with acquiring, maintaining and selling rental homes, apartments, land and other real estate, second trusts—particularly when purchased through a reputable professional broker—can be as simple to handle as a low-yielding passbook bank account. You choose the sort of loan you want to make, examine the key property-related documents in advance, and write your check. About a month later you begin receiving your monthly payments from your borrowers. The broker periodically lets you know how much interest you've received—for federal and state income-tax purposes—and how much principal has been repaid. The broker's fees are taken care of by the borrower, not by you.

Balance to Realty Portfolio. Because second trusts provide net income flows, many real estate investors use them to produce the cash they need to cover out-of-pocket monthly cash losses on other properties, such as rental homes. A house that "loses" $100 a month, for example, can be balanced out by a $5,000 second trust that yields $100 a month in interest and principal amortization.

RISKS

The opportunities for profit with ease are seductive in seconds. But sobering realities go along with any investment offering such high yields. The higher the yield, in fact, the riskier the investment.

Defaults. Reality number one is that at any moment the nice little $10,000 trust note bought for $7,500 may make the buyer a landlord facing angry tenants, broken water pipes in the night, eviction proceedings and the police, among others. Rare though it may be, that innocent-looking speculative note may also involve you in the personal lives of total strangers—their marital spats, their financial struggles, their births, deaths and bankruptcies. And nightmares in the second-mortgage trade don't happen just to novices, but can haunt the most seasoned investors.

When borrowers default on their first and second trusts, the *second*-trust holder may have to step in, try to get the home-owners back on schedule, or even assume their payments. That can happen when husband and wife split, leaving inadequate funds to cover both mortgage payments plus a rental apartment for the spouse who moves out. Or it can happen through loss of employment by one or both spouses, injury or reckless piling up of consumer installment debts.

As the junior lien holder, *you* are second man on the totem pole in case of foreclosure. If the house sale isn't likely to produce enough to pay off the first-trust holder, plus the lawyers and real estate brokers involved in the sale, it's in your interest to do whatever is necessary to forestall such a sale and avoid a judgment action. As a result, second-trust holders often are looked to by the first-trust holder to "cure" a homeowner's defaults or to take over the property entirely.

Inadequate Underwriting. Some time-tested standards govern second trusts or mortgages all over the country. When they're not followed, through ignorance, incompetence or outright fraud, investors can lose every cent they put into a deal. For example, most professional loan brokers and experienced individual investor-lenders prefer to have a minimum 20 percent security "cushion" between the combined debt of the first and second trusts and the appraised value of the house involved. That means that the owner of a home appraised at $100,000 with a $65,000 first mortgage against it could not expect to get

more than $15,000 in the form of a second trust ($65,000 +
$15,000 = $80,000 = 80 percent of the appraised value of the
house).

The reason for the 80 percent limit is that it allows plenty
of leeway for appraisal errors (that $100,000 house might only
be worth $90,000 in the real market), unexpected local prop-
erty value decreases (for example, the county government votes
to turn the vacant farmland across the street from the $100,000
house into an eighteen-hour-a-day landfill dump, rendering the
property unsalable at anything above $80,000), undetected seri-
ous structural problems with the house requiring large repair
expenditures, or unexpected declines in the real estate market.
In any of these situations, the second-trust holder would be
exposed to potential loss if the market value of his underlying
security—the house—dropped precipitously. The 20 percent
cushion normally would be sufficient to protect both lenders
(first- and second-trust holders) from undue risk of loss, but
not all brokers or investors follow that conservative guideline.
Some are quite willing to cut the margin to 10 or even 5 percent.
The risk is far greater this way, though, and you as an investor-
buyer of notes ought to be sensitive to the increased dangers
involved. Notes secured by property with "thin" equities should
come with higher yields and deeper discounts. Otherwise, stay
clear of them. They perform well in rapidly appreciating strong
housing markets; they can be unreliable in recessionary markets.

Fraudulent   Documentation. Unsuspecting   investors   are
bilked of tens of thousands of dollars a year by fraudulent
second-trust notes unsecured by any real estate. Sometimes the
"notes" are written against a single piece of property four or
five times and sold at attractive discounts to four or five different
individuals. Investors who shell out cash without checking on
the validity of the lien at the local recorder's office or obtaining
title insurance are easy marks for mortgage-market con men.

Statutory Variations. Purchasing or making second trusts on
properties beyond your immediate state can involve additional
risks. Lending rules vary so widely from state to state that what

is legal and acceptable in one jurisdiction may be illegal in another. Prepayment clauses, usury limits on interest, licensing of loan brokers, foreclosure procedures and "redemption" rules can cut your yields or tie you up for years in court if you don't check them out in advance. The "opportunity costs" of having your dollars tied up for extended periods can wipe out your apparent profits.

Tax Treatment. Unlike other investment mediums discussed in this book, second mortgages offer no real tax shelter or favorable tax treatment. The income generated through seconds is taxable like other interest—as ordinary income at your ordinary rates rather than as capital gains. In fact, if you build up a sizable, high-income-producing portfolio of notes, you may need to acquire more tax-loss-producing real estate to shelter your new source of wealth!

GETTING INVOLVED

How deeply and rapidly you get involved with seconds depends upon your investment strategy and resources, and to some degree upon where you live. Not all metropolitan areas or states offer the combination of favorable laws and vigorous economic growth that are ideal for this form of investment. Not all jurisdictions permit the relatively high interest rates that make second mortgages such attractive investments. And not all areas of the country have real estate traditions among homeowners, buyers and brokers conducive to high volumes of junior liens. An estimated 50,000 to 60,000 Californians a year, for example, take out second or even third trusts on their houses to generate cash for investment or pleasure. An estimated one out of six homeowners in some California communities have second liens against their homes—a ratio far beyond the estimated one out of thirty owners nationally, and well beyond the estimated ratios for such active housing communities as Miami, Houston, Dallas, Phoenix, Washington, D.C., and Chicago. On the other end of the spectrum, more financially conservative areas, such as smaller communities in the Midwest and New England, produce insignificant volumes of second trusts and mortgages. In other words, the prevailing social and legal attitudes toward debt in your area may be key determinants of the opportunities open to you in junior real estate liens.

Probably your best bet for learning how active your area is in second trusts or mortgages is to check with several experienced real estate *brokers*—not real estate salespersons or associates but the brokers who employ them. Brokers are often brought into housing-sale transactions involving special wrinkles, such as junior financing, to make them "go." Brokers stay in touch with individuals, generally higher-income clients or referrals whom they know are interested in buying high-quality "purchase-money" seconds at discounts. And many brokers buy and hold second trusts for themselves. If there are any seconds to be had locally—either purchase-money or hard-money loans— you can be sure the top brokers in your city know about them. So do title and escrow companies, and active real estate attorneys.

Usury Limits. An important factor in the volume and nature of second-loan activity in any state is the prevailing limit on interest rates, or usury ceiling. States with low ceilings for most categories of real estate loans, such as New York (9½ percent), tend to generate lower volumes of seconds and also tend to be short of capital for first mortgages during tight-mortgage-money periods in the national economy. States with more competitive limits (such as 10 percent in California, 12 percent in Arizona, and 18 percent in Utah) tend to be more fertile for investors. There are exceptions to this rule, of course. High usury ceilings on their own don't guarantee a good market. For instance, Massachusetts allows second mortgages to be written at 18 percent annual interest, and many loans carry that high rate. But Boston's market in seconds is far quieter than the market in seconds in small cities in California, where the limit is 8 points lower, or even in northern Virginia, where the limit is 10 points lower for consumers. The reasons are those stated above, plus the added factors of high property taxes in Massachusetts as a whole and lower than average growth rates for real-property values.

Deeds of Trust versus Mortgages. In states where deeds of
trust are more common than mortgages,* you're likely to find
a much greater volume of second liens available for purchase,
because deeds of trust carry inherent advantages for investors.
The fundamental difference between a mortgage and a deed
of trust (also known as a trust deed or simply a trust) is that
in a mortgage only two parties are involved (lender and borrower), whereas in a trust there are three (lender, borrower,
and an intermediary called the trustee). A deed of trust con-
veys title to or interest in real property to the intermediary
(often an individual or a corporation, like a title company),
who holds the title as security on behalf of the lender. An accompanying promissory note specifies the debt and the terms of
the debt. The trustee simply transfers the title to the borrower,
via a deed of reconveyance or release deed, when the debt is
fully paid to the lender and the note returned. The form and
language of a trust deed are basically the same all over the United
States (thus their widespread salability).

If a borrower defaults by missing a payment, the trustee is
empowered to (a) record a notice of default in the county
recorder's office; (b) announce to the public, via published
notice, that an auction of the property will be held on a specified
date; and (c) pay the lender the debt with the proceeds of the
auction. The *power of sale* that comes with the trust deed permits a relatively rapid, inexpensive foreclosure upon default.
From an investor's or a lender's point of view, this *nonjudicial
foreclosure remedy* and the *lack of a statutory redemption
period* for the defaulted borrower to reacquire his property are
extremely important when the loan goes sour. They guarantee
swift, final disposition of the property and payment of the note.
In California, for instance, trust-deed holders can expect sale
of the defaulted property within about four months.

A mortgage, in contrast, often entails legal complexities for
the lender beyond those of a trust deed. The mortgage usually
does not carry a power of sale, and in most states is covered by
a statutory redemption period ranging from six months (in

* Use of deeds of trust and mortgages generally is determined by state
law and local real estate custom. Many states permit the use of either; a
few states allow only one.

South Dakota) to thirty-six months (in Rhode Island). The time and costs of foreclosing mortgages in some states could wipe out your returns as a noteholder.

Nonetheless, second mortgages can yield just as much income and be just as solid investments as second trusts. The thousands of banks, credit unions and other lenders who make them coast-to-coast to the tune of $2 to $3 billion a year certainly think so. As an investor in mortgages, you've simply got to recognize, as the professionals do, the added risks you take on when you buy a junior lien with a long redemption period and no power of sale by a third party.

BUYING YOUR FIRST NOTE

In California the beginning investor in seconds probably has the most favorable situation in the country. Not only is there a highly organized and highly regulated group of lenders who produce large volumes of loans, but their investment packages tend to be easy to understand, uniform and very safe. Since the majority of you readers, however, don't intend to invest in California real estate, what are the typical first steps to buying a note elsewhere in the country?

Your first opportunity to purchase a second trust or mortgage will probably come via a real estate broker (or attorney), as noted above. The note will more than likely be a purchase-money second that originated in the course of selling a home. A broker may call you up, for instance, and tell you he's got a $10,000 second trust for sale at a discount that will yield you 16 percent a year. The note was made seven months ago, he says, by a locally employed husband and wife, and is secured by a piece of prime local real estate—their home in a fine neighborhood of your town. The broker suggests you come down to his office and take a look at some documents he's got on the note, and mentions that he's alerting other interested investors as well.

What criteria do you use in judging the broker's offer? What are the essentials of a good purchase-money second-trust note and the prudent steps for any prospective buyer of a note? Let's run through them.

The Broker. The first question on your list ought to concern the middleman in the note transaction—in this case, the realty broker. What do you know about him or his firm? Do they have a longstanding, first-rate reputation in your community— a reputation the broker would be loath to damage by palming off a bad loan to an investor? Do you know other individuals who have successfully purchased a note through him? What compensation, if any, does he stand to receive in the deal? (Some real estate brokers, in contrast to professional loan brokers, perform this matchmaking service gratis, to help a client or a salesperson. Others take the cash equivalent of a portion of the discount on the note—for example, three percentage points of an eighteen-point discount.) What connection, if any, does the broker have with the original lender on the note? If you're dealing with a marginal fly-by-nighter who is looking for a sizable, quick commission, you stand a much greater risk of buying trouble. A pillar of the local real estate or legal community, on the other hand, is a much better bet.

The Borrower(s). The broker referred to a working couple as the "makers" of the note; the couple, in other words, bought their house with not one mortgage but two. Who *are* these individuals? What do they do for a living? What are their salaries and other income? How long have they been employed locally, and how long have they lived in the community? Why did they not put more equity into the house when they purchased it? Was it simply a shortage of cash? Or are they rental-home investors looking for and getting high-leverage, low-cash residential property deals? How well have they performed thus far (in terms of payments) on the note for sale? Who is the primary (first-trust or mortgage) lender on the property, and how well has the couple done in meeting that lender's payment deadlines? How thinly are the borrowers stretched in other financial areas? Do they pay their non-real estate debts in timely fashion?

A good broker will have most or all the answers to these questions on hand. Ideally, you should see a credit report on the borrower before going ahead. Sometimes, however, only a fact sheet covering most of these key points will be available, with the promise of an acceptable credit report prior to the closing of the sale. If you're dealing with a reputable middleman, that should be sufficient.

Why all the concern about the makers of the note? After all, you might think, the property will be there as security for the loan; if necessary I can always foreclose and be paid in full. But you don't really want the hassles of late payments, penalties, defaults or foreclosure. Far wiser to turn down borrowers who are skating on thin financial ice and wait for more solid customers.

The Property. The centerpiece of your prospective investment is the house that serves as collateral for the note. If it's got inherent problems—because of location, structural soundness, underappraisal, or declining market appeal—your actual security may be less than the amount of the note. To judge accurately whether the underlying property offers you full protection against loss, consider the following while analyzing the loan package:

1. Is the appraisal report by an independent professional fee appraiser, and does it indicate that the property's current value is well in excess of the combined first and second trusts? Is there *at least* a 10 to 15 percent equity cushion on the part of the borrower for your margin of safety? (Purchase-money seconds on investment properties, such as rental homes, should be analyzed with special care. As was discussed in Chapter 2, some popular investment techniques involve combined trusts or mortgages that may *exceed* the real market value of the house, in the expectation that inflation will quickly fill in the gap. That's fine for the rental-house investor, but it presents an added risk for you as a trust-deed purchaser. Note also that nonowner-occupant rental property may be exposed to greater likelihood of damage, or poor upkeep, which may affect the value of security over a period of years.)

2. Are you *personally* familiar with the neighborhood in which the property is located? Is it a rapidly developing, quick-growth area where market appreciation will indeed cover up

any appraisal errors, or is it a stagnant neighborhood, where growth rates are glacial?

3. How does the property's value stack up against prevailing average sales prices in the neighborhood? Remember, as noted in Chapter 2, high-cost properties in low-cost neighborhoods are inevitably held back by the midgets around them. (Reviewing the rental home/neighborhood analysis criteria on pp. 30ff would be a good idea, too. For instance, you ought to make absolutely certain there are no public projects or plans in store for the immediate vicinity that could depress the value of the house.)

4. Don't rely on the photograph accompanying the appraisal report. Drive by the property and inspect it yourself. Look at it as potential real estate of your own—it just might turn out to be that, in the event of default.

"Seasoning." Buy "used" notes if you can rather than brand-new ones, because then you will know better what you're getting. The longer a loan has run toward its maturity without default, the safer it is. Loan brokers call this a note's "seasoning." A well-seasoned note—say, a seven-year trust deed that has already run for three years—carries a lower risk for the purchaser than a green thirty-day-old note. In the former case, not only do you know that the makers have a history of on-time payments, but you also know that their property has probably appreciated enough to provide a thick equity cushion for your protection. In the latter case, you can't be so sure.

Terms. Every trust note carries a bundle of terms with it—amount of loan, pay-back method, interest rate, and so forth—all of which have important bearing on its market value and on its specific value to you as an investor. Terms that deviate from accepted norms in the local or national marketplace almost always *reduce* the attractiveness of the note; a high degree of conformity to those norms improves the note, making it more salable in the event you need to turn it into dollars. A note with a face principal value of $10,000 may "sell" for only $5,500—55

percent of its actual value—because its terms aren't adequate
for the going market. On the other hand, a note with a similar
face value may sell at only a small discount—say, 4 to 5 percent
—because its terms offer a low-risk good deal for investors.*

Here are the key loan terms to scrutinize before buying a
purchase-money second trust:

1. Size of loan. Purchase-money seconds ranging from $5,000
to $25,000 constitute the most easily salable notes. Anything
much below $5,000 isn't worth the trouble for most investors;
anything much beyond $25,000 has a smaller market of potential
buyers and will probably require a steeper discount than the
norm. There are no limits on the size of trusts, however, that
a seller of a house may agree to provide to a buyer. In the case
of expensive residential properties, you may encounter $30,000,
$40,000 and larger notes that are in most respects highly at-
tractive, solid investments. Don't turn your nose up at them.
Size alone shouldn't be the determinant of whether you buy or
not—with the exception of the tiny under-$5,000 class of loans.

2. Length of pay-back period. Here again the range of terms
you find in purchase-money seconds will astonish you. As discussed in Chapter 2, purchase-money seconds are "deal-makers"
in home transactions. A seller may be so eager to get rid of his
house—or so poorly counseled—that he offers the buyer a large
second with a pay-back period comparable to a first trust. When
that noteholder (the home-seller) turns around and seeks to
sell it for cash, however, he'll find that few second-trust investors
are interested in a note that matures in twenty-five years. The
desired norm, in fact, is far below that—three to seven years.
Notes carrying substantially longer terms go for lower prices
and larger discounts. On the weakness of its long pay-back
period alone, a twenty-five-year purchase-money second might

---

* Notes in this regard are virtually identical to their financial marketplace distant cousins, corporate and tax-exempt bonds. Low-interest-rate,
long-term bonds of financially weak cities suffer as investments during
periods of high market interest rates. The discounts necessary for their
resale get bigger and their prices get lower in order to provide new buyers
of those bonds the yields they need for current conditions. Triple A bonds
with high-interest-rate, in contrast, require little discounting in a high-
interest-rate market. They are the safest, best alternatives around, and their
prices reflect their superior terms.

start out with a thirty-point discount (i.e., a $10,000 note would bring only $7,000). Any other unfavorable terms would depress its cash value even further.

3. Type of pay-back. Purchase-money notes generally employ one of three pay-back formats: direct amortization of principal and interest; interest only, with a balloon principal payment at the end; or a mixed schedule of partial principal and interest pay-backs, followed by a balloon payment of the remaining principal. All three are acceptable; none *in itself* determines the value of a note in the market. But certain types of amortization make more sense for certain investors.

Direct Amortization. If you want your money back fast, this may be the choice for you. Here you are in the position of the typical mortgage-lending S&L or bank, receiving equal installments of principal and interest monthly (or quarterly or annually) from the borrower. A $10,000 five-year note written at 10 percent annual interest would thus require sixty monthly payments of $212.48 to be fully amortized. During the course of the pay-back you would receive $10,000 in principal and $2,748.80 in interest. Since you would be getting your principal funds back rapidly, you would presumably be able to put your funds to work earlier (e.g., into other second trusts or real estate investments).

Interest Only. As mentioned in Chapter 2, an interest-only second offered by the seller is a highly prized bargaining chip in many rental real estate transactions. It offers the property buyer maximum leverage by cutting his out-of-pocket costs to the bone—no principal pay-back until the final day of the loan. The five-year $10,000 note above would require only $83.33 a month ($1,000 a year) in payments for five years, followed by a lump-sum payment of the $10,000 principal.

From the point of view of the noteholder—either the original lender (the seller of the house) or an investor who has purchased the trust deed—interest-only has distinct advantages as well. First, it offers the highest total payment of interest of the three common alternatives. The 10 percent is assessed against the unreduced $10,000 annually; in the other two methods the principal is reduced periodically, and the interest collected declines over time.

Purchasers of notes also like the interest-only option because of its relative simplicity at tax time. Uncle Sam taxes only interest, not your principal repayments. The other two methods produce varying monthly (or quarterly or annual) mixtures of principal and interest that have to be sorted out mathematically for tax purposes. Most small-scale investors pay their accountant to do this, although some California brokers prepare statements automatically as part of the service. Interest-only pay-backs require no formulas to determine what is taxable income and what isn't.

The drawback of this technique, of course, is that it takes the longest time to repay your principal. If you're particularly concerned about the *time value* of money—and expect to have higher-yielding speculative uses for your capital before the loan term is up—you might prefer the direct amortization approach.

Partial Principal Pay-back. Many purchase-money second trusts are written to return 1 or 2 percent of the principal debt per month, at the face interest rate. The monthly payments on the $10,000, 10 percent five-year note above at 1 percent would be $100 a month, $1,200 a year. At 2 percent, the payments would be $200 a month, or $2,400 a year.

At the end of the five-year term, under 1 percent pay-back, 87.09 percent (or $8,709.00) of the principal debt would remain unpaid. Under the 2 percent method, 9.66 percent ($966.00) would still be owed the noteholder, via a balloon payment.

Noteholder Protections. Read over the note package you're being offered to make certain it contains these important features:

1. A *"due-on-sale" clause.* This makes the full face amount of the note due and payable if the borrower transfers, sells or puts additional liens on the property. (This is a common mortgage or deed-of-trust provision aimed at safeguarding the lender's security from harmful transfers of ownership, but it isn't found in the "standard" forms used in all states.)

2. A *prepayment penalty.* Although many purchase money notes *do not* carry language defining a penalty (e.g., three to six months' interest) for early payoffs, those that do are worth

a small premium in price. A large proportion of junior liens are paid off before their terms ends, and any penalty assessment merely increases the *yield* of the noteholder.

3. *Fire insurance.* The note should contain language requiring the borrower to maintain adequate coverage to protect the security of both you and the first-trust lender. You should insist that you receive a copy of the policy prior to completion of the sale of the note.

4. *Statutory factors.* Beware of value-depressing state laws that may affect your prospective note. Such rules as burdensome foreclosure procedures and lengthy mandatory redemption periods won't be spelled out in the documents at the broker's office. You've got either to know them in advance for trusts or mortgages originated in the state where the property is located, or to question the broker. This is still another reason to *buy where you know*; don't fool around with out-of-state trust deeds or out-of-state property unless you're highly familiar with the particular property involved.

Discount and Yield. Now we've gotten to the bottom line— the price of the note. Here's where you have to determine, in view of all the factors above that influence market value, what *you* are prepared to pay for the purchase-money trust being offered by the broker. What size *discount* off the face value of the note are you going to accept or demand? Your answer will inevitably depend on the interest-rate conditions prevailing in the market at the moment, as well as on your personal investment objectives and financial capacity.

Keep these tips in mind, however, about the slippery subjects of discounts and price.

• Discounts can do incredible things to yields on the dollar. The five-year, 10 percent note for $10,000 paying $100 per month, for example, will yield you 16 percent because it is selling at a discount of 19.54 percent, or a price of $8,046. Sold at a 25 percent discount, the same note would yield 18 percent. A 10 percent discount would yield 12.85 percent over the remaining term.

• Discounted notes that are paid off earlier than scheduled can also do wonders for your final yield. (It's always worth inquiring of the note seller whether the chance of a prepayment appears especially high.) A 9¾ percent note for $10,000 that is fully amortized over ten years (paying $130.77 per month) that is purchased at a 20 percent discount (a price of $8,000) yields a very attractive 19.43 percent if prepaid without penalty in three years. The same ten-year note, if purchased at a 10 percent discount, would produce a 14.3 percent yield if paid off in three years, 12.5 percent if paid off in seven years. California investors regularly get 12 percent or higher on undiscounted second-trust deeds—in spite of the 10 percent state usury limit—because of early payoffs. Buying the same loans at discounts up front would magnify these yields even further.

• Many investors in seconds approach a prospective purchase with a *minimum yield* in mind. They calculate what they'll need to get from the note—a yield of 14 percent, 15 percent, 20 percent—in order to justify investing their capital in paper rather than in real estate. With a preset yield and access to some financial tables, they can tell the seller the exact price they'll pay for his note.

Let's say you've decided that you must have at least a 15 percent yield on whatever notes you purchase. A seller offers you a five-year, $10,000 trust note with a 10 percent face interest rate and a $100 per month (1 percent) partial principal payback. You check one of several commercially available financial publications, and you find that the top price you can offer is $8,337 (a discount of 16.63 percent.)* The seller can either agree to your price and sell you the $10,000 note for $8,337, or come back with a counteroffer—say, a price of $9,000, a 10 percent discount. At that point, the transaction becomes like any other real estate bargaining process. You haggle, bob and weave, and maybe buy. Or you walk.

---

* Among the best known are the Financial Publishing Company, Boston, Massachusetts, and Professional Publishing Corporation, San Rafael, California. Financial Publishing Company will prepare custom discount, yield, and pay-back tables on request. Professional Publishing Corporation markets the *Realty Bluebook*, a compendium of useful yield and discount tables.

DOCUMENTATION PRIOR TO SETTLEMENT

Your note purchase won't be complete until you (or your settlement attorney) receive the documentation that proves you're the new owner of a legally recorded lien secured by a specific piece of real estate. These documents include:

• An acceptable *title report* and *title insurance policy*, with you as the insurance beneficiary in the event of title challenge. The title report is essential; never purchase a note without receiving one. It is your best protection against fraudulent, worthless second trusts. The title report should state clearly that there are no outstanding liens against the property senior to yours, other than the first-trust holder's; and that in all other respects the title is clear, of good record and freely marketable.

• Verified copies of the signed settlement papers from the sale of the house, showing the first- and second-trust positions.

• A credit report on the borrower(s) and verification of the first-trust principal balance.

• The original note, plus copies, with an assignment to you.

• The original fire insurance policy, if one was taken out specifically for you, or a copy of the original policy held by the first-trust lender. Make certain the coverage amounts are more than adequate to handle the first- and second-trust note balances in combination.

• A copy of a request sent to the local recorder's office asking for notification of any announcements of default received from the first-trust holder.

• A recorded deed of trust from the local recorder's office indicating that your lien against the property has been received and duly placed on the jurisdiction's books.

HARD-MONEY LOANS

If you have the opportunity to purchase a hard-money second trust or mortgage, should you do so? Are there any differences in the steps for analyzing hard-money loans in comparison to a purchase-money trust? The answer to both questions is an emphatic yes. California's largest dollar volume in second trusts involves hard-money loans, and as an active investor you'll find chances to pick up loans like these at discounts in many other states as well.

The key steps in analyzing hard-money notes prior to acquisition are basically the same as those we've just covered on purchase-money seconds. The differences between the two types of loans, however, produce differences in discounts and risks that should be understood in advance. Hard-money trusts or mortgages are almost always originated by *professional* lenders. They are business-purpose or personal-expenditure loans secured by homes, and tend to carry relatively high interest rates (15 percent to 22 percent is not unusual). They also tend to be (but aren't always) conservatively underwritten. The "pros," whether New Jersey's Money Store or Allstate Equity in California, prefer low risks and high equity cushions. When they agree to loan $20,000 to a homeowner-businessperson to purchase restaurant equipment, they are very particular about the strength of the security backing their money. As a result of their generally solid underwriting and advantageous interest rates, many hard-money loans sell at lower discounts than purchase-money seconds. California's mass-market second-trust originators, as a case in point, sell their loans at par or full value, with no discount.

By the same token, when you see a hard-money loan being offered at a substantial discount, look doubly closely. Check out the borrower and his possibly shaky business enterprise. (One hard-money lender admits that "about a third of the people I lend to are involved in business ventures with such high risks that essentially they're rolling dice with what I loan them.") Look hard at the broker/originator of the loan, at his reason for wanting to dispose of the note, and especially at the property securing the loan, which may be falling apart, in the path of public acquisition, or worse. Look closely for odd terms —present or absent. The absence of a prepayment clause, for example, will cut the market value of some business-purpose trusts and make them tougher to resell.

HANDLING YOUR PORTFOLIO

After you buy a note—whether of the purchase-money or hard-money variety—get in touch immediately with the two other parties on the line with you: the borrower and the first-trust holder. It's a good practice to write a note to the borrower, not only to let him know where to send payment checks but also to establish a cordial business relationship. In the letter or by means of a follow-up phone call, you may also want to discuss possible voluntary term changes in the note's pay-back schedule. For example, if the note was written on an interest-only basis, you can point out to the borrower that by paying back at least a portion of the principal, he can cut his total interest payments significantly over the life of the loan. Doubling a $100 (or 1 percent) pay-back per month on a $10,000 loan (2 percent) might be easily within the borrower's financial capacity, and a change he'd make without fuss in order to cut total interest payments. For your purposes, the idea would be to speed up return of your capital, and possibly to increase your yield by encouraging early payoff.

The importance of getting and staying in touch with the first-trust lender can't be emphasized enough. Although you may be protected by a notice-of-default request filed by the county, don't depend on it solely. Ask the loan department of the first-trust holder to contact you before the lender takes *any* action with respect to the borrower. Let the S&L or bank know that you may be prepared to step in and try to cure whatever default occurs, including taking over payments on the first trust in the unlikely event the borrower stops making all payments whatsoever. Of course, if you're holding a loan with a huge equity cushion protecting both the first-trust holder and you, your concern needn't be so great. The proceeds of public sale may be more than enough to satisfy your debt.

Keeping Records. If you purchase and hold just one or two notes at a time, your record-keeping requirements will be relatively simple. All you need to do is keep track of the payments you receive and the principal and interest composition of each. You may want to use a four- or five-column ledger (which you can buy at any stationery store), with additional entries for late fees, monthly due dates, total payments due for the year, and the expiration date of the loan.

When you begin to get into higher quantities of notes, you'll need to step up your bookkeeping sophistication or risk losing track of the varied payments that you're receiving. You may, as many note purchasers do, wish to engage periodic accounting help to sort out your records for tax purposes.

Group Investing. One method of investing in and managing portfolios of notes efficiently is through clubs or groups of small-scale buyers. For a fee tied to the overall annual performance of a portfolio of say, ten, fifteen or more notes of $5,000 to $20,000 apiece, a group of friends can afford to have professional help in selecting and maintaining its second trusts. The arrangement can be something like a personalized mutual fund or bond fund. A group can ask a local individual who has experience with notes—probably a real estate broker, salesperson or attorney—to help create and/or manage its portfolio. The individual may have the authority, by telephone approval of the other members, to add new notes to the portfolio, sell notes at discount, or even originate new loans directly. He may be a full-fledged member of the group with the responsibility of visiting and appraising the properties before purchase of notes, dealing with delinquent borrowers, arranging property sales if necessary, and keeping the originals of all notes and other important documents under lock and key. Like a Wall Street bond-fund strategist, the note-portfolio manager can select a mix of high-yielding, higher-risk green trusts or mortgages to pull up the low-risk, lower-yielding seasoned investments already in the pool.

Deliquencies. You may never have to confront a nonpaying borrower face to face as a second-trust note investor, or you may do it the sixth week after you purchase the paper. How you handle delinquencies will depend upon the specific situation, but in general your approach will be similar to the way a rental-home investor handles delinquent tenants (see Chapter 2, p. 64). First you find out the nature of the problem. If the borrower has been sick for a month and earning no money, you forbear a little. You give him a decent chance to get back on his feet and catch up with his responsibilities.

Sometimes, the problem may simply be one of communication. The borrower may not have understood that a due date of the first of the month meant the first of the month, and that late charges would be assessed after the tenth. Or he may have had a temporary cash crunch and hoped to get a check to you before the end of the month. Whatever the reason, approach delinquencies sympathetically—until it's clear your patience and sympathy aren't going to turn the borrower around. At that point you're forced to file a notice of default with the local recorder's office, and you may be on your way irreversibly to the ultimate step.

Foreclosure. Avoid it, but don't fear it. If you've bought a properly secured note with a power-of-sale provision for the trustee or mortgagee, you will come out of a foreclosure unscathed. Since foreclosure will involve early repayment of your debt, you may even *increase* your yield on your investment. Once you have filed your notice of default, consult competent legal counsel for advice on what your state or local laws require next. Do-it-yourself foreclosure can be similar to do-it-yourself brain surgery. Far better to let someone with professional training conduct the operation.

SHOULD YOU ORIGINATE SECONDS DIRECTLY?

Absolutely, but *only* after you've been in the second-trust investment field long enough to know its complexities, the byzantine statutory restrictions on various types of lenders, and the mathematics involved, and you can bring in enough business to make the extra paperwork expenses worth your while. There is a potentially vast market waiting to be tapped in many parts of the country for hard-money second-trust originators who will take a slightly *lower* initial interest rate than the professional lenders—who always ask and get top dollar. Rather than 18 percent loans in a state with an 18 percent usury ceiling, small-scale originators can offer 15 to 16 percent and flexible terms, and can still get a very attractive return on their money.

4
Land

From George Washington, who speculated unabashedly in home-building lots on Capitol Hill, to John Jacob Astor, who wowed Manhattan with his bold land grabs in the early 1800s, to the corporate developers who turned Florida's mangrove swamps into Miami, no investment has been quite so appealing to Americans as land. Land is the stuff they're not making any more of. Land is "not only the best way, the quickest way, and the safest way, but the only way to become wealthy" (Marshall Field). Land, indeed, offers the biggest potential gains, along with some of the highest constant risks, of any real estate investment medium today.

There is no other field—with the possible exception of certain commodities options, natural gas exploration, and currency speculation—where highly leveraged small investments can turn into lifetime windfalls. There is no other medium where a shrewd (or just plain lucky) small-scale investor can buy, say, 80 acres of scrub outside a city for $1,200 (as one man did in Miami in 1950) and resell it eleven years later for $565,000. The same parcel went for over $3 million a decade later and is valued at more than $5 million for industrial usage today. Far bigger splashes have occurred in every metropolitan area in the United States and will continue as long as demand for residential and commercial acreage keeps outpacing inflation.

Look at what's been happening nationwide in land valuation trends in the 1960s and 1970s.

• Average farmland—not your premium crop-producing land, not especially well-located land, but simply *average* land—increased in market value at an annual pace of close to 20 percent between 1971 and 1977, a rate which, when compounded, produces a doubling roughly every four years. Many farm areas have witnessed far higher rates of appreciation in 1977–78, ranging from 25 to 35 percent in prime producing areas like Illinois, Indiana and Iowa. One analyst has calculated that if present average national rates continue, land that today sells for $1,000 per acre will be worth $33,535 an acre in the year 2000. Sounds unlikely, but twenty years ago you wouldn't have believed that today you would sell for $87,000 a house you paid $21,000 for then.

• Land for residential development in many areas of the country has seen astonishing jumps in market value in the past decade—outpacing even prime farmland by several percentage points. Outside Los Angeles and San Francisco, for example, orchard land that in 1974–75 went for top prices of $20,000 an acre is selling for $90,000 today. Tracts outside fast-growing cities like Dallas-Fort Worth, Houston, Phoenix and Washington, D.C., have tripled, quadrupled or in some cases quintupled within the decade. The cost of a typical single-family residential building lot now exceeds $15,000 in a number of major metropolitan areas, and exceeds $30,000 in scattered high-cost communities. Residential land investments haven't duplicated some of John Jacob Astor's coups—he once bought a 70-acre farm in mid-Manhattan at a distress sale for $25,000, and the identical property was valued at $20 *million* later in the same century by his heirs—but judicious purchases in the path of future growth can still be spectacularly profitable.

• Commercially developable frontage land has performed well in this decade, rising at 13 to 20 percent a year in many areas. Sunbelt communities experiencing net migrations of jobs and new industry have chalked up price doublings and triplings within four- to five-year periods. Prime development acreage astride Route M-150 near Detroit reportedly has jumped tenfold in selling price since 1970 alone, as have properties outside Louisville, Kentucky, Frederick, Maryland, Chicago, Albuquerque and other cities, according to realty brokers.

• Raw rural land has the widest variations in prices, ranging from $2 or $3 per acre for government surplus cactus tracts in the Southwest to $2,000 to $15,000 an acre for land in outlying areas of eastern California, New York State, North Carolina and Florida with recreational potential. Almost 150 counties in the

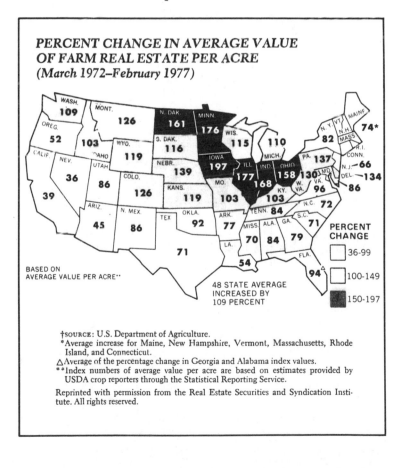

PERCENT CHANGE IN AVERAGE VALUE OF FARM REAL ESTATE PER ACRE
(March 1972–February 1977)

BASED ON AVERAGE VALUE PER ACRE**

48 STATE AVERAGE INCREASED BY 109 PERCENT

PERCENT CHANGE
36-99
100-149
150-197

†SOURCE: U.S. Department of Agriculture.
*Average increase for Maine, New Hampshire, Vermont, Massachusetts, Rhode Island, and Connecticut.
△Average of the percentage change in Georgia and Alabama index values.
**Index numbers of average value per acre are based on estimates provided by USDA crop reporters through the Statistical Reporting Service.

FARM REAL ESTATE VALUES**

1977 Rank	State	Average Per-acre Value February 1977	Average Per-acre Value March 1971	1971 Rank
1	New Jersey	$ 2,051	$ 1,135	1
2	Connecticut	2,024	1,034	2
3	Rhode Island	1,852	854	3
4	Illinois	1,450	494	7
5	Maryland	1,371	688	4
6	Delaware	1,322	553	6
7	Iowa	1,228	392	12
8	Indiana	1,167	423	9
9	Massachusetts	1,143	623	5
10	Ohio	1,131	416	10
11	Pennsylvania	1,000	393	11
12	Florida	783	378	13
13	Michigan	782	333	16
14	California	686	471	8
15	North Carolina	684	372	14
16	Virginia	677	309	17
17	New Hampshire	669	286	19
18	Minnesota	664	231	29
19	Kentucky	603	268	22
20	New York	591	288	18
21	Wisconsin	591	255	25
22	Louisiana	590	350	15
23	Tennessee	556	277	20
24	South Carolina	541	277	21
25	Vermont	530	256	24
26	Missouri	529	236	28
27	Arkansas	527	255	26
28	Georgia	524	256	23
29	Washington	500	224	31
30	Alabama	437	227	30
31	Idaho	419	188	32
32	Mississippi	411	238	27
33	Nebraska	407	157	39
34	Maine	405	187	33
35	West Virginia	401	151	37
36	Kansas	381	162	38
37	Oklahoma	374	183	34
38	Texas	298	156	36
39	Oregon	288	168	35
40	Colorado	262	103	40
41	North Dakota	258	95	42
42	Utah	246	111	41
43	South Dakota	188	85	43
44	Montana	154	63	45
45	Arizona	129	77	44
46	Wyoming	105	42	48
47	New Mexico	95	46	47
48	Nevada	94	60	46

* Source: Questor Associates and U.S. Dept. of Agriculture.
** Listed in order of 1977 ranking.

United States—all of them west of the Mississippi—have *average* per acre rural land selling prices under $100. You can still buy chunks of Vermont woods for $150 an acre, or entire small mountains in rural West Virginia for $200 an acre. Undeveloped waterfront lots along the protected coves of Chesapeake Bay, on the other hand, go for $25,000 to $40,000; but these are mere fractions of similar plots in southern California or on Long Island, which bring $100,000 to $150,000.

Nationwide appreciation rates in undeveloped land are impossible to generalize, however. Raw land depends heavily for its value on its expected eventual use. If that $20-per-acre tract you bought in New Mexico ten years ago is still forty years away from any commercial use whatsoever, its real value may have been stable over the years, or may possibly have declined. If the McCulloch Corporation, however, decides that your acreage is right smack in the middle of a new desert city it plans to build, complete with the Eiffel Tower and a bridge imported from the Thames, your percentage jumps in value could be astronomical. Raw land is the speculator's sandbox: fantasy castles can rise and become real—or you can end up with the same old sand you began with.

PROS AND CONS OF LAND

Land investment as an inflation hedge has to be measured against the alternatives—other forms of real estate, stocks, bonds, gold, objets d'art.

Pros. Chapter 1 discussed real estate versus non-real estate to beat inflation; let's take a look at land versus other real estate. The pros include:

1. *High leverage and high-yield potential.* More so than rental houses, second mortgages and real estate securities, land holds the possibilities of mind-boggling dollar-for-dollar returns. Land investments can often be highly leveraged, with only a small fraction of the cash value of the property required for acquisition. This is especially true in the case of seller-financed land parcels, where a shrewd investor can negotiate 5 to 10 percent down payments and generous terms; or in the case of land options, where a token outlay on a parcel about to be rezoned

can produce incredible returns. Twenty thousand dollars down to acquire a $125,000, 180-acre piece of farmland on the metropolitan fringe *can readily return 500 percent or more* within several years if the land is subdivided for residential or commercial development.

2. *Wide variety of investment types and sizes.* As much or more so than other real estate, land offerings in any given metropolitan region tend to be highly diverse—with acreage ranging in prices from the low hundreds on the far fringes to the millions in the central city. Investors can try their hand with relatively small initial expenditures or can plunge in with a splash, like the petrodollar-financed Middle Eastern land buyers have in every region of the United States.

3. *Relative ease of management.* Owning vacant land, unlike owning a vacant duplex in a central-city neighborhood, tends to be pretty simple. You pay the taxes once a year or every six months, pay off your mortgage, and visit now and then. Raw land generally doesn't need maintenance, repairs or special coddling; it just sits there growing trees or growing in value. If you buy land suited for an interim use—an enterprise aimed at cutting your outlays during ownership, such as farming, timber, miniature golf, or whatever—things do get more complex, but only by your choice.

4. *Relatively inflation-proof.* With the exception of rip-off recreational acreage, most land investments that have been conservatively researched and financed are inflation-proof. That is, the historical odds are strong that the value of the property you buy will outpace the rate of inflation by a respectable margin. Farmland during the early 1960s and early 1970s is a good example. While the overall inflation rate from 1960 to 1970 averaged about 3 percent a year, average farmland jumped 7 percent a year in sales value. In the years from 1964 to 1974, the land-value rate rose to an average 9 percent a year versus about 4.5 percent for inflation in the national consumer price index. As long as land values maintain a ratio of 1.5 to 2 times the overall rate of inflation—and nothing in sight suggests they won't—well-chosen land will continue to make eminent good sense for the wise investor.

5. *Capital gains treatment.* Unlike interest payments from second mortgages or the profits from buying, rehabilitating and selling large numbers of central-city houses, your profits on landholdings of a year or more are treated as capital gains rather than as ordinary income. For what is often the most passive, quiet, uninvolved form of real estate investing—simply acquiring and sitting on some land for a period—the IRS accords you the same favorable tax treatment as the most harried, headache-prone landlord. Three-fifths of your profits go tax-free; only two-fifths are subject to taxation.

Cons. Despite these advantages, the negative aspects of buying land for investment should not be ignored.

1. *High risks.* Many land purchases are essentially speculative gambles. They involve educated guesses that development will or will not proceed in a particular direction, or that rezoning or sewage connections or utility tap-ins will or will not be feasible for a particular tract. Guess right, and you may be a millionaire. Guess wrong, and you're a loser—perhaps a big loser.

The risks of poor research on soil composition, timing of economic swings, suitability of land for eventual development, legal title, exposure to natural hazards like floods, or the direction of community politics tend to be more drastic in land than in improved property. If you bought a parcel at a price predicated upon eventual residential development, and you ultimately can't build houses on it or otherwise develop it, you could lose far more than what you put into it, to say nothing of what you could have been doing with that money invested elsewhere.

2. *Immediate tax advantages tend to be less* than from investments in houses, apartments or commercial buildings. As was discussed in detail in Chapter 2, land can't be depreciated for tax purposes—and that eliminates the principal annual shelter it would otherwise offer against your regular income. Business enterprises you run as an interim activity on your land may of course generate tax deductions beyond the usual mortgage interest and local property tax write-offs—particularly farming. But they may not be large, dollar for dollar, in comparison with rental residential property.

3. *Income from land investments is often small* measured against carrying costs. Raw, unsubdivided or unimproved land generates nothing but red ink: taxes, principal and interest payments (offset perhaps only by an occasional rental fee you might charge campers or hunters). Farmland or dairy land bought and operated by nonfarmer investors often runs at an economic loss; vacant commercial land sitting on highways may be great for grazing cows, but the fees rarely support the monthly carrying costs for the property owner biding his time waiting for developers to drive up.

4. *"Opportunity costs" can be high* in land investments, and often are ignored on balance sheets. Since holding land may be a long-term cash drain, the capital gains had better be big when they come. Otherwise, you've had your money tied up less productively than it could have been elsewhere. Ten percent per year jumps in market value may sound good, but given the opportunity costs and your out-of-pocket expenses in a double-digit inflationary economy, it's the rock-bottom *minimum* return you'll need in land. Reasonable expectations of 20 percent or higher annual growth make the costs worth it; a doubling in value within four years is worth it.

5. *Land can be tougher to finance and to sell* than improved property. That's an important factor to weigh carefully before jumping into land. S&Ls, banks and other customary sources of financing for buildings consider land a much higher loan risk because it has debatable value (benchmark properties may be hard to find) and produces no income. These institutions tend to be very picky about what they finance in the land field—and prefer not to finance land except immediately prior to construction on it. As a result, owners of land often partially or wholly finance the buyers of their property. That can be a serious drawback for an owner who needs to cash out of a property quickly, or who simply can't afford to be a long-term lender.

LAND STRATEGIES

You can shoot for quick, splashy returns in land—concentrating solely on farm or wooded acreage at the edge of the urban area that will double or triple in value within three to four years if you get the zoning you need and can attract developers. Ralph Shirley, a prominent Houston land broker and consultant, says speculative acreage ought to have the potential of 100 percent gains in value in six to twelve months, or the land may not be worth the risk. Or you can, as many small- to medium-scale investors do, look for raw land located well beyond the metropolitan confines, and plan to sit on it for four to five years.

Whatever you choose to do, determine in advance the full cash outlays for acquisition, transfer taxes, mortgage or contract costs, property taxes and interim business related costs. Professor Maury Seldin, author of *Land Investment* (1975), and chairman of American University's graduate real estate program, says that most failures in real estate investments by nonprofessionals arise from insufficient capital to "feed" the property during long holding periods prior to development.

For example, say you purchase a ninety-acre farm sixty miles from your home in the city, at a price of $165,000. Your objective is to hold it for several years and then subdivide for tract housing if you can convince the county government to grant sewer and utilities permits, and rezoning. Subdivided for housing, you calculate the land will be worth at least ten times what you paid for it. You negotiate a low down payment with the seller—$15,000. The $150,000 balance of the price is to be paid to him in an installment contract of ten years at 10 percent interest. This will require $1,982.28 per month in principal and interest amortization, or $23,787.36 per year. Local taxes will add another $3,000 per year to the carrying costs, to say nothing of the expenses related to the farm business itself.

Your out-of-pocket costs, while you are awaiting the opportunity to strike it rich by subdividing and developing, could make your *pretax* balance sheet look something like the outline on page 126. Though tax considerations will lessen the burden of this annual cash drain, the costs of acquiring a "dream farm" for investment and then holding it for several years can be staggering. You need to confront them realistically before you run head-on into them in a panic sale situation later.

PROS AND CONS OF ALTERNATIVE LAND INVESTMENTS

Type of Land Investment	Advantages	Disadvantages
Raw land—speculative holding for future urban growth	High gain potential, low cost. Taxes and other carrying expenses low compared to metropolitan area averages. Interim uses include recreational, timber harvesting, campgrounds, and so forth. Long-term usage may be residential or commercial, depending upon path of growth.	Risk of low yields or loss if development doesn't follow expected path, or if local authorities restrict land usage. Offers little or no tax shelter, relatively low income possibilities for interim. Financing difficult if parcel is unusually large. Requires high average annual appreciation rate—doubling every three to four years—to make sense as speculative investment.
Farmland	Can have high potential for residential development if within commuting distance of urban center, employment. May have good to excellent interim use as farm, depending upon soil, location and management. Current average annual price increases far above historical levels—15 to 20 percent versus 3 to 5 percent—causing new farmland boom among U.S. and foreign investors. Working farm can generate tax benefits via expense deductions, depreciation of buildings and equipment. Financing more plentiful for income-producing farm than for raw land.	Large minimum acreage for working farm may require high initial capital investment, high long-term carrying costs, especially in high-tax Northeast. Rezoning for residential or commercial use more difficult, more costly than five to ten years ago in many areas. IRS will expect proof that farm operated as a business rather than as a hobby, or may disallow deductions, depreciation.

Subdivided, rural, recreation-oriented lots	Modest annual growth in capital value possible in well-located developments where promoter has made substantial front-end investments in club, pool, tennis court, and so forth. Most offerings required by law to be registered with U.S. Office of Interstate Land Sales Registration (OILSR, of Department of Housing and Urban Development). Rules allow cooling-off period for buyers, other consumer protections.	The least advantageous land investment category—unless you are the subdivider or promoter. No tax advantages. Often difficult resales because seller is in competition with promoter.
Subdivided, developed urban area building lots	High demand for housing pushing up values of such lots rapidly in many metropolitan areas. provided location is convenient to employment, buffered from nuisances, traffic. Suburban lots that offer buyers residential *and* recreational convenience—near lake, bay, ski slopes, for example—make particularly good annual price jumps. Waterfront acreage in economically sound metro areas likely to see large gains in coming decade.	Like recreational subdivisions, big benefits may have gone to first subdivider. Taxes much higher than outlying land, particularly in Northeast. High carrying costs; negligible, if any, tax benefits. Risk of poor return if development location, other aspects, cannot attract housing types intensive or expensive enough to produce yields you need.
Commercial/industrial acreage	For experienced investors who have done extensive research, can offer excellent returns. Local government agencies interested in economic development may actively help you to attract purchaser/lessee. Interim farming/other uses can generate net income.	Not for beginners or small investors. Usage and value depend heavily on corporate moves, active brokerage by professionals. Holdings in economically sagging area can require substantial resources, long-term view of return.

Year 1

Down payment	$15,000
Mortgage principal and interest	23,787
Property taxes	3,000
Settlement costs	3,500
Insurance	400
Farm-related expenses and other	12,000

$57,687 *Outgo*

Income from leasing of acreage, miscellaneous sales and rental activities	$11,020 *Income*

($46,667) Negative Cash Flow

Year 2

Mortgage principal and interest	$23,787
Property taxes	3,200
Insurance	400
Farm-related expenses and other	9,000

$36,387 *Outgo*

Income from leasing of acreage, miscellaneous sales and rental activities	$13,400 *Income*

($22,987) Negative Cash Flow

Small land purchases can also require substantial staying power for anyone on a tight budget. The $30,000 piece of land you buy with $10,000 down may require $3,000 to $5,000 a year in outlays—with no offsetting income whatsoever. Are you prepared to feed your land long enough for it to mature into the excellent investment you imagine it to be?

Keep these points about objectives and strategy in mind:

• *If you're primarily after tax shelter* for your ordinary business income, you ought to stop and ask yourself whether you really want to purchase land. Except for investors who have the cash to acquire a working (or workable) farm, orchard, or cattle- or timber-producing spread, land isn't a particularly good tax shelter. Residential property is far better suited to that objective.

• If you've already got adequate tax shelter from other investments and *now are simply looking for capital growth*, any of the alternatives in the table on pp. 124–125—with the exception of subdivided recreational land—should fit. A good example of this strategy is the case of three Washington, D.C., physicians who in 1975 paid $59,000 for a 200-acre farm in northern Maryland and leased it out to local farmers for short-term income. In 1978 the physicians sold the farm for $200,000—over fifteen times their initial cash outlay. Within several months the new owner subdivided the tract into four plots for a total of $260,000. He got his price, and two sets of investors took away handsome, rapid capital gains.

• If you're looking for a *combination of opportunities*—investment potential *and* a spot for a retirement home or a second house—subdivided acreage near or on waterfront, or adjacent to some other finite natural attraction, is a solid bet if it is well researched and financed. But instead of buying a piece of land that's already been subdivided, why not buy a tract and subdivide it yourself? Take the best lot or lots for yourself and sell the remainder to people you'd like for weekend neighbors. By dint of a little extra effort, you personally become the key ingredient to big capital gain from your land purchase (see the section on subdividing below).

LOCATING AND ANALYZING LAND

Where you search for acreage depends entirely on your overall investment objectives, but some basic, unfailing principles hold sway whether you're speculating in inner-city commercial parcels or farmland.

Buy Only Where You Know. As in rental houses and apartments, your odds for investment success are highest in the
community or metropolitan area where you live, work, and/or
take your vacations, and whose economy you understand best.
Large-scale real estate–related operations—hotel/resort chains
such as Marriott, or tax-ridden Europeans looking for safe
U.S. farmland havens for their cash—buy all over the country, but *never* without professional local appraisers and economic consultants to steer them. You may not be able to afford
the high fees of consulting economists, so you've got to depend
upon your own research and local market savvy—perhaps but-
tressed by competent legal counsel and one or two real estate
brokers. Inside knowledge about a community, its politics and
plans, is so critical in land that you ought to stay away from
any purchase where you can't qualify—either by virtue of the
people you've hired to represent you, or by virtue of your own
personal knowledge—as something other than an outsider.

Have well-defined interim and end uses in mind for the property you go after. Purchasing fifty acres simply "to hold" isn't
sophisticated investing; it's roulette. Analyze your interim-use
options—mobile home park, campground, skeet-shooting range,
marina, and so forth—in terms of projected income over your
expected holding period. And project your end use—a planned
residential community, a vacation resort, industry—even if it's
fifteen to twenty years down the road. By calculating the expected reasonable returns on equity from these two categories of
uses, you can determine how sensible the investment is for you.
Projecting interim and end uses also forces you to consider such
factors as current and future utilities services and employment
centers and residential and commercial developments in the
immediate vicinity.

Take advantage of all the research tools available to you, including the many supplied free of charge by government agencies. Maps are readily obtainable from local and state government
highway departments, forestry and agricultural departments,
economic development agencies, and chambers of commerce.
The U.S. Geological Survey's offices are a good source of topo-
graphical maps, scaled to your needs. Write for the U.S.G.S.'s

maps index at Map Distribution, U.S. Geological Survey, 1200 South Eads Street, Arlington, Va. 22202 for areas east of the Mississippi River. For areas west of the Mississippi, write to Map Distribution, U.S. Geological Survey, Federal Center, Denver, Col. 80225.

For aerial photos of your prospective timberland or farmland acreage, write to the appropriate regional U.S.G.S. office:

U.S. Geological Survey	U.S. Geological Survey
1109 North Highland Street	Building 25, Federal Center
Arlington, Va. 22210	Denver, Col. 80255
U.S. Geological Survey	U.S. Geological Survey
Box 133	345 Middlefield Road
Rolla, Mo. 65401	Menlo Park, Calif. 94025

Some local government maps offer such valuable specialized information as parcel-by-parcel ownership, topography, soil composition and surface coverage of specific tracts of land. Make it your business to obtain county or regional master plans defining permitted and projected land uses; water supply data; and utilities supply data. Check with federal or state highway agencies to determine projected new construction or improvement of existing roads or freeways. (Land that roads touch turns into money; land that roads don't touch remains dirt.) Anyone truly interested in beating inflation with land has to be truly interested in highways, bridges, exits and anticipated traffic counts. Inside urban areas, rental vacancy rates compiled by housing and community development departments can be important indices of where housing may be needed, or where there is an excess.

Real estate brokers, title companies, local bankers, tax assessors, businesspeople, gas-station operators, farmers, village clerks, and absentee owners of neighboring tracts are essential research sources. Better than anything, such people can tell you why the present owner is *really* selling; what your property tax will be after the proposed sale (it may be five or six times what it was before the contract of sale); where the area is headed in terms of growth or growth control; and the area's economic facts of life.

Be acute to land characteristics—soil composition, surface topography, percolation, mineral composition, presence or lack of
trees—that could turn your prospective purchase into a bonanza
or a dud. Is the soil you're considering buying saline, rocky,
loamy, adobe, alkaline, sandy? Does it have too high a clay composition to meet minimum local percolation tests for residential
development? Does it have gradients of slope that rule out or
are particularly favorable for housing, commercial or farm-
related interim uses? Does it have water-related characteristics
that may be long-term pluses (such as ponds or streams) or
flood hazards that periodically turn it into a swamp? Find out
what's underneath the dirt you're buying—potential or proven
mineral deposits or geological formations—and make certain
that you're buying the mineral rights along with the land. Does
the property breed insects or other pests that could put a damper
on your projected usage? Northern Michigan's tiny no-see-ums
fly right through screens, for example, and don't help vacation
property values. Neither do Oklahoma's famous chiggers or
Louisiana's or New Jersey's mosquitoes.

Get documentation on all easements and rights of way. Don't
wait for the formal title search to learn that there are eighteen
rights of way and easements scattered all over the fifty acres
you're buying that may tie up your development alternatives.
Demand to know in writing from the seller about all easements,
rights of way, unrecorded liens, and squatter's uses, in advance.
Easements are a special hazard out in the country. Farmers traditionally have given permanent easements to utility companies
for underground cables, pipelines, or above-ground lines for
token payments. Cables don't bother the farmer, but they are
a definite drawback for certain forms of development. Easements or rights of way may also permit owners of land-locked
parcels within or astride your acreage permanent access through
your property, and may grant rights for maintenance of bill-
boards, grazing or other activities. Check to make sure that
legally binding easements haven't been created anywhere on
the property through *adverse possession*—continuous, open use
of the land for some purpose by persons with no formal title to
it (such as squatter's housing, or a neighboring farmer's long-

standing use of another owner's field, without compensation)
beyond the state code's statutory minimum.

Hire local talent. A little ole country lawyer and a little ole
country real estate broker will protect your interests on their
home turf and will keep an eye on each other far better than
any city slicker you can employ. Have the slickers do your appraisals, surveys, soil tests and accounting, but hire a local to
handle negotiations, title work and contract details.

Avoid buying from a speculator or short-term investor unless
you've got information about usage potentials, local zoning
change opportunities, or future highway locations that he
doesn't.

Don't overemphasize price in your acquisition strategy; price
is just one element in the overall package you're negotiating.
Favorable mortgage finance terms (for example, a small down
payment; assumption of settlement costs, survey fees, and related acquisition expenses by the seller) may outweigh the
seemingly high price the seller is demanding. Give a few thousand on price, but save at least that amount with concessions
from the seller in other areas. If the land is as good an investment as you think it is, what's a few thousand dollars against
the tens of thousands you're going after in capital gains?

Consider options contracts in lieu of binding initial contracts of sale, particularly where the economics of the purchase
are dependent upon a zoning or other governmental land use
change. Options are written agreements provided for a fee to a
buyer by a seller, giving the purchaser exclusive right to buy a
piece of property and the right to bail out, under specified
conditions. Say you're interested in an 11.5-acre $260,000 parcel
next to a highway in an expanding metropolitan area, but only
5 acres of the tract are zoned for shopping-center use—which is
your ultimate aim. The remaining 6.5 acres are zoned residential.
You check with the county planning commission, and the staff
suggests a rezoning might be possible, although some local
homeowner-group opposition might lead to a legal challenge.
Rather than involve yourself inextricably in a multi-year fight,
you go back to the seller. You point out that his $260,000 ask-
ing price is only reasonable if a rezoning can be obtained, and

that the parcel is worth only half that price if developed for housing. To protect both parties' interests, you propose an option contract—for a $5,000 nonrefundable fee—for purchase of the land at $260,000, provided the necessary rezoning is accomplished within two years. If the zoning change does ultimately come through, the owner gets his full price, and you get the valuable commercial property you sought. But if in two years the zoning change hasn't come through, you have an escape hatch and all you've gambled away is $5,000, rather than $260,000.

Options come in an endless variety of shapes, including what are known as rolling options. These involve sequential actions by the buyer and seller. One section of the contract may allow the buyer to take title to 100 acres of a 500-acre tract for development; the second part may open up 300 additional acres within three years; a third section of the contract may permit acquisition of the balance any time within the first four years, and so forth. If development plans go awry somewhere along the way, purchaser and seller can stop the deal at the next acreage segment and avoid wasting time and money. A crucial acquisition tool for large-scale land buyers, options can work very advantageously for small-scale investors as well.

Consider leasing acreage with an option to buy, rather than outright purchase. This could be a relatively painless way to move into a farming, orchard or cattle enterprise for the interim. As when you lease a business car, most of your out-of-pocket expenses can be deducted at tax time. You might also look at the possibility of purchasing land for immediate leaseback to the seller. This has tax benefits for him and produces instant income for you.

FINANCING

Your local S&L, bank or mortgage broker may greet you with open arms and competitive interest rates when you walk in for a rental home or vacation condominium mortgage. But ask for money to buy a piece of acreage in the hinterlands, or even for a vacant lot in your metropolitan area, and you will probably be greeted less effusively. Commercial banks and S&Ls are permitted by their federal regulatory agencies to make loans on raw, unimproved land, but most avoid doing so. They see the land business as an area of high risk and high potential loss—unless construction of housing or commercial development is about to occur on the property you're buying, or unless you're exceptionally solid financially.

Far more than unimproved real estate, land is highly vulnerable to such factors as government decisions about zoning and environment protection, and the swings of the national economy. The interest-rate peaks of 1974 and 1975 and the shock waves following the oil embargo ruined billions of dollars' worth of "prudent" land investments across the United States. The banks that lent money to those developers and real estate investment trusts who couldn't afford to hold on to their properties for the duration of the credit crunch are still smarting from the experience. S&Ls, which by tradition and law prefer to stick to residential finance in their local areas anyway, never took the early 1970s land plunge and are glad they didn't.

Given this institutional reluctance, where do you look for financing for land? The two main sources are commercial lenders who are willing to buck the trend, and the owner of the property you want to purchase.

Some local lenders, particularly commercial banks, can be convinced by their depositors to take a chance on a land investment. It helps if you're a substantial depositor and if you have substantial assets elsewhere, particularly income-producing real estate. And it helps if you can put together a strong loan application package for the bank, showing what a shrewd investment your purchase will prove to be when it's subdivided for housing years from now.

The bank loans you negotiate for land generally won't carry ideal terms—ten to twelve years might be the maximum length of mortgage you'll be able to obtain, and the interest rate may be several percentage points over the bank's prime lending rate (i.e., up to 12 to 15 percent). The loan-to-value ratio may also be relatively low—75 percent or less, requiring a down payment of 25 to 35 percent.

These stiff terms have the drawback of greatly increasing your carrying costs. A $50,000 ten-year mortgage on a piece of acreage at 11 percent simple interest requires monthly principal and interest amortization of $688.76. Add that to property taxes of $800 to $1,000 a year in a metropolitan area plus insurance, and you've got a sizable cash drain.

Loans for development lots are generally easier to obtain than loans for raw land or farm acreage because of the expectation of construction in the near future. Banks and even your neighborhood S&L may be willing to offer 85 percent loans (with 15 percent down) at several points over the prime rate for short terms. A northern Virginia bank, for example, has financed hundreds of individual-investor homesite lots between $30,000 and $50,000 in suburban Washington, D.C., at rates of 10.25 to 11 percent with ten-year terms. Creative banks elsewhere in the country offer alternative financing packages, some with steeper rates, some with longer pay-back periods. For speculative, subdivided lots that appear to be on the verge of development, many banks lose their nightmare of being stuck with unsalable cow pastures.

For larger land projects, life insurance companies, real estate investment trusts and commercial land brokers are worth trying. For farmland purchases, some lenders may be willing to participate in loans under a variety of U.S. Department of Agriculture programs, but you've got to be prepared to do serious farming. The Veterans Administration's GI loan program also permits the acquisition of land, as long as there's a house on it, or one about to be built.

The second major source for financing—and often the most advantageous—is the seller. Presumably no one is more motivated to dispose of the property than the person trying to sell it. No one is likely to be more creative and flexible—guided by you, according to your investment objectives—than the seller. And in the land field, seller participation in financing is more common than in virtually any other segment of real estate.

What sorts of deals can you readily negotiate?

First, you can ask for an *option contract,* as discussed above. That has the effect of cutting your ultimate risk exposure to

the option fee amount, and offers the possibility of increasing
your leveraged return sharply.

Second, you can push for a loan *interest rate* well below what
might be charged by a commercial bank. Institutional lenders
have overhead costs that account for two points or more of
their quoted interest rate. The least a seller can do is go two
points below the prevailing market. If your bank would offer
you 11 percent on a ten-year loan, press the seller for a rate
no higher than 9 percent. With true grit, you can push him
even lower than that.

Third, you can seek *extended pay-back* terms—fifteen or
twenty years rather than five to ten—or *interest-only* payments
(no principal amortization at all). You can arrange for annual
or quarterly payments rather than monthly, or set up a non-
amortizing mortgage that simply calls for a lump-sum balloon
payment at the end of the term.

Fourth, you can negotiate exceptionally *low down payments*,
5 percent or 10 percent, and point out to the seller the significant tax advantages of an installment loan over a period of
years (see p. 266).

Land Contracts. A common land-acquisition financing technique used throughout the country is the contract-for-deed, or
land contract. The form of the contract differs somewhat from
jurisdiction to jurisdiction, but the net effect is the same. Unlike mortgages or deeds of trust, where title passes in the transaction to the purchaser or a trustee, in a land contract the title
remains with the seller until either a specified percentage of
the debt has been paid, or until the entire sum has been paid.
Land contracts typically allow the seller or owner to cancel the
sale and retain all payments to date if the purchaser misses one
or more payment deadline. Some unscrupulous Florida and
Southwest land promoters have used land contracts to bilk
tens of millions of dollars from unsuspecting small investors. In
numerous cases recorded by federal and state legal authorities,
these promoters have sold virtually worthless acreage via land
contracts over and over again to out-of-state purchasers. Commonly the same lot was "sold" simultaneously to several buyers.

The buyers learned of their mistake, stopped making payments, legally forfeited their investments to date, and ended up with nothing. The promoters then resold their lots to still more investors.

The legitimate usage of land contracts, however, far outweighs their role in scandals. When properly drafted for the buyer by competent counsel, land contracts can offer an exceptionally low down payment, extended-term route for buying acreage.

SALES CONTRACTS AND FINANCIAL DOCUMENTS

The written "offer" you casually hand over to Farmer Brown for his eighty acres will turn into a legally binding contract if he puts his signature on it. So think out your negotiating tactics, your need for protective clauses, and your development plans *before* you fill out that innocent-looking "bid" form the real estate broker provides for you.

Sales contracts come in all sorts of standard and no-so-standard types, depending upon area of the country. Your concern as a buyer should be that whatever format the sales contract takes, it should adequately address at least the following:

Precise Description of the Property. When you buy a house or an apartment building in a built-up urban area, there's normally little question about the legal description of the property you're buying. But property descriptions of raw land, farmland, or even unsubdivided acreage located inside major metropolitan areas tend to be more complicated. In general, the farther you go out from the city into rural areas, the less precise are the existing descriptions in deeds. For example, say you've taken a quick drive around a piece of partially farmed, partially wooded rural property, whose owner describes it as consisting of 56 acres. You've agreed verbally on a price of $100,000 for the tract, or roughly $1,800 per acre. The reality, though, may be that the owner has only the foggiest notion of how many acres he's really got, and that his deed describes the property with phrases like "twenty feet south of the oak tree on Agatha's Bluff" or refers to granite rock piles, stream beds, wooden bridges, log cabins, dirt roads and the like. The seller, who inherited the land and never had it properly surveyed, may really own only forty acres, thus raising the per-acre price to $2,500, far beyond market values in the vicinity for similar land.

How do you ensure you're protected from the very serious potential problems arising from inadequate descriptions?

First, the contract should be contingent upon a survey, conducted by a licensed professional surveyor acceptable to you, providing precise boundary descriptions, locations of all easements, encroachments, alleyways and streets, and an accurate acreage count. If price is to be set on the basis of the acreage fixed by the survey, that should be stated in writing. If you as purchaser are to have the right to cancel the contract if the survey turns up problems, inadequate acreage or unacceptable permanent easements, that should be stated plainly.

Second, you may want to insert a "mother hubbard" clause to be certain you're going to take title to everything you expected. The clause—as appropriate to the particular situation—can specify that the property description embraces "all real property owned by the seller" in the town of _____ , or all the real property owned by the seller known as the Hatfield Farm, etc.

Third, the contract should be highly specific as to the mineral rights you are or aren't getting (a crucial point historically in many oil- and gas-rich areas of the Southwest), water rights, and full development rights consistent with local laws.

Composition of Property. In tracts composed of multiple parcels with varying acreage valuations, it will be advantageous for tax purposes for you to structure the contract so as to spell out these variations and their relation to the total price being paid. In other words, if you are buying a 500-acre, $100,000 tract composed of 300 acres of hilly timberland, 100 acres of commercially zoned highway frontage, and 100 acres of working farmland, the contract should break out the parcels in detail. This gives you varying tax bases for computation of gains or losses later on varying segments of the property, and provides you with flexibility in tax planning you wouldn't have if a simple $2,000-per-acre flat value was assigned to the tract.

Financing. Where purchase is to be contingent upon your ability to obtain financing from an institutional lender, the contract should give you plenty of time to get it. If the money market is tight for housing, it will be even more so for unimproved land finance, so add in extra time—two to three weeks extra, if necessary—for shopping around.

Where financing is to be provided in whole or part by the seller, the contract should include detailed descriptions of note terms, repayment schedules and the nature of the security. To protect yourself, always insert (if the contract doesn't already have one) an exculpatory clause making it clear that the real property involved will be the noteholder's *only* security for the loan. That means the seller-financer can't come after your personal property or other real estate in the event you default and the proceeds from the land aren't adequate to retire the debt. All he can do is reclaim the property he sold you.

Other worthwhile finance-related points your contract ought to include are language prohibiting any prepayment penalties should you choose to retire the note earlier than scheduled; and language requiring the seller-financer to notify you when he believes you are in default. In some states, trust deed documents routinely include "acceleration" clauses allowing the noteholder to foreclose immediately after the purchaser defaults.

Releases. Both the mortgage (or deed of trust) and the contract should state that portions of the property may be released from the lien created by the mortgage at later dates, according to the development plans of the purchaser. This is extremely important, for it allows you to prepay segments of your debt as you proceed with your development project(s)—e.g., turning 30 acres of your 120-acre tract into a mobile-home park, leaving the remainder as a farm—and to use pieces of land for streets and other required local purposes. The contract should also state the lender's willingness to subordinate his lien (make it junior in standing) to whatever bank or S&L construction or development financing you may need to secure later on for construction of a subdivision on the land. The original lender's express willingness to do this is a valuable advance concession to negotiate.

Authority of Seller. Routine as it may seem, before you sign a contract for purchase and spend money preparing for acquisition, are you certain the seller has the authority to dispose of the land? In the case of a corporate owner, for example, a vote of the board of directors may be required for legal disposition of such assets as farmland. Numerous deals have fallen through at or before settlement because the purchaser hadn't really made sure he was negotiating with a party authorized to sell.

Title. The contract should be contingent upon receipt by you of an abstract of title indicating the property to be free of all liens or claims, or of probable lawsuits against the owner. You should also obtain title insurance from a reputable firm, particularly in cases where the seller is your lender. Try to get the seller to pay for all title-related charges; after all, he should be willing to deliver a property free of liens.

Mortgage Moratorium Clause. In cases where you plan immediate development, consider inserting language in the contract and the note allowing postponement of the debt and interest payments during any period of direct government action delaying your intended development activity. In an age of environmental constraints, you have to buy and plan defensively. Your attorney can draft adequate protective language.

Warranties Against Undisclosed Government Actions or Plans. As an additional safety precaution, include express warranties by the seller that he knows of no zoning changes, condemnations, or other land-use-related regulatory changes underway or contemplated by government authorities that would endanger the stated development plans of the purchaser.

SUBDIVIDING: WHOLESALE INTO RETAIL

Whatever your interim or long-range plans may be for your land, someday you probably will want to *subdivide* it into smaller parcels. Subdividing is the customary first step to turning landholdings into huge capital gains. No one really gets rich in land without knowing at least the brief, basic steps in the subdivision process in advance.

Subdividing simply means taking a parcel of raw land, surveying it, marking out on paper a series of *plats* with lots, blocks, roads and easements, and then presenting it in proposed form to local governing authorities (see the example opposite). If the plans are acceptable to the local officials, they will permit them to be entered on the public land records as the proposed eventual use of your land. At this point in the process, you may not want to do anything further. You may want to let the property sit, zoned and ready for development by residential or commercial builders, or for purchase by land speculators. You may already have gone to considerable expense in pursuing the subdivision: in addition to the costs of surveying, you may have had to spend thousands of dollars in legal, planning, architectural and market-research efforts. Or you may have had to battle local growth-control forces for a zoning change.

Whatever the case, the mere act of recording a subdivision at the local courthouse means you've transformed what was a wholesale commodity into a retail commodity—and you've almost certainly increased the value of your holding. Your thirty-acre tract may still be filled with timber or still be a working vegetable farm, but to potential investors it suddenly looks very enticing. They may want to buy it as it is, leaving your street and lot outlines undisturbed, or they may buy it with plans to alter it prior to actual development.

Of course, nothing should prevent you from acting as *developer* of your own land, reaping benefits not only from the increased value of the acreage, but from construction of houses or commercial structures as well. But that's a whole book in itself. A good introduction to the subdivision development process, covering all the permits, fees, licenses, red tape and market-

SITE PLAN FOR A SUBDIVISION

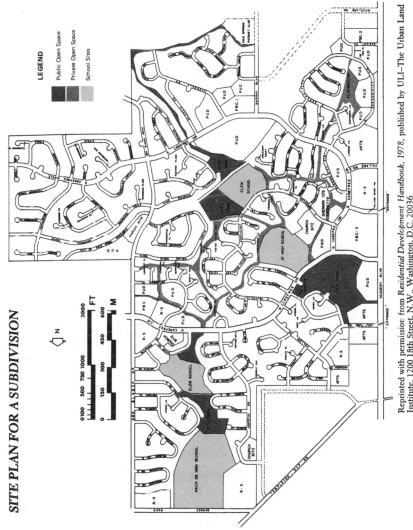

LEGEND

Public Open Space
Private Open Space
School Sites

Reprinted with permission from *Residential Development Handbook, 1978*, published by ULI–The Urban Land Institute, 1200 18th Street, N.W., Washington, D.C. 20036

ing costs that development entails today, is the *Residential Development Handbook*, published in 1978 by the Urban Land Institute, Washington, D.C.

TAX TIPS

The same capital gains and depreciation rules of the U.S. tax system apply to you as a prospective land baron as they apply to your rental property holdings. (See pp. 76ff for a detailed discussion of basic terms and principles.) The key difference is that unimproved land is a non-depreciable asset and can't provide you with the annual income-sheltering tax write-offs of other real estate investments.

Land held for twelve months or more, and which isn't traded as business inventory, qualifies for favorable capital gains treatment. Note, however, that land deemed by the IRS to be held for personal use, as opposed to investment—for example, for a hobby that is intended to make no profit—qualifies for no expense deductions whatsoever, other than interest, property taxes and casualty losses. Property taxes that can be construed by the IRS as having been assessed by local authorities as repayment for special benefits, such as construction of a public road to the property or some other unusual public service, are not deductible. They must be taken as long-term capital improvements to the property, and used to adjust the land's tax basis for capital gains purposes.

Depreciation is permissible, naturally, on any business-related capital improvements, existing or newly constructed, on the land. For example, say you bought a fifteen-acre tract of land that had an old farmhouse on it. If you rent out the house, you treat it for tax purposes exactly as you would a rental house (see Chapter 2). You can depreciate the building (minus the land value and anticipated salvage value, if any) on a straight-line or 125 percent declining-balance basis over the course of its economic life.

All expenses related to your rental of the house (ranging from ads in the paper to property taxes) are deductible in the year they occurred. All routine maintenance and repair work also qualifies for deduction. Anything that fits the IRS's definition of a capital improvement must be capitalized and added to the tax basis of the rental house.

Tax treatment of the *interim uses* you choose for your land gets progressively more complex as your business enterprise on the property gets more complex. For example, citrus orchards and almond groves have been used for the high tax shelter deductions and depreciation-loss write-offs they provide during their early nonproductive years, and their long, profitable fruit-bearing lives. Certain expenses of farming in general qualify for favorable federal tax treatment (for example, the immediate deductibility of costs for fertilizers, soil conditioners and water conservation payments, and expenses for erosion control) and may qualify for special local property tax incentives as well. Farming, incidentally, includes poultry, cattle, fish, fruit and vegetable cultivation, among other forms. Timberlands qualify for preferential federal taxation, too, via capital gains treatment of timber harvests by investors and rapid amortization of road-construction expenses.

The specific tax wrinkles you can take advantage of on your interim land business—whether it's skeet-shooting ranges or a drive-in movie theater—should be examined thoroughly with your accountant or attorney. *Think taxes before you acquire* property. Tote up what a piece of land will do to your taxes in the year of acquisition (undeveloped), year two (developed), and so on during the period of your holding.

Thinking taxes will also help you calculate when to *sell* your property, or perhaps convince you to hang on to it indefinitely. The same ownership strategies that are open to you in rental properties are open to you with land. These include *tax-free exchanges* and *pyramiding* of your equities, using second mortgages and purchase of new lands. (These options are discussed in detail in Chapter 10.) Note that one of the dangers of high-volume investment activity is also present in land: being classed as a dealer for tax purposes. Before subdividing a tract, or selling off parcels of it, consult your attorney about the possible impact on your status in the eyes of Uncle Sam.

5

Vacation Houses

Sugarbush. Lake Tahoe. Vail. Outer Banks. Laguna Beach. Taos. The Hamptons. Freeport, Bahamas. Costa del Sol. Hilton Head. The names alone are enticement enough to lure buyers in droves to vacation and second-home properties. One in every twenty American households—3.5 million—now owns a housing unit at a resort or on a lakefront, mountainside, river, or ocean beach somewhere in the United States or abroad. One in twelve families now owns *either* a lot or a recreational home in addition to a principal residence, and the number is rising fast.

Vacation property in the economy of the late 1970s is viewed less as a luxury than as a natural extension of residential real estate ownership and an inflation hedge. Over ten million second-home lots have been subdivided in the past decade, assuring the construction of at least 75,000 to 125,000 additional units a year.

Price movements in second-home properties are difficult to generalize because of their diversity of structural type and location, but the direction most definitely is up. For example, ocean-front cottages in Outer Banks, North Carolina, that went for

$30,000 to $35,000 four years ago sell for $70,000 to $80,000 today. Condominiums in Vail, Colorado, that cost $50,000 in 1975 went for $75,000 and up in 1978, and prices are rising at least 15 percent annually. Units in Killington, Vermont, that sold for $45,000 in 1974 bring $65,000 to $70,000 today. Beach area prices in pre–Proposition 13 California were rising at 12 to 18 percent a year, despite high mortgage rates. Today, thanks to lower property taxes, the annual percentage jumps may be even higher. The average *national* price of a newly constructed second home *doubled* between 1974 and 1977; currently the average is over $30,000, with huge variations on either side of that figure.

How do vacation or second-home properties such as these perform as investments? How do they stack up against alternative real estate purchases? What are the risks involved in vacation property, and what are the tax consequences?

PROS AND CONS

In *pure* investment terms—comparing yields on the dollar, liquidity, and tax advantages—the nod almost always would have to go to rental houses, second trusts, syndications or income-producing commercial property over vacation real estate. The combined advantages of high leverage, rapid appreciation and tax shelter that you can obtain from the typical central-city or suburban rental unit simply can't be touched by the typical vacation home. The tax consequences in particular—as discussed below in some detail—are quite lopsided.

Sometimes the opportunity to buy a vacation house or condominium apartment at a distress-sale price negates the general rule. Hundreds of condos and townhouses in South Florida and in East Coast mountain and shore resort areas were auctioned off for bargain basement prices in 1975 and 1976, when their developers foundered financially and creditors foreclosed. Buyers walked away with three- and four-bedroom $29,000–$35,000 oceanfront units in Maryland resorts, for example, that would bring nearly double that price in 1978.

Other possible outstanding vacation property moves, in

competitive investment terms, are purchases in the early development stages of boom resort towns, or the acquisition of unusually choice sites that someone later will pay you an arm and
a leg to get. Natural waterfront property, for example, is in
finite supply; it has higher than average appreciation potential
for the years of 1980 to 1990, when the baby-boom generation
of the late 1940s and early 1950s hits its highest income-earning,
highest discretionary spending years. A particularly well-situated
piece of waterfront property, with boat dockage or access, could
prove to be an exceptional investment in terms of real capital
growth.

   The risks of vacation properties, like their benefits, stem from
their distance from cities, their removal from the economic
mainstream. When the mortgage market sneezes, the vacation-
property finance market catches a full-blown cold. When the
Arabs clamp an embargo on oil shipments to the West, the
cities are merely inconvenienced, but developments out in the
mountains come to a shuddering halt and property values freeze
or plummet. During the 1974–76 period in many parts of the
United States, for example, gasoline prices shot up, people were
less willing to make the long haul to the mountain lakes, and
the recreation-home field went fizzle.

   A good example of what can happen to vacation property in
the midst of a recession took place in the mid-Atlantic Gold
Coast communities of Delaware, Maryland and Virginia that
serve as the playgrounds for the cities of Washington, D.C.,
Philadelphia, Baltimore, and Wilmington. From the mid-1960s
until the early 1970s, buyers of cottages and duplexes in Bethany
Beach and Rehoboth Beach, Delaware, and Ocean City, Maryland, picked up what often turned out to be extraordinary investments. Cottages that sold in the $10,000-to-$15,000 range
doubled or tripled in value during that period and returned
handsome summer rental fees and tax deductions. Michael
Sumichrast, a Washington area resident and chief economist
of the National Association of Home Builders, was one of the
many wise buyers. In 1965 he paid $11,000 for a three-bedroom,
two-bath rental house at the beach, and in 1973 he sold it for
$33,000—a handsome capital appreciation by any standard.

Yet the very economic forces that produced Sumichrast's windfall also created the condo boom that plunged real estate at the seashore into a depression during 1974 and 1975. The massive overbuilding at Ocean City and elsewhere during the go-go years of the early seventies—combined with the high mortgage rates and the Arab oil embargo—threw prices into a freeze that only recently has begun to thaw. Buyers of real estate at the shore who were anticipating 10 to 20 percent appreciation per year in their property values were badly disappointed. Values stagnated or dropped. In 1975 and 1976 owners who tried to sell their units found themselves in competition with the large banks holding the mortgages on foreclosed condominium projects, who were auctioning everything off for a song.

It may not be really fair, of course, to judge vacation property *purely* in investment terms. Most people don't buy it on those terms; most people don't ask themselves, "Well, should I put my last $15,000 into that rehab rental house in the city or into one of those cedar two deckers on Lake Minniwattie?"

Sharp buyers don't go after vacation real estate until they've invested in other, more advantageous real estate that will provide them better leverage, greater tax shelter, or net income. They can then afford to take a lower-yielding route for the sake of pleasure—and not feel that they're losing ground to inflation.

THINGS TO LOOK FOR IN VACATION PROPERTY

Whether you plan to rent out or not, there are a number of basic, investment-related considerations you ought to give to your choice of vacation property. Just as you don't buy your principal residence on a whim, don't let yourself buy a second home on the spur of a moment in the middle of a vacation in the mountains or at the beach. At least you ought to have a mental checklist and "walk through" your decision logically, in advance.

Community/Geographic Area. What do you really *know* about the community, town or county in which your prospective second home is located? Have you been going to the area for recreation for years? Do you read its newspapers, know its future development plans or its current restrictions? Do you know its tax and voting rights treatment of nonresident property owners? (Some resort communities prevent nonresidents from participating in local politics and decision-making.) Does the locality rise and fall economically with the tourist/resort trade, or does it have an ongoing self-sustaining economy that acts as a buffer during recession periods when tourism weakens? Does it function as a *year-round* community for a growing number of people? Year-round resort communities tend to have more stable property values and more dependable financing, and involve less risk than single-season towns that close up when the snow melts or after the Labor Day crowds head home. Does the local government provide adequate or better public services that make sense in comparison to your projected level of property taxes? Does the community itself or a neighboring community offer a *variety* of things to do, thereby widening the attraction to different age groups and to people with different tastes in recreational activities? Resort areas limited to a single attraction are more vulnerable to economic swings or to changing tastes in leisure activities. A community with multi-season cultural and entertainment opportunities will attract higher gross rentals per year and will have higher, more dependable resale values than less diverse communities will.

Immediate Neighborhood/Vicinity of Property. Can your property be reached easily by some form of transportation throughout the year? Is the community close enough to your primary residence to make sense as a place to get away? If your proposed second home is a cabin deep in the Maine woods (and you're getting fifty acres of the woods along with the cabin), you may not need to worry about development plans on the tract next to yours. But if you're interested in a $60,000 waterfront house and the four large lots next to yours are zoned (or could be rezoned) commercial, you could end up with an eighteen-hour-a-day miniature golf course or a twenty-story condo as a neighbor. You must find out what's in store for the immediate area, or risk loss of value relative to inflation. Call or visit the municipal planning office (or county/regional planning commission) and ask how your area fits into the long-term master plan for land use; ask whether any attempts have been made to rezone vacant tracts nearby from low density to high, or from residential to commercial/industrial, and find out what the end result was. Your real estate broker may be able to furnish some of this information as well, but not without potentially losing you as a buyer.

Special Locational Advantages. In vacation property, siting can create and accelerate value unbelievably; it can also hold it back depressingly. Waterfront property, whether on a river, ocean, bay or pond, commands top dollar in most areas of the country, and *rises in percentage terms* faster than other property. Although it is more costly to begin with—and sometimes carries with it a special risk of flooding, erosion or storm damage—waterfront second-home properties are a good investment bet. So-called semi-waterfront property (near the water, with direct access) or property with unusual, spectacular natural views comes next in appreciation potential.

The Unit Itself. Reviewing the structural points in the house-analysis form on pp. 30–35 or the investment guidelines for condominiums in Chapter 6 would be a good idea. In the case of a detached one- to two-unit dwellings in resort areas, pay special attention to the following.

1. *Sleeping space.* Does your proposed unit sleep at least four adults, and preferably a total of six to eight people? Vacation property commands substantially more in rentals, produces higher occupancy rates, stays in better shape, and is worth more at resale time if it has room enough to sleep more than one family comfortably. Experienced owner-investors and agents across the United States will testify that units with enough room for the average-sized family—plus plenty of extra room for relatives, friends and other guests—are better investments than more cramped quarters.

2. *Layout and equipment.* Does the unit make sense in terms or room arrangement and layout? In particular, are the bedrooms sufficiently separated from the living and dining areas to afford privacy and quiet for adults? Is there plenty of dining space,

FEATURES OF AN ENERGY-EFFICIENT HOME

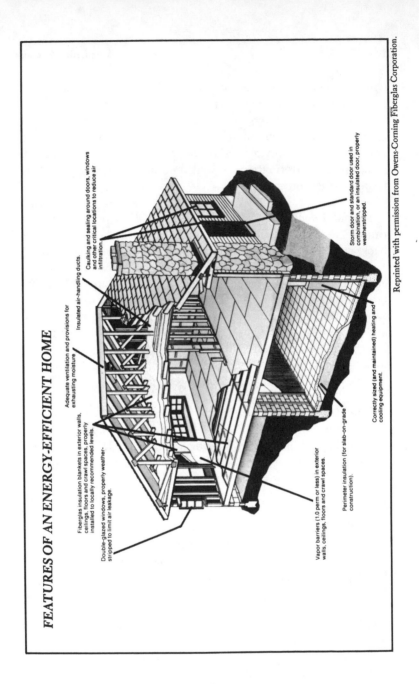

Adequate ventilation and provisions for exhausting moisture

Insulated air-handling ducts.

Caulking and sealing around doors, windows and other critical locations to reduce air infiltration.

Fiberglas insulation blankets in exterior walls, ceilings, floors and crawl spaces, properly installed to locally recommended levels.

Double-glazed windows, properly weather-stripped to limit air leakage.

Storm door and standard door used in combination, or an insulated door, properly weatherstripped.

Vapor barriers (1.0 perm or less) in exterior walls, ceilings, floors and crawl spaces.

Perimeter insulation (for slab-on-grade construction).

Correctly sized (and maintained) heating and cooling equipment.

Reprinted with permission from Owens-Corning Fiberglas Corporation.

cabinet space, and storage space? Are there enough bathrooms, and in the case of beach-area cottages, is there a shower outside to keep sand out of the house? Does the unit contain—or have room for you to add—the sorts of amenities you or renters may seek on a vacation: washer, dryer, dishwasher, fireplace(s), air conditioning, telephone, at least a fifty-gallon hot-water heater? Is the parking space adequate? Is there enough cross-ventilation to keep the unit comfortable on hot summer days?

3. *Utilities.* Sewage, water supply, gas and electricity are things you may take for granted at home, but they are of vital importance in vacation property. If you've got to drill a well and/or install a septic tank, you may be talking about thousands of dollars and lots of headache. Well-drilling charges can run from $5 to $10 a foot, depending on the amount of piping required. A septic tank and field for a four-bedroom house can run $1,100 to $2,000—or even thousands more in distant resorts like the U.S. Virgin Islands. Rapidly developing recreational areas, particularly in mountain or ski areas, sometimes pollute their own streams and brooks because of poor placement of septic fields and usage beyond the soil capacity. A federal study of second-home communities in 1976 pinpointed this as one of the most severe challenges posed by the recreational boom.

The availability of gas or oil for heating in a recreational community is a definite plus in terms of monthly utility bills. Many new developments have only electrical services, however, and that generally means higher heating costs, particularly with baseboard units. Be certain to obtain copies of a year's worth of monthly utility bills from any seller of an existing resort area home, and get firm estimates from the builder of any new unit. The seller may be getting rid of that charming ski chalet because he can't take the $400-per-month electric bills on top of the mortgage.

Is the unit adequately insulated for the usage pattern you anticipate? If the dwelling has extensive glass surfaces, are they thermally efficient? If the seller tells you the attic and wall insulation is just fine, ask him for its R-value (resistance to heat flow) and check it against the accompanying minimum regional levels recommended by the National Association of Home Builders Research Corporation (see p. 152)

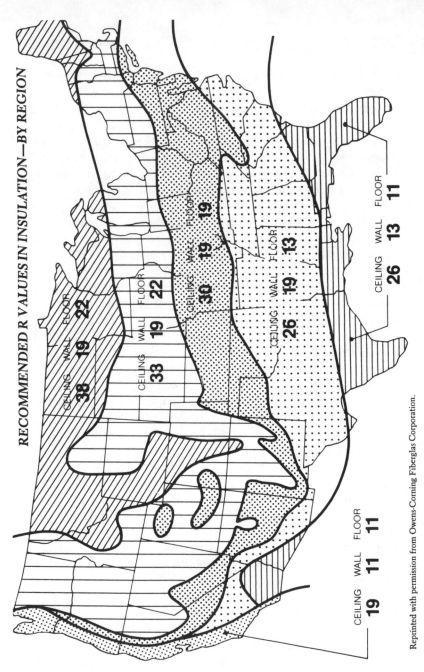

RECOMMENDED R VALUES IN INSULATION—BY REGION

CEILING WALL FLOOR
38 19 22

CEILING WALL FLOOR
33 19 19

CEILING WALL FLOOR
30 19 19

CEILING WALL FLOOR
26 19 13

CEILING WALL FLOOR
26 13 11

CEILING WALL FLOOR
19 11 11

152

4. *Maintenance-free features.* The last thing you need for vacation property is a house that requires a lot of fixing up and maintenance. Think about this *before* you buy. Does the siding have to be repainted every year or two because of the salt air, or is it a salt-resistant natural finish that requires little care? Is the carpeting you bought with the unit long-lasting and easy to keep clean, or is it likely to need replacement in two to three years? How about the cabinets, tables, chairs and other furniture (if they come as part of the package)? Are they highly durable and functional, designed to withstand use over a number of years, or are they easily damaged? Is the kitchen equipment of good quality, or is it bottom-of-the-line stuff that will break down with the first large, demanding bunch of renters? (If your mortgage on the unit *includes* financing for these furnishings, think twice. You could easily end up paying for a refrigerator or stove long after you had it hauled away.) Will you need to employ help to keep the landscaping and other aspects of the exterior in good shape, or are they essentially maintenance-free?

5. *Restrictions on use.* Many second-home developments have permanent covenants in individual property deeds that restrict what buyers can do with their units. This is *always* the case with condominiums, whether high-rise or townhouse, and is common in "planned unit developments" (PUDs), where homeowners' associations are incorporated, own common property and exert architectural review rights. Better read through the standard restrictions before buying. You may find yourself prevented from installing solar power equipment, a swimming pool, or a TV antenna or from even changing the color of your house's finish without your absentee neighbor's okay. Homeowners' covenants and rules can preserve property values by maintaining high standards of upkeep and appearance, but they can also lead you into court or cut down on rental income.

6. *Price.* Nothing is more variable, and *less* worth splitting hairs over, than price. Sellers often fixate on price; sharp buyers see the entire package, which includes financing terms, settlement costs, and other fees partially or wholly assumable by the sellers. Agree to the full price, but cut your short-term outlays by *more* than what you gave up on price. Let him take one or

more of the loan discount points imposed by the lender. Let him
pay most of the settlement fees.

You should, of course, do the same careful check-outs on
price that you'd do for a rental house or for your own residence.
Talk to several different brokers and examine their multiple listing files, if available. Visit comparable properties and note selling prices. In the case of larger properties, consider a professional

CASH-FLOW PROJECTIONS ON VACATION HOUSE

Year 1

Outgo	Down payment (25 percent)	$15,000
	Settlement related costs, 3 percent (including title, transfer taxes, legal)	1,800
	Principal and interest (based on $45,000 loan at 9.5 percent over 25 years)	4,720
	Casualty insurance	120
	Utilities—electricity	750
	Water and sewage	120
	Property taxes	600
	Maintenance and repair	200
	CATV	85
	Furnishings	1,000
	Rental ads, licenses, signs, etc.	100
	Travel	200
	Homeowners' association fee	125
	Telephone service	200
		$25,020
Income	(Rental based on ten weeks total, marketed and managed by owner, at average rental charge of $350 per week, plus three holiday off-season weekends at $150 each)	$ 3,950
	Cash Flow:	(−$21,070)

Year 2

Outgo	Principal and interest	$ 4,720
	Insurance	120
	Utilities—electricity	920
	Property taxes	630
	Maintenance and repair	220
	CATV	85
	Furnishings/equipment	350
	Travel	80
	Homeowners' association fee	125
	Telephone service	225
	Advertising, mailings, signs	200
		$ 7,675

Income (Based on twenty weeks of rental at an
average $300 per week, plus four off-
season holiday weekends at $150 each) $ 6,600

Cash Flow: (−$ 1,075)

Year 3

Outgo	Principal and interest	$ 4,720
	Insurance	135
	Utilities—electricity	1,050
	Property taxes	630
	Maintenance and repair	200
	CATV	100
	Furnishings/equipment	400
	Travel	80
	Homeowners' association fee	125
	Telephone service	225
	Advertising, mailings, etc.	200
		$ 7,865

Income (Based on twenty-two weeks at an
average $375 per week, plus four off-
season holiday weekends at $150 each) $ 8,850

Cash Flow: +$ 985

appraisal to determine the limits within which your negotiations can take place.

7. *Cash flow.* Calculate in advance what you're going to have to spend on the place for at least the first two years; then calculate possible offsetting income and tax breaks, and assess the bottom line. Your pretax projections on a $60,000 town-house in a recreational community might look something like the table on pp. 154–155. Obviously, some of these figures will vary widely according to the type of unit and its geographic location. Outgo for utilities may be higher or lower according to seasonal usage, construction quality and insulation. The figures here do not include brokerage or management charges by realty professionals—which can cut rental income by anywhere from 10 to 35 percent, depending on services rendered. Many owners set aside a cash reserve in local banks for emergency repairs or maintenance, and many incur higher maintenance costs than the owner in the example. The post-tax outcome will vary widely according to tax bracket and degree of usage by the owner.

Clearly, however, vacation property can be a substantial cash drain, and you ought to face that squarely in advance. It can also turn around and produce a positive cash flow within a couple of years.

TAXES AND INVESTMENT OPTIONS

In the area of vacation property, more so than in the case of any other kind of real estate investment, federal tax law will help you determine whether you really want to rent, where you buy, how many days you rent, and how you treat income and expenses. The 1976 Tax Reform Act revolutionized the vacation-property business, and you ought to understand what it permits and disallows *before* you buy that ski condo or the four-season hideaway in Florida.

Tax-Law Fundamentals. If you've got some notion of creating a tax shelter on your vacation place by renting it out, you'd better take a second look at your figures. Unless you're planning not to use it much for your own fun, you'll find it difficult to deduct your expenses come April 15, and virtually impossible to register a tax loss on the property.

Under the old, easy rules governing vacation-home investments you could do that, or at least try. You could claim incredibly high expenditures against your rental "business"—including the magic paper expenditure known as depreciation—while simultaneously enjoying rapid capital growth and having a ball in your place in the mountains or at the shore.

The 1976 act changed all that. Accountants around the United States active in the real estate field report that a large percentage of their vacation-property clients still haven't familiarized themselves with the provisions of the law, and could lose thousands of dollars needlessly on their returns in 1979 and beyond. One tax specialist for a national accounting firm said a client of his lost $3,500 in deductions by unknowingly staying at his shore home one day beyond a limit imposed by the new tax law—possibly the most soberingly expensive vacation day the man will ever spend.

For prospective buyers and current owners, here is a quick rundown of the revised tax treatment of vacation real estate investments. Read slowly; it can save you money on your next tax return.

• *If you make personal use of your vacation house no more than 10 percent of the total days it is rented this year (or fourteen days, whichever is greater),* you can deduct as expenses such items as property maintenance costs, utilities, fees paid to brokers, depreciation, insurance premiums, mortgage interest, property taxes, casualty losses and other costs legitimately attributable to your efforts to generate rental income. Under these circumstances, the property is not considered a residence but a business enterprise similar to any commercial rental property. However, you'll have to be able to demonstrate under the so-called hobby-loss section of the Internal Revenue Code (Section 183) that the property is indeed a profit-motivated venture. This can be done by showing that it has turned a profit in at least two years during a consecutive period of five years, or by providing other proof convincing to the Internal Revenue Service. You must also reduce deductions for expenses claimed, proportionate to the number of days—up to the fourteen days or the 10 percent limit—during which usage was for your own personal purposes.*

The range of expenses you can claim for deductions in this type of rental property is as wide and creative as in the case of urban rental homes (see Chapter 2). Allowable deductions include travel to and from the unit, management and upkeep, entertainment, telephone, and of course any business functions, meetings or dinners you conduct there. Allowable depreciation rates on beach structures tend to be slightly more generous than on urban-area properties. IRS concedes that such factors as salt air, high winds and lower-quality construction do tend to cut useful life. Therefore, thirty-year lives for new dwellings and fifteen- to twenty-year lives for used properties may be acceptable. Check with your accountant before doing so, nonetheless.

• *If your personal use of the house exceeds 10 percent of the rental time or fourteen days,* your unit will be considered to have been used as a residence for some portion of the tax year (and you'll be governed by a new Section 280-A of the tax code). If you rent your property for fewer than fifteen days, you needn't worry about reporting your rental income (which theoretically should be very small), and you can't deduct any expenses other than mortgage interest, property taxes and casualty losses.

If your personal use goes beyond 10 percent of the total days the house was rented or the fourteen-day ceiling, your deductions for expenses can be no greater than your gross rental income, reduced by the portion of mortgage interest and property-tax expenditures that can be attributed to the rental use. In other words, once you exceed the 10 percent/fourteen-day threshold, you're not going to be able to take tax losses on the property because you're using it for personal pleasures.

---

* Incidentally, in the IRS's book, "personal use" includes such things as occupancy by brothers, sisters and grandparents, even at nominal rentals— or rentals to anyone else at concessionary rates in exchange for something of value.

To show how this works, let's take the hypothetical example of a New York man who rented out his Nags Head, North Carolina, beach house for 100 days in 1978, generating $5,000 in gross income. But he calculates that he had $10,750 in total costs, including mortgage interest, property taxes, utilities, maintenance, licenses and ads, and so forth. The owner used the beach house himself 25 days. He can therefore attribute only 80 percent of his mortgage interest and property-tax expenses to his commercial rental activities (100 days of rental use divided by 125 days of total rental and personal use), and he gets socked with a $1,000 limit on his $3,750 worth of other allocable expenses (see the outline on p. 160).

MAXIMIZING RENTAL INCOME

Can you picture owning an oceanfront house or a ski-resort condominium that generates $10,000 or more a year in gross rental income and offers substantial tax write-offs as well as an excellent spot for your own summer or winter vacation? Ask most second-home owners that question and you'll probably get an incredulous stare. How *do* you keep a unit far away from the city so filled with renters that it generates gross income comparable to or greater than that generated by urban property? After all, a three- to four-bedroom house rented out in the suburbs or in the city for $500 a month only grosses $6,000 a year; an in-town duplex rental at $400 per unit per month only grosses $9,600. How do you squeeze so much out of a vacation home?

The answer is in the multiples: First, you purchase a unit that has *four-season* potential. Second, you *equip* it for four-season usage. Third, you actively *market* it year-round. Fourth, you *manage* it, either on your own or with professional help, so well that you build up a solid repeat business and steadily cut marketing costs. And finally, you set your *rentals* at levels that generate profits to you after no more than two years of trying.

Let's take a look at each of the five. There's nothing magic about making money from vacation property; all it takes is a little flair and sensible organization.

A. INCOME AND EXPENSES

 1. Gross rental income $ 5,000
 2. Expenses
  a. Property taxes   1,000
  b. Mortgage interest   4,000
  c. Maintenance and utilities   2,000
  d. Depreciation   3,750

  Total expenses   10,750
 3. Profit/loss   (−$ 5,750)

B. CALCULATION OF LIMIT ON EXPENSES

 1. Gross rental income $ 5,000
 2. Minus prorated portion of realty taxes and
   mortgage interest allocable to rental usage
   —i.e., 80 percent or four-fifths of 2(a)
   and (b)   4,000

 3. Adjusted rental income and limits on
   deductions for expenses   1,000

C. ACTUAL EXPENSES

 (which normally would be fully deductible as
 business expenses under Section 162 of the
 Internal Revenue Code)
 1. Maintenance and utilities $ 2,000
 2. Depreciation   3,750

               $ 5,750

 3. Allocable to rental business
   ($5,750 × .80 = $4,600)

D. ALLOWABLE DEDUCTIONS FROM THE
 VACATION PROPERTY

 1. Real estate property taxes and mortgage
   interest attributable to rental use* $ 4,000
 2. Other expenses†   1,000

               $ 5,000

* Owner can deduct the remaining $1,000 in property taxes and mortgage interest as an itemized personal deduction.

† These are the expenses in C that are mainly wiped out as deductions by the new limit.

Four-Season Potential. Not every vacation property has it, of course. That log cabin in the wilderness of northern Minnesota may be a charmer in August, but once the blizzard season sets in in October, its market appeal drops precipitously. Sharp second-home buyers consider the seasonal rent performance potential well in advance of signing any sales contracts.

The units with greatest potential, obviously, are those in or near resort communities that hum every month of the year. These may be mountain resorts—offering skiing, indoor and outdoor swimming, platform and regular tennis, hiking, entertainment, and so forth, à la Vail or Lake Tahoe—or they may be ocean communities with special attractions in the colder months (such as Atlantic City, Sanibel Island or St. Thomas). Gross rents in well-chosen, twelve-month areas like these can easily outstrip urban properties. The per-week rates tend to be impressively high for top-of-the-line units, with no vacancies. For example, beach-house rental rates in Ocean City, Maryland, rise to $600 to $700 a week in the height of the season, and drop off to $95 to $150 for weekends in the dead of winter. Small, investor-owned Hawaiian beach houses go for $500 to $800 a week year-round, depending upon amenities. Vail and Sugarbush units bring in $500 to $700 a week in high season, somewhat less in the warmer months. Caribbean condo-villas rent for $100 to $150 a day, and often gross $18,000 to $20,000 a year.

Equipment for Multi-Season. Don't freeze your tenants or they won't come back. And don't make them sweat if they'd prefer to be cool. You can't fill your Outer Banks or northern Oregon retreat in January without providing dependable heat and blankets. Tenants don't feel at home in the off-season if you don't provide good kitchen equipment, the pots and pans necessary for three meals a day, and plenty of lights and chairs for reading. Picture yourself cooped up in your vacation house in the middle of an off-season rainstorm or a snowstorm; then furnish your place with whatever *you'd* need (within reason) to stay happy as a guest.

Year-round Marketing. Owners of resort homes who turn out annual positive cash flows do it either by marketing their property year-round or by signing the unit up for rental brokerage by a realty firm. Below is a sample seasonal letter (for fall and winter) used by a highly successful multiple-unit vacation-property owner of Atlantic beachfront townhouses. The owner has built up an extensive list of over three hundred guests who come back year after year and tell their friends about his units. He no longer needs to advertise, relying strictly on his mailings.

For less established owners, an inexpensively printed mail-out to friends, relatives, business acquaintances, and neighbors, plus some initial advertising in a metropolitan daily newspaper, will be necessary. Put up bulletin-board notices with color snapshots at work, in churches and at the meeting places of large social organizations. The notices and mailings should be seasonally oriented. In the fall mailing, stress the fantastic ski and platform-tennis facilities your unit enjoys—and all the extracurricular things to do and see in the area. In the spring and summer mailing, sing the praises of your community's swimming, surfing, skin diving, boating, and so forth.

By the way, if you are part of a small development or group of condos/townhouses, perhaps you should join with your co-owners in a loose promotional arrangement. Some groups of owners pool names and print up small brochures that go out

Dear Guests: August ___, 197__

It is again time to send out our fall off-season rate sheets to our previous guests, like yourselves, whom we would be most pleased to have return. We also welcome those of you who have not rented from us before but have expressed an interest in our "vacation" homes.

Although the summer season is not over, we already have several reservations and some inquiries for the Christmas holiday season. If you do have an interest in an off-season relaxation on the oceanside, we suggest that you check with us as soon as convenient.

Sincerely,

OFF-SEASON FALL RENTAL RATES

Summer Rentals	Sea Splash II-V and Pilot House #9 Townhouses	Bimini #204 Apartment
Sept. 3–10	$300 per week	$200 per week
Sept. 10–17	250 per week	150 per week
Sept. 17–24	200 per week	125 per week
Sept. 24–Oct. 1	175 per week	100 per week

Off-Season Rentals

	Sea Splash II-V and Pilot House #9 Townhouses	Bimini #204 Apartment
Oct. 7–10	$125 per weekend	$ 80 per weekend
Oct. 14–18 Columbus Holiday	150 " "	100 " "
Oct. 21–25 Vet's Holiday	150 " "	100 " "
Oct. 28–31	125 " "	80 " "
Nov. 4–7	125 " "	80 " "
Nov. 11–14	125 " "	80 " "
Nov. 18–21	125 " "	80 " "
Nov. 23–28 Thanksgiving	150 " "	100 " "
Dec. 2–5	125 " "	80 " "
Dec. 9–12	125 " "	80 " "
Dec. 16–19	125 " "	80 " "
Dec. 23–26 Christmas Holiday	150 " "	100 " "
Dec. 30–Jan. 2 New Year's Holiday	150 " "	100 " "

Note 1. September weekly rentals are from Saturday 2:00 P.M. to Saturday 11:00 A.M. Weekend rentals from Friday noon to Monday noon.

Note 2. Add 5 percent to the above rates for state sales tax and 3 percent for county tax for a total of 8 percent.

Note 3. Above weekend rental rates do not include cleaning services and are based on the assumption that guests will clean upon departure. However, cleaning service can be arranged with advance notice at an additional charge.

twice a year to a large, cooperative master mailing list—thereby offering maximum cost-effective exposure for each unit.

Should you market your unit through a professional realty broker? That can be advantageous, as discussed below, but find out in advance whether (1) the broker owns or controls a large number of units in the immediate area (he may use your property primarily as a come-on for his own); (2) his rates are in line with those common in your area (anything over 12 percent of gross rents for brokerage alone should be carefully scrutinized); (3) his reputation among long-term owners stacks up well; and (4) he shows you proof that his mailing list really draws.

Some condominium developments, usually those registered with the federal Securities and Exchange Commission (SEC), offer "rental-pool" marketing services to purchasers as part of their overall investment package. For a prearranged percentage fee, the developers/realty brokers will guarantee you pro rata shares of the net rental income from your unit and others "pooled" with it in the development. This may or may not totally offset your unit ownership carrying costs, but it certainly can remove the headaches of marketing and managing your property all by yourself. Have your lawyer or accountant look over the prospectus of any condominium you're considering purchasing that comes with a rental-pool option. The developer/promoter may not in fact have the marketing track record to fill his project consistently with enough renters to make the pooling arrangement really work well. In such a case, you'd probably do better marketing the unit on your own.

Effective Management. The principles of good multi-season resort rental management are pretty much the same as those for rental homes in Chapter 2. Some additional tips:
• Make certain to collect rents well in advance. If you're signing up a tenant in the winter for a two-week stay in the summer, get one-third of the projected rent at the signing of the contract. Arrange for a second third to be paid at the start of the season, and the final third no later than several days before the renter is due to arrive. This way you avoid no-shows and inexplicable vacancies.

• Don't simply take *anybody* who'll pay your rent. Discriminate on all legal bases. That can mean no kids, no pets, no unrelated groups of high school or college students, no subleases, or whatever. If you decide to rent to such high-risk tenants as students, do so at a rent significantly higher than normal to cover your higher risks. And insist upon security deposits as high as local ordinances permit.

• Provide brief, typed informational brochures in your unit that tell people how to operate appliances, where they can locate food stores, restaurants, hardware stores and hospitals, and how they can get in touch with fire, police and other emergency services (and with you or your agent).

• Be assiduous about cleaning and upkeep—and require that your renters do the same. During off-season months, ask renters to do a thorough cleaning before they leave. During the busy season, ask the tenants to keep the place neat, but engage a local cleaning service (if one is available, or clean it yourself if you're around) to tidy up before each new tenant arrives.

• Professional management—including leasing arrangements, collection of rents, advertising, bookkeeping and clean-up—can be worthwhile, particularly if you live far from the property. Costs will vary according to the extent of services rendered and are 100 percent deductible if you use the property within the fourteen-day/10 percent IRS guidelines.

• The maximum rent you can charge is a function of demand for the locale as well as for your unit. You should aim for rent levels over a two- to three-year period that get you to break-even or better in terms of cash flow. That doesn't mean, however, that you should ask $500 a week in a $400-a-week market. Far better for the long run to ask $475 a week in a $500-a-week market—but extend the high season at both ends and stay fully occupied year in and year out.

FINANCING VACATION HOUSING

The sources of finance for your second home investment fall into four basic categories.

First, the conventional lending institutions you deal with in your home community. These include your commercial bank, your savings and loan association, and your credit union. All three may be willing to provide mortgage money for a single-family house or condominium within a reasonable driving distance (say, a hundred miles). The terms will almost certainly be stiffer than on your primary home or on rental-investment property. Down payment minimums may be 25 to 30 percent rather than 10 to 20 percent; interest rates will probably be a notch or two higher than those quoted for prime owner-occupied home mortgages. And repayment terms are likely to be shorter— fifteen to twenty years, rather than twenty-five to thirty.

Second are the same types of lending institutions, but in the community or area where you plan to buy. S&Ls in resort communities know their home turf, lend for construction purposes all the time, and may be a better bet for advantageous terms than their confreres in your hometown. These institutions are likely to be especially concerned (or impressed) with your rental plans. If you're going to bring in income that completely offsets the annual principal and interest before taxes, an S&L or bank will be far more inclined to lend you cash for the purchase.

Third, the developers of many resort-home projects nail down large financing packages for consumers in advance of construction through mortgage bankers, thrift institutions, insurance companies and other sources of long-term funds. Often the terms available via this "wholesale" method are far better for the buyer than conventional alternatives—for example, down payments of only 10 percent rather than 25 percent, mortgage rates under the prevailing rates charged by S&Ls, pay-back periods of thirty years. The only dangers with package deals such as these are in the fine print. Watch for big prepayment penalties, nonassumption clauses, and clauses prohibiting secondary financing on the property by you at a later date.

Fourth, as with all real estate, the seller (excluding developers) may be the very best financing source. Look for properties with seller financing. (See page 46 for a discussion of seller-financing terms and tips.) You may well be able to negotiate surprisingly favorable terms in exchange for meeting the asking price. Far better to get a 10 percent down, thirty-year seller-financed loan at one or two percentage points below the going market on a beach house or mountain estate than to haggle over whether the sale price should be $59,500 or $57,500. Go with the higher price overall—inflation and your excellent management of the property will take care of that disparity in a year or two—but get the low financing costs. It's pennies a month more on price, but big dollars a month less in out-of-pocket expenses.

TIME-SHARING

Undoubtedly the hottest vacation real estate concept in the United States today is time-sharing, or fractional ownership or leasing of resort property, usually condominiums. Time-sharing requires relatively low initial outlays for consumers who want long-term guaranteed vacation spots; it offers the possibility of periodic swaps of property-use rights among unit owners in various resorts. Time-sharing is also spreading rapidly, however, because it produces financial bonanzas for resort developers. It enables a condominium unit that might be sold conventionally for $60,000 to be sold for two and a half to three times that— by selling it to different people for fifty weeks of the year at an average of $2,500 to $3,000 a week. It has brought some badly ailing resort developments back from the brink, turning them into highly profitable ventures.

Whether time-sharing makes any sense whatsoever as an *investment* for the individual unit buyer—as opposed to the developer/promoter—is unclear at this point. Unit fractions have moved up in selling price in some locations and have stayed flat in others, but reliable national data is lacking. Moreover, the resorts, involved are so new that the long-term impacts on unit value of management and construction quality, and the legal standing of unit ownership under state real property laws, are years away.

As a way to spend money on vacations, time-sharing can be diverting. An owner of a time-share unit can join Resort Condominiums International, Inc., an Indianapolis-based swapping network, and have access to tens of thousands of units located in 150 resort developments around the globe. Or an owner can join R.C.I.'s rival, Miami-based Interval World, Inc., which links units with owners in ninety other international resorts. For a small annual listing fee to stay in the pool, owners' time-share units are advertised internationally and can produce swaps at nominal costs with owners in Mexico, Spain, Morocco, the Austrian Alps, Hawaii, Virginia, the Bahamas and so on.

Some purchasers rarely if ever stay in their "own" unit. They buy into the time-share game to have access to the international pool, and may spend a week a year in Mexico, a week in Vermont, a week at the Maryland shore. Meanwhile, their unit in South Florida is being occupied by a succession of foreign and American unit owners—or to renters, in some resorts.

Time-Sharing Variants—and Problems. Before going into a time-share real estate purchase, be certain whether you are getting a time-span ownership (TSO), interval ownership (IO), or one of several types of *non*ownership interests, such as vacation licenses, club memberships, or vacation leases.

Time-span ownership, a concept pioneered in Europe, provides you with what is known legally as an undivided tenancy-in-common with a group of other owners, and a contractual agreement with them reserving a specific time period for your exclusive use of the property. For $4,000, for example, you might get ownership of 1/26 interest in a resort townhouse, with a guarantee of one week's use in the summer-fall season and one week's use in the winter-spring season. By arrangement with other owners, you would draw lots or agree to annual assignments, plus set aside periods and money for maintenance costs. An important drawback to TSO is that under common law any owner can sue for *partition*—not only liquidating his or her share but possibly forcing sale of the unit and distribution of proceeds among all owners. Some developers require purchasers to waive their right to partition, but this waiver is of questionable legal enforceability on future unit owners, and in some jurisdictions creates title insurance problems. Because it provides an undivided common ownership, time-span ownership also raises the (at least theoretical) possibility of forced sale of the unit due to a federal tax lien against a fractional owner.

An alternative time-share legal format is *interval ownership,* which provides you with a "tenancy in years" for a specified period (thirty to forty years), followed by a "remainder-over" as a tenant-in-common with other unit owners. Interval-ownership deeds assign specific segments of time to specific unit owners; the real estate interest a purchaser receives in a piece of property is therefore already divided and not subject to further partition. Tax liens brought by the government would not force sale of the entire unit, displacing all co-owners. At the end of the stated period of interval ownership—the remainder-over—the unit is owned as tenants-in-common by all owners, and they can arrange to dispose of it or to run it as they agree. Presumably the condo would have reached the end of its useful life as a resort by that point.

A major problem with both TSO and IO forms of ownership is their still-foggy legal status under the laws of many states. Is interval ownership *really* a lease until the thirty- or forty-year initial period is up, rather than *ownership* of property? Can you obtain title insurance to guarantee your legal claim to "your" 1/12 interest in Unit 556A on the third floor of the Sunset Island Beach Club? If not, who'll buy your share in the property if you want to sell? Are time-shares legally classifiable as "securities," requiring complete financial disclosure by developers or promoters? States that have tough condominium disclosure rules already enforce such a requirement for time-share developers who wish to market units there.

Condominiums have been a legal and management challenge in their own right in a number of states during the past decade. Time-share ownership introduces still greater potential management problems—if not in the first few years of a development, then later on when equipment begins to wear out and needs replacement.

Nonownership time-sharing options such as vacation licenses and club memberships don't even constitute real estate—except for the developer, who essentially gets his cake and eats it too. Purchasers receive no real estate title, tax or other benefits, aside from the unit-use times specified in the license or long-term lease. These options are a clever travel-marketing tool, sold by travel agents, not real estate dealers. Occasionally, however, purchasers think they're getting an actual ownership interest and an investment; they're actually getting neither.

6
Condominiums and Cooperatives

The hybrids of residential real estate—condominiums and cooperatives—are enigmas to many otherwise sophisticated American investors. Compared with tracts of raw land, single-family rental houses, duplexes or apartment houses, they seem legally complex, financially more risky, and only marginally worth the trouble of getting involved. Yet in dozens of urban areas—from Chicago's Gold Coast to central-city Los Angeles to Manhattan—condos or co-ops are producing stunning hedges against inflation. Condominiums, in particular, have the potential in some large cities of becoming the *rental* and ownership wave of the future, filling the vacuum left by uneconomic or rent-controlled apartment projects. Cooperatives are a major investment vehicle only in New York City, but their sheer numbers there, as well as their potential role in other cities, command attention.

Let's take a look first at the investment aspects of condominiums—the dollars and cents of individual units, as well as conversions of investor-owned rental buildings—and then go on to co-ops.

CONDOMINIUMS, CONDOMANIA, AND CAPITAL APPRECIATION

Whither condominiums?

• In Chicago, individual investors who bought one- to two-bedroom condominium units in 1976 for $38,000 to $42,000—with just $4,000 to $7,500 down—sold them less than two years later for $75,000 to $85,000, *double* what they paid. Their returns on the dollar, before tax and rental-income considerations, "have been out of sight by any investment standards," in the words of Jaqui Rosenthal, director of operations for the Howard Ecker Residential Organization. Rosenthal says she knows of dozens of investor-owners who have done as well or better in that city's booming market, where thousands of apartment units a year are converted to condominiums. Many investors have taken their capital gain from one condominium purchase and sale and have bought two or three more—creating a small pyramid of units in one or more buildings. One Chicago investor has built up a staggering portfolio of close to *two hundred* units, "scattered here and there around the city," Rosenthal says, "which he sells, trades, borrows against, or holds—all very profitably." Ten to 15 percent of all purchasers of individual condominium units in the city, according to several Chicago brokers, are investors who intend to rent them out, not live in them.

• In prime suburban bedroom communities of Westchester County, New York, and Norwalk, Connecticut, condominium units that sold for $39,000 to $50,900 new in 1976 resold for $70,000 to $90,000 in mid-1978. Specialized firms such as the Condo Mart in Westchester find they can sell two-bedroom units at $75,000 to $80,000 as fast as they can list them—and one out of every fifteen buyers is an investor who plans to rent the unit out. "That proportion is growing," said Condo Mart sales head Rita Cohen, thanks to the rents of $600 to $800 a month that transient executives of large, suburban-based corporations are willing to pay for well-situated "high amenity" condos.

• In South Florida's Miami/Dade County area, which had an unsold glut of 40,000 condo units in 1975, investors (including a significant number of European or Latin buyers) have helped turn the market around completely. Almost any condominium put up sells out rapidly. Even those high-rise buildings that were developed as condos in the early 1970s and went untouched until they were turned into rental units are now being profitably "reconverted" into condominiums and sold.

• In Southern California communities, "theme" condominiums are the rage with investors, small families and retirees. Developers spend hundreds of thousands of dollars to create waterscape settings or to build on difficult sites with stunning views —and pass the steep engineering and construction costs on to the eager buyers of $100,000-and-up units.

• In metropolitan Washington, D.C., in-town conversions sell for as high as $150 a square foot. Developers don't even bother to advertise any more, because condo buyers will sign contracts on units in projects still in blueprint. In 1978 one large project of $90,000-and-up units was sold out in several hours, without any advertising, fourteen months before planned occupancy! Realtors estimate that one out of every eight condo purchasers in the nation's capital is now an investor, prepared to rent the unit, sell it (or a sales contract) for a quick profit, or hold it for long-term gain.

Reports from elsewhere around the country—Houston, Dallas, Atlanta and Seattle, to name just a few—differ only in price specifics, not in substance. Condominiums finally have come of age in the United States, not only for people looking for a home but for investors looking for tax shelter and capital gain. *One out of two* mid-rise or garden apartment–type condos five years or older is now occupied by a tenant—and owned by an absentee investor, according to the Community Associations Institute.

In the early 1970s, by contrast, the only investors interested in condominiums were the real estate developers and apartment-building owners who saw the immediate profit potential inherent in individual sales of high-density housing. During that period state laws defining and regulating condos typically did not include important legal guarantees for purchasers, thus exposing unit owners to a wide range of abuses. A burst of development activity between 1968 and 1973 produced nearly 1 million new or converted condominiums around the country, but it also triggered consumer complaints and investigations by state and federal agencies. The investigations documented abuses by developers in some states ranging from fraudulent "low-balling" of anticipated monthly costs for unit owners to extensive self-dealing of long-term high-cost management contracts. Studies also documented what many condo buyers in 1970–71 feared most after they made their purchase: the resale market for units in many areas of the country was poor. Lenders were reluctant to hand out mortgage money on high-rise "subdivisions in the sky," and were only slightly more favorably inclined toward low-rise condominium townhouse developments. The big drawback of condos, in lenders' eyes, was the massive amount of paperwork and research involved in analyzing and appraising a unit within a larger project. S&Ls were willing to take the trouble to do the necessary research and paperwork, but only if they could be guaranteed a large number of loans— possible only in the early sales campaign for a new condo, not in the later resale "spot" loans on individual units.

The turnabout in the market since 1974 has in part been the result of state and federal actions to end these problems. At the state level, most legislatures have now followed the examples of New York, Illinois, Virginia and Michigan: they have beefed up the consumer-protection and disclosure requirements of their condominium laws to such an extent that purchasers are often better safeguarded today, and have access to more pertinent information at no cost, in buying a condo than in buying an existing single-family home. Under the so-called second-generation condo laws of the post-1975 years, the purchaser is not overwhelmed with hundreds of pages of prospectus but is provided with easy-to-understand information about the developer, his finances, the express warranties he is offering, the physical condition and projected expenses of the building, probable mortgage finance costs for the buyer, and other useful data. Most of the new laws prohibit the marketing abuses that gave

condos a bad name, and restrict self-dealing arrangements between the developer and the condominium association while it
is under the developer's control.

At the federal level, the resale problem has been eased by the
creation of secondary mortgage finance programs by two corporations. Both the Federal National Mortgage Association and
the Federal Home Loan Mortgage Corporation now purchase
condo-unit mortgages in large numbers. These programs, plus
the gradual build-up of lenders' and appraisers' familiarity with
condominiums, have brought condos virtually on a par with
conventional housing as security for long-term loans.

All of this naturally has done wonders for condominium
sales, their appreciation rates, and their attraction to investors.

INVESTMENT PROS AND CONS OF CONDOS

Before plunging into the pluses and minuses of condominiums
as investment vehicles, let's be certain of the nature of the
property we're discussing. *Condominium** is a form of real
estate ownership, traceable back at least to the Romans, that
provides individual deeds to individual units within a multi-unit
structure or subdivision, plus undivided interests in common
facilities and property shared among a body of co-owners. An
owner receives a recordable title to a specific subdivided piece
of ground or space—which may be an apartment on the thirty-
fifth floor of a building or one of fifteen townhouses on a
cul-de-sac. He or she also receives ownership, jointly with all
deed holders to units, of predefined common elements of the
building or subdivision, which may be hallways, vestibules, pools,
tennis courts, a marina, garages, elevators, exterior lighting, air
ducts, wires, shrubbery, sidewalks, fire escapes, roads or whatever, depending upon the specific case. Co-owners share not
only in their use but also in the expense of their upkeep. While
the rights of unit ownership are in most respects like the rights
of any conventional single-family ownership, this common

---

* The term is derived from the Latin word *dominium,* meaning "right
of ownership, dominion," and the prefix *con* ("with"), indicating sharing
of ownership.

ownership of facilities gives condominiums their unique strengths and drawbacks.

Condos can take *any* outward form imaginable; although popularly pictured as mid- and high-rise projects, condominiums often are single- or two-floor townhouses, small suburban patio homes, office buildings, warehouses, and even double-decker combinations of two types of condos. For example, the 57-story Galleria in Manhattan contains a 16-floor commercial, retail and garage condominium, plus an independent 41-story, 253-unit residential condominium on top of it, complete with an indoor-outdoor restaurant and lounge.

Investment Advantages. Condominiums are attracting a growing number of small-scale investors because they offer both the benefits of detached single-family rental units and some important extras.

• *Condos can offer rapid capital growth, high-ratio leverage and tax shelter*—a tempting combination. In a number of metropolitan areas during the 1976–78 period, well-chosen condominium units have kept pace with or exceeded average appreciation rates of detached single-family and duplex units. Some central-city brownstone conversion projects in such cities as Chicago and San Francisco have had 35 to 50 percent and higher yearly appreciation rates. California quadriplexes (or quadrominiums) have jumped 25 to 40 percent a year in some locations. Although these specific cases may be temporary phenomena caused by below-market prices at initial offering, condominiums in general are solid vehicles for capital growth.

With high-ratio 5-and-10-percent-down loans readily available for some projects, the leverage potentials through purchase of individual units are impressive. Moreover, the tax benefits of condos are identical—via deductions for depreciation, mortgage interest, taxes and expenses—to those of other property held for rental. Condos can work out even better tax-wise for investors, since the nondepreciable land component of a condominium tends to be much smaller than the land-value component of a single-family house. With more to depreciate, you get more tax shelter.

• Condominiums come with a built-in *ease of management*. The owners' association contracts for many of the key maintenance items affecting your unit—from the exterior to the roof to the hallways. You still need to keep track of windows and built-in appliances, and you must be concerned with how tenants treat your apartment, but a lot of your worst potential headaches as a landlord are under professional care. Investors find that purchasing more than one unit in a large building— and then living in the building in a unit purchased as a principal residence—makes rental management even more efficient.

• In cities with tight apartment rental markets, *condominiums often are easier to keep at full occupancy* than competing real estate investments. Dollar for dollar, central-city condominiums, particularly those with such amenities as pools, saunas and racketball courts unavailable elsewhere, can produce more in rent than suburban tract houses.

• Condominiums offer a *wide range of scale* to investors. You can do well with a $6,000 investment in a $45,000 suburban condominium townhouse, a $10,000 investment in a $55,000 one-bedroom apartment, $50,000 split up among several units in your area, and so on up the ladder. Like conventional rental houses, condominiums don't require a lot of sophistication or long experience in real estate. All you need is common sense, an ability to understand market trends, and some professional help at key intervals (legal assistance prior to the initial purchase, and accounting aid at tax time).

Disadvantages. A major drawback of condominiums, compared with virtually any other form of real estate, is their legal complexity. Condominiums create interrelationships among a body of co-owners that can be chaotic if leadership isn't adequate. Condominiums hand over effective control of complex multi-million-dollar structures to untrained boards of directors; the official decisions of a board of directors about expenditures, maintenance, repairs, reserve funds, annual budgets and security can make or break your investment, and can cost you thousands of dollars in unexpected assessments over a period of years.

• *Condominiums—particularly those with management or structural problems—can involve greater investments of your time* than other forms of real estate. Larger condominium projects involve frequent meetings, the creation of numerous committees, and other responsibilities that you may not *want* to avoid as an owner because the market value of your investment is so vulnerable to bad decisions on the part of others. Condominium politics, especially in cases where you not only own one or more units but live in the building as well, can take up a lot of your time and wear you out emotionally.

• *Condominiums as rental investments rarely break even* or turn a positive cash flow. Their out-of-pocket cost per month is swelled by the charges for common elements assessed by the board. These charges can range from $20 a month in a low-density townhouse development to $500 or more in a luxury building in a city—and can take quantum leaps from year to year. Negative, pretax cash losses of $200 a month are not uncommon for rental investors in urban condos. This creates a greater dependence on continued high rates of inflation in the economy.

• *Eight or nine out of ten home-buying Americans, according to authoritative surveys, eventually want to live in a detached single-family dwelling.* This deep-set traditional preference underpins the capital safety and appreciation potential of single-family rental-home investments. Their ultimate market value is in their attraction as homes for this majority of buyers. Condominiums are generally viewed as *transitional* homes, and are thus more vulnerable in sales-value terms to swings in the economy than conventional detached homes are.

• Although *financing conditions for condos* have improved greatly over the past several years, lenders in a credit crunch are likely to go with the lowest-risk and least complex form of housing—and that won't be condominiums in all but central-city areas.

CHOOSING AN INVESTMENT CONDO

Certain basic principles of real estate acquisition hold for condominium units as well as they do for detached single-family rental units; these are detailed at length in Chapter 2. The big differences in investing in condominiums versus other types of housing-unit ownership derive from the unique legal status of the condominium and its high-density form of living. The purpose of the following guidelines, therefore, will be to supplement the basics in Chapter 2 by examining those special characteristics.

Location . . . and Convenience. "Location, location, location" are the mantra-like bywords you hear constantly from real estate agents. In choosing an investment condominium property, however, amend their formula slightly by thinking "convenience, convenience, convenience." The condo unit you purchase for rental purposes should above all offer convenience to single people or couples (childfree or with a child or two), because they make up your market, and a relatively trouble-free life is what they want from their shelter. Convenience requires a location well served by public transportation and close to employment, cultural and entertainment centers. The only exception to this would be in the cases of suburban townhouses or quadrominiums, where your market is families with children who intend to buy a house as soon as they are financially able to do so.

Facilities. The higher the "amenity package," as real estate promoters are fond of calling facilities in a condo project, obviously the greater attraction to prospective tenants. Swimming pools, saunas, social rooms, handball courts, and so forth are tremendous draws—but don't forget the bottom line as an investor. Condominiums with exceptionally attractive facilities may also have unbelievably large monthly assessments. As an owner-occupant making heavy use of these amenities, you may not mind the heavy cost; as an investor, you've got to examine the costs and benefits of facilities in relation to the rent you can command.

For example, take two competing condo projects in a Midwest metropolitan market. Project A is in the middle of the city and offers you the possibility of buying a luxury $61,950 one-bedroom "executive" unit, a corner apartment on an upper floor of a 26-unit mid-rise, with a 10 percent down payment. The building is a rental project conversion, architecturally distinguished and well located, but it offers little in the way of special amenities. Besides a small social room in the basement, there is a part-time clerk/manager at the front desk. An itemized breakdown of your expenses during the first year can be found below. You may be able to get $500 to $550 a month rent on this unit because of its exceptional location and its fine views of the city. This produces a pretax cash loss of $100 to $150 a month. The unit may be growing in resale value at 15 percent a year.

Project B is in the suburbs, and for the same $61,950 offers a newly constructed two- to three-bedroom high-rise luxury apartment, with a similar down payment and similar financing terms. The complex offers three swimming pools, several tennis courts, a sauna, and extensive, well-landscaped grounds. You can get close to the same $500-plus rent as you can in the city, but the condominium fee is $100 more—thanks to the cost of maintaining and repairing all the facilities. Your monthly net pretax loss is also $100 more. And the rate of appreciation is estimated at only 10 percent a year because of lower demand and a larger supply of competitive units.

	Project A	Project B
Acquisition price*	$61,950	$61,950
Down payment	6,195	6,195
Mortgage or first trust	$55,755	$55,755
Principal and mortgage interest (thirty-year 9½ percent loan)	$ 469.27	$ 469.27
Mortgage insurance premium	8.02	8.02
Taxes	94.47	94.47
Condominium fee	85.49	185.49
TOTAL PER MONTH	$ 657.25	$ 757.25

* Closing costs paid by the seller.

This is *not* to suggest you look for units in buildings with spartan facilities and rock-bottom condominium fees. In some markets, the "high amenity" package may be necessary to compete with rental opportunities, and in-town locations may not produce such disproportionately high rents. You've simply got to look at facilities in terms of their likely net impact on your bottom line. Condo fees for leisure-oriented developments can act as a drag on long-term capital appreciation.

Condominium Legal Documents. If you are in a jurisdiction requiring detailed disclosure statements before any new or conversion condo can go on sale—and the most active metropolitan condominium markets now generally do—your analysis of the legal foundation of a prospective unit purchase will be much easier than an analysis done in a less progressive jurisdiction. The essential declaration establishing the condominium as a legal subdivision and the by-laws of the condominium unit owners' association are provided to you in the sales process. So too are the structural engineers' reports by independent outside experts on the condition of the building, its units and all common elements; statements detailing all warranties and warranty limitations; a proposed or actual operating budget of the condo association; disclosures relating to any lease arrangements or management contracts negotiated in advance between the developer/converter and the condominium association; disclosures relating to planned expansion or other changes to the structure or on adjacent lots or tracts; financial statements regarding the developer and its principals; disclosures of any encumbrances—existing liens, covenants, easements, leases or licenses—that may affect title to the property.

In jurisdictions where such information is not required, or in resale transactions, ask for and obtain these key pieces of information. Have your attorney or other competent real estate counsel review them before you sign any sales contracts.

Items in these documents of particular concern to you as an *investor* with plans to rent out your unit(s) include the following:

1. A precise definition of your prospective unit's percentage allocation of undivided ownership of the common elements,

expenses (and profits, should any occur). This should be contained within the condominium declaration, and should be based either on the square footage of the unit in relation to the combined square footage of all the units, or on the original sales price of your unit, expressed as a percentage of the total of all the original sales prices of all the units within the project. (See page 182 for an extract from an actual condominium offering prospectus for a typical listing of allocations.) The allocation will control your voting power within the association, the amount of your monthly condominium fee, and your share in the cash proceeds from the structure if it is ever acquired by condemnation by a government agency. In condominiums containing units that vary widely in interior area or in initial selling price, a system of voting based on one vote per unit probably won't fairly protect the interests of the owners of the larger units. On the other hand, projects with fairly uniform units should do fine with this system of voting. Condominium by-laws requiring much more than a simple majority of the unit owners present (or by proxy) to make virtually any decision will be unwieldy, and will tend to stay under the developer's control for a long time. Better to stay away from poorly organized, excessive democracies.

2. By-laws allowing you adequate flexibility as a landlord-owner. Excessive restrictions by a condominium board of directors on the leasing of units can make it difficult for you to attract and keep tenants. Requirements that all leases be submitted to the board within seven days of execution, or that tenants conform in all respects with house rules regarding interior maintenance, noise, pets, storage and the like, are reasonable and prudent. On the other hand, if a by-law states that you must have prior approval of the board or of specific tenants before leasing your unit, this can create real problems.

By-laws permitting tenants to serve on association committees or to be elected as members of the board are a good idea. Condominium investors around the country have found that their rental units stay in better shape, and their tenants stay happier, if the tenants are encouraged to feel like partners in the condominium, rather than like second-class citizens looked down upon by the owners surrounding them.

CALIFORNIA HOUSE CONDOMINIUM
(*Extracted from Prospectus,* 1978)

All units listed below have the street address of 2205
California Street, N.W., Washington, D.C.

Identifying No. (Unit No.)	Approximate Size	Percentage of Undivided Interest in the Common Elements, Expenses and Profits
1	1199 sq/ft	3.273 percent
2	1257 sq/ft	3.431
101	1133 sq/ft	3.093
102	1451 sq/ft	3.961
103	1268 sq/ft	3.461
104	1473 sq/ft	4.021
201	1464 sq/ft	3.996
202	1451 sq/ft	3.960
203	1268 sq/ft	3.461
204	1588 sq/ft	4.335
301	1464 sq/ft	3.996
302	1451 sq/ft	3.960
303	1268 sq/ft	3.461
304	1588 sq/ft	4.335
401	1464 sq/ft	3.996
402	1451 sq/ft	3.960
403	1268 sq/ft	3.461
404	1588 sq/ft	4.335
501	1464 sq/ft	3.996
502	1451 sq/ft	3.960
503	1268 sq/ft	3.461
504	1588 sq/ft	4.335
601	1464 sq/ft	3.996
602	1451 sq/ft	3.960
603	1268 sq/ft	3.461
604	1588 sq/ft	4.335

100.000 percent

3. Insurance. Make sure the by-laws require that the board maintain full-replacement coverage for the building against fire and other hazards, and adequate liability coverage for the association, board members and all unit owners as a group. The by-laws will probably also encourage unit owners to maintain individual hazard insurance policies; as a landlord you should obtain add-on liability coverage for your specific unit.

4. Annual budget projections must be realistic and verifiable, or you'll risk falling into a "low-balling" situation that will hurt in the future. A typical first year's budget estimates in a medium-sized urban project can be found on page 184. Ask your real estate agent or your attorney for the name of a local property manager, structural engineer or builder who'll look at the projections blind and tell you where they may be unrealistically low.

5. Management. Take a hard look at the management contract that's been negotiated, or is in existence. Ask the same professionals mentioned above about the reputation of the professional management firm—if one is under contract—or the performance of the converter/developer in that capacity to date. Beware of *any* long-term contracts for management services if they involve the developer, promoter, or any entity they may control. Bear in mind the sobering experience of the unit owners at North Miami Beach's Point East Condominium, who found themselves locked into a multi-year management agreement with the developer. Unhappy about the quality of his management services and about the sweetheart nature of his contract, the owners finally agreed to pay the developer $60,000 a year for *not* managing their property!

Management arrangements for small condominiums also require special scrutiny on a cost-per-unit basis. Buildings under a hundred units may not be able to afford top-flight management, or such firms won't take on small projects, and this tends to raise monthly management costs per unit in small-scale projects. "Our managers have to spend three or four hours per association committee meeting whether the building has fifty units or sixteen hundred," explained the head of a major condominium management firm. "Obviously there are going to be economies on management fees in larger developments."

Proposed Budget for the First Twelve Months of the Condominium's Operation
(*Extracted from Prospectus, 1978*)

Expense Item		Total Annual (first twelve months of operation)
Administrative Expenses		
Audit	$1,000.00	
Office supplies	300.00	
Legal counsel	500.00	
Miscellaneous administrative expenses	180.00	
Licenses	100.00	
Insurance	2,400.00	
Total		$4,480.00
Personnel Expenses		
Building superintendent	4,800.00	
Payroll taxes	500.00	
Workmen's compensation insurance	500.00	
Total		$5,800.00
Utilities		
Electricity, common areas	2,900.00	
Oil	2,100.00	
Water	2,000.00	
Total		$7,000.00
Contracted Operating		
Exterminating	180.00	
Trash removal	1,080.00	
Security telephone	300.00	
Management fee	7,200.00	
Elevator	1,140.00	
Total		$9,900.00

6. Parking problems can lead to extra costs, inconvenience and tension within a tightly packed residential society. Make certain of your (or your tenant's) right to at least one parking space (preferably two, one of which is under a roof). And find out how additional spaces beyond this are allotted or rented.

7. As an absentee landlord, you will find income-producing facilities an obvious plus to have in your building, since they can decrease your monthly carrying costs and can possibly even provide additional services to your tenants. Many high-rise condominiums lease units or space on their lower floors for stores or for business or professional offices. Some condominiums charge rent on parking spaces or lease portions of their land for commercial enterprises.

Interior Locational Factors. Just as purchasers of townhouses pay premiums for end units—and often experience appreciation rates higher than those of their neighbors—so investors in multi-story condo units should go for the best-located units. You may have to pay more, but the long-term value increment will more than compensate for this extra cost. For a mid- to high-rise building, this normally means you should take into consideration the following: (1) Units on higher floors are preferable to those on lower floors, because they're farther away from street noise and command higher rents. (2) Units near elevators, garbage chutes, commercial offices or stairwells should be avoided. (They command lower prices and rents because they're noisier.) (3) Corner units with views on two sides draw raves and yield high rents, whereas units without views go begging.

Buy where you know best, and buy in quantity if you can swing it. Ideally you should buy a unit in a newly converted or constructed condominium in which you plan to live. Rather than simply purchasing one unit, buy one or two more with high-ratio (90 to 95 percent) long-term loans. In such a strategy you get the advantages of the first buyer (many condo units and conventional houses in good locations take extraordinary value jumps in the first two years), as well as management efficiency via concentration of your rental and primary residential properties.

FINANCING INVESTMENT CONDOS

The mortgage finance sources for condominium unit investors are the same as those outlined in Chapter 2 (pp. 42–51) and in the chart on pp. 44–45. These include conventional loan sources (S&Ls, credit unions, banks, mortgage bankers), as well as the sellers of individual units. In rare cases, the financing may involve assumption of an FHA-insured or VA-backed loan.

Since many initial purchases are in newly built or converted projects, financing often comes as part of a large-scale package deal arranged by the developer with a particular S&L or bank. Such terms can be favorable in comparison to retail "spot loan" financing; the lender is willing to give a slight break on the interest rate or on other terms in exchange for the prospect of a large volume of loans arising out of one piece of property.

Lenders may expect a premium—via slightly higher rates or points—from you if you identify yourself as an absentee investor with plans to rent. Many investors do not identify themselves as such and sign loan applications attesting that they plan to reside in the mortgaged unit themselves indefinitely. An investor who is not honest with the lender, however, runs the risk of having the loan "called" (made payable in full immediately) if the lender discovers that he or she isn't living in the property.

Both the Federal National Mortgage Association (Fannie Mae) and the Federal Home Loan Mortgage Corporation (Freddy Mac) want to purchase mortgages in predominantly owner-occupied condominiums on the theory that owners take better care of the lender's underlying security, while heavy concentrations of tenants in projects lead to trouble.

Condominium mortgages available from S&Ls or banks have no statutory size limits, but loans that are eligible for resale to either Fannie Mae or Freddy Mac must be no larger than $75,000, with up to 90 percent ratios. Mortgages with up to 95 percent loan-to-value ratios generally cannot exceed $42,000. All mortgages with greater than 80 percent loan-to-value ratios must also carry private mortgage insurance.

The typical income standards for loans on condominiums that will be sold to Freddy Mac or Fannie Mae are as follows:

borrowers (investors) must have an annual gross income of at
least 48 times the total monthly payments, consisting of principal, interest, taxes, condo fees and private mortgage insurance
premium. Total payments for housing expenses cannot exceed
25 percent of a borrower's effective monthly income.* That
means, for example, that if you wanted to buy a $91,250 condo
unit with a 10-percent-down, 9½ percent thirty-year loan, you'd
need about $46,174 in annual income. If you wanted a $77,000
unit with similar mortgage terms, you'd need $38,700. For a
$62,000 unit, the lender would require $31,550. Of course in
cases where you can demonstrate to a lender that your *effective*
cost per month on a unit, before taxes, will be, say, $100 (your
cash loss on the rental of the unit), and that you have every
reason to expect full occupancy of the unit because of high
demand for rental apartments, you will not need anywhere near
$31,550 in additional income for each $62,000 unit you buy.

TAXES

Condominiums used for business purposes, such as residential
rental units held for income or capital gain, qualify for the same
favorable tax treatment as conventional rental houses (see pp.
76ff). An investor-owner may take deductions for depreciation,
calculated according to his unit's tax basis or cost, using a
schedule appropriate to the economic life of the building as a
whole. (Note that in the IRS's view a new multi-family apartment building may have an economic life of forty to forty-five
years.) An investor may also take deductions for insurance, utilities not paid by the tenant, repairs and routine maintenance
inside the unit, and all other expenses associated with rental
activities. Investors can also deduct the portions of the
condominium-fee assessments which are not for capital improve-

---

* For more details on the requirements and standards for unit finance
under the FHLMC and FNMA programs, contact either a participating
lender (S&Ls generally prefer to deal with FHLMC), or mortgage banker
(they deal mostly with FNMA), or either corporation directly. FNMA is
at 1133 15th St., N.W., Washington, D.C. 20005 Attn: Corporate Relations. FHLMC is at 1700 G St., N.W., Washington, D.C. 20006.

ments or capital reserves. The percentage of the monthly condominium fee which is deductible will differ from building to building; you'll need advice each year from your condominium board of directors on the specific mixture of deductible and capitalizable costs, year by year.

In the case of newly constructed projects, where you are the first user of a unit and you rent it out upon acquisition, you may qualify for accelerated depreciation up to 200 percent declining balance. For all other existing residential buildings, the maximum depreciation schedule for which you can qualify is 125 percent declining balance.*

CAN YOU PROFIT BY CONVERTING YOUR RENTAL APARTMENT BUILDING INTO A CONDOMINIUM?

You bet you can—provided you do adequate research on your local market, know your local and state laws regulating conversions (which are getting stickier in many jurisdictions), and do a complete feasibility study, projecting rehabilitation costs, interim financing costs, and a realistic cash-flow schedule based on a realistic marketing plan. Conversions are booming today because they make a lot of sense to owners and developers, as well as to tenants. Conversions offer a method for you as an owner of a heavily depreciated building, or as one whose rents provide only marginal net operating income, to get out of the rental business with a significant capital gain. It also offers your tenants a genuinely good method of cutting their after-tax monthly housing expenses, and turning their outlays into an investment.

For a rough idea of the numbers involved for both the developer/converter and the tenant/unit purchaser, see page 190 for a summary of a hypothetical conversion from rental to condo, suggested by southern California real estate developer Ken Wilson, president of Ken Wilson and Associates, Studio

* For more information, get a copy of IRS Publication No. 588, revised October 1975.

City, California. The building involved was a 25-unit suburban mid-rise producing an average of $325 per month per unit in gross rent. As a rental project, it was estimated to have a market value to its owner of $682,689. As part A suggests, the net pretax income from the sale of the project and pay-off of the first trust deed would have been around $153,555. Converted to condominium, with an average sales price per unit of $39,000, the project produced a gross sales value of $975,270. As summarized in part B, the combined costs of rehabilitation of the project (upgrading of a small pool, putting down new carpets, doing some interior remodeling, adding a storage area, and so forth) and sales commissions came to roughly $158,584. Retirement of the first-trust deed and compensation of the professional converter/ consultant hired by the building owner to handle the project cut net pretax income to $307,552.

The bottom-line difference between A (rental project) and B (converted condo) is one reason why conversions have become so popular. Wilson estimates the conversion would also be highly profitable to an outside investor who purchased the 25-unit building at the full $682,689 asking price with the intention of converting. The sales, less costs, would produce a nearly $100,000 pretax profit. In some urban markets, where rental vacancies are 1 to 3 percent, investors are buying even small five- to ten-unit rent-controlled structures with the intention of converting them into individual-ownership units.

The entire conversion process might take as little as forty weeks, or as long as a year and a half to completely sell out. Those already living in the converted project would be likely to purchase their units because the monthly pretax costs of ownership are only marginally greater than the costs of renting a unit in the project, following rehabilitation. The post-renovation rent would have been $350 a month. As part C on page 191 suggests, the $388 out-of-pocket costs of condo ownership are close enough to the original rent to convince tenants to buy. The real costs of ownership for each unit would of course be lower, because of the deductibility of interest and property taxes.

A

Value of project as rental apartment building	$682,689
Disposition costs:	
Realty sales commission	34,134
Prepayment penalty on loan	17,813
Closing costs (assumed)	2,187
First-trust deed (assumed)	475,000
Net pre-tax income from sale of rental project	$153,555

B

Total sales price of individual condominium units	$975,270
Costs of conversion:	
Engineering fees	4,375
Legal fees	3,125
Title fees	4,375
Local filing fees:	
Condo subdivision	450
Maps	259
Loan points (interim and permanent)	16,802
Remodeling:	
Swimming pool	10,000
Garage doors	7,500
Storage	3,750
Pergola area	3,000
Exterior painting	4,000
Model decoration	2,000
Unit interiors	37,500
Total marketing costs	29,258
Rent loss during marketing	8,127
Prepayment penalty	17,813
Miscellaneous	6,250
(Total conversion costs = $158,584)	
Net sales price	$816,686
Less first-trust deed (assumed)	475,000
	341,686
Less converter/consultant's fee	34,134
Net pretax income from sale of project in condominium format	$307,552

C. Renting Versus Condo Ownership

Rent per unit after remodeling (if building remained rental project)	$350.00
Estimated typical monthly mortgage, tax and condo fees after conversion*	388.43
Principal and interest	269.90
Real property taxes	73.90
Condo fee (per month)	44.63

* Based on the assumption of a $39,000 typical purchase price, with a 10 percent down payment and an 8.5 percent, thirty-year loan. Higher prevailing interest rates would raise the principal and interest costs, but would also increase the monthly deduction possible for the unit owner. If we assume that 90 percent of the first year's monthly mortgage payments are tax-deductible interest, a taxpayer in the 30 percent bracket would save $103.14 a month of the $388.43 payment.

Conversion Pointers. Investors can do very well on conversions, but they shouldn't ignore the common-sense rules of the game. Among the most important:

• *All apartment units are not potential successful condos.* Sometimes a building simply lacks the basic structural configuration, a convenient location, the physical condition or the minimal facilities necessary for conversion within a feasible budget. Buildings with balconies, porches or patios, for example, lend themselves to condo conversion far better than buildings without. Buildings with adequate interior and exterior space for the required amenities—a meeting room, extra parking space, adequate room inside each unit for a stacked washer/dryer, and the like—convert more economically than those without.

• *Rental projects in predominantly single-family ownership residential areas do better than those in mixed-use (commercial or industrial as well as residential) areas.* The single-family market locally should be exceptionally strong, and the median-priced houses should be selling for 20 to 30 percent *more* than your anticipated converted units. You'll be competing with the existing and newly constructed detached units in the area, and one of your strongest marketing cards will be your lower price.

• *If you can't count on selling at least one-third of your units to their present tenants—whether because of low income, abnormally high rents, or ill will toward you or the developer/converter—think twice about converting.* Some local laws require minimum tenant approval levels before conversion can be carried out. A 40 to 50 percent sale to tenants is an excellent target, and will speed the sale of the remaining units—even if the sales to tenants are at rock-bottom concessionary prices.

• *The selling price of your converted, remodeled units should be a multiple of at least 125 to 150 times the current monthly fair rent.* Anything less and you're not realizing the full benefits of conversion. A $400-a-month unit, in other words, might sell for $70,000 to $80,000 or more in a good market. A $300-per-month unit shouldn't bring much less than $40,000. "Fair" rent isn't necessarily *current* rent; it means the appropriate rental value of the unit per month after rehabilitation of the building.

• *Don't try a do-it-yourself conversion* unless you've done it yourself several other times. Hire professionals with verified track records to do your marketing feasibility study and to handle the conversion from start to finish. Make sure that the law firm you use specializes in the byzantine ins and outs of your local condominium and cooperative statutes. Hire competent engineering and architectural consultants early in the process; they can save you, your tenants and the future unit owners in the building thousands of dollars and a lot of grief.

COOPERATIVES

Housing cooperatives constitute the second mixed form of residential real estate: they provide ownership, but not of individual units within a building or subdivision. A co-op, as distinct from a condominium, is a corporation owned by stockholders; the corporation in turn owns a building or a complex of buildings. Individual stockholders receive proprietary leases giving them the right of occupancy to specific units within the building or subdivision. For tax purposes, membership in a housing co-op is essentially similar to ownership of a house or condominium. The co-op member deducts a proportional share of the entire building's blanket mortgage interest and its property taxes, rather than deducting against individual mortgages (which do not exist).

Like condominiums, cooperatives can take any shape or size. They range from New York City's luxury high-rises to entire suburban subdivisions of detached single-family homes sitting on spacious, fenced yards. The key element is in the property's legal structure, not its physical characteristics. Co-ops are most heavily concentrated in New York City, where they developed and prospered from the 1880s on as both in-town "country clubs" for the rich and housing for middle-income workers (after World War II). They are also spread around the country, however, and exist in every state (see the table on p. 194).

CO-OPS AS INVESTMENTS

Unlike condominiums, co-ops have a built-in mechanism restraining speculative investment. Co-ops overwhelmingly are bought by people intending to live in them, not rent them out. These purchasers normally hope that the market value of their share(s) of stock and their proprietary lease will increase during their period of ownership. But absentee ownership is often ruled out by the legal structure of co-ops, under which the corporation's board of directors traditionally has substantial powers to control use of specific units, and veto rights over leasing. Most New York co-ops simply won't admit a purchaser who intends to rent out to others for income, or one who will leave the units vacant for extended periods of time.

Pros and Cons

• Co-ops have been spectacular, albeit volatile, capital assets for many owners in New York. Manhattan cooperative apartments that were difficult to sell for $40,000 to $50,000 during the period from 1972 to 1975 sold quickly for $200,000 to $300,000 in 1978. According to Saul Clateman, head of co-op sales for the Charles H. Greenthal Company, in 1978 the average sell-

SUMMARY OF HOUSING COOPERATIVES IN THE UNITED STATES

By Types and Estimated Numbers of Dwellings

I. Privately Financed Cooperatives:

  a. Conventional conversions by profit-motivated owners and brokers, mostly in New York City, for higher-income families   180,000

  b. Conventional middle- and moderate-income cooperatives built by United Housing Foundation, labor unions, and nonprofit organizations   35,000

  c. Membership-sponsored cooperatives of all sorts, mostly small, one-time affairs by potential residents   5,000

  d. Conversions and rehabilitations of abandoned and semi-abandoned rental buildings, including programs in formation at this time   5,000

                                                        225,000

II. HUD Programs:

  a. Section 213—multi-family management type, market rate   71,663

  b. Section 213—individual mortgage—"sales type"   34,732

  c. Section 221(d)(3)BMIR—multi-family, moderate income   35,795

  d. Section 221(d)(3)Market Rate   2,080

  e. Section 236—lower and moderate income, multi-family   23,249

  f. Section 202—senior citizen high-rise   902

  g. Cooperatives created by transfer of physical assets, sale of stock to residents—all programs with HUD insurance (estimated)   10,000

  h. Co-ops organized with local assistance through HUD Community Development Block Grant Assistance   1,000

  i. Cases closed since 1976, estimated   5,000

                                                        184,500

III. Other Federal and State-Aided Programs:

a. Conversions of World War II housing under Lanham Act and the Colonel Westbrook program, estimated	35,000
b. Public housing without cash subsidy converted in New York, plus a few scattered cases like Buffalo and Chicago	12,000
c. Rural area cooperatives, primarily self-help	3,000
d. New York State and City programs, mostly Mitchell-Lama	60,000
e. Other known state housing development agency cooperatives (Connecticut, Illinois, Michigan, South Dakota, New Jersey, Massachusetts)	3,500
	113,500
TOTAL	523,000 units

SOURCE: National Association of Housing Cooperatives, September 1978.

ing price of a cooperative apartment in the city was *100 to 125 percent* above the price in 1975. Some owners of spacious apartments who in the early 1970s thought they had white elephants on their hands have made 300 to 400 percent capital gains upon selling them more recently.

• Volatility in value may not be what you really want in a long-term investment, however. Had you been forced to sell (as many owners were) in the New York doldrum market of 1973–75, you could have lost your shirt, as well as the equity you needed for your next home purchase. New York's co-op boom hit its last peak in 1969, the end of Wall Street's go-go phase, but then hit the skids. The plummeting sales values were caused by the city's declining economic fortunes, as well as an exodus away from the central city by middle- and upper-income people. New York's market has bounced back with vigor, but no one can be sure for how long.

• Co-ops have all the convenience, physical amenities and economies of management enjoyed by condos—with some extras thrown in. As a condo owner-occupant or absentee investor, you don't really have tight controls over who (or what) moves in next door; in a cooperative, you may well have an effective veto power. By-laws in some co-ops require 100 percent approval of all new stock purchases. Thus you can control the use of your environment and preserve its value to a greater extent than you can in any other form of real estate. Co-ops are *exclusive* by nature; condominiums can't be.

• Outside New York State, lenders in some areas are not always so favorably inclined toward cooperatives. New York City savings banks will happily provide a loan up to 85 percent of the appraised value of an apartment share, but in states with few cooperatives, banks don't want to be bothered. In some metropolitan areas, co-op sellers are forced to provide financing to their purchasers, since local S&Ls don't trust the security of proprietary leases. This inevitably holds back appreciation rates in the market value of cooperatives, and can cost owners thousands of dollars a year in unrealized potential gains.

7

Apartments

During the past ten years, apartment buildings have been the subject of more get-rich-quick books than any other form of real estate investment. Successive waves of formula books have promised fortunes to those following in the authors' footsteps.* But due to their heavy focus on apartment buildings, some of these books have less and less relevance to the real economics of the small-scale investor of the 1970s and '80s. Apartment buildings *can* be excellent investments; however, you've got to confront some sobering realities in apartment investing if you're going to realize the potential returns that are indeed there:

• During the last decade, the American economy has been extremely generous to owners of small one- to four-family dwellings—as annual housing cost and appreciation data confirm—but has been stingy to owners of apartment complexes. Rental income is the principal objective in investing in apartment build-

* William Nickerson's *How I Turned One Thousand Dollars into Three Million—in My Spare Time*, Richard F. Gabriel's *The Complete Guide to Building a Real Estate Fortune Investing in Older Multiple Dwellings*, and Albert J. Lowry's *How You Can Become Financially Independent by Investing in Real Estate* are just a few examples.

ings, yet during the past eleven years average apartment-rent levels nationwide have lagged badly behind inflation. According to the federal government's consumer price index, from 1967 to 1978 rents went up 61.4 percent; meanwhile, fuel costs have doubled or tripled in many parts of the country, and property taxes, mortgage-finance costs, and material and supply costs have outrun rents. As a result, the cash profits in rental housing are smaller today than they have been in many years. Tax losses and long-term negative cash flows may be acceptable in the field of rental houses, where the property is appreciating rapidly in value and can be readily turned into cash, but they are warning signs for apartment-building owners, who cannot look to high rates of annual appreciation for their ultimate return.

• A good gauge of the profitability of rental apartments is new construction. Despite a national vacancy rate of about 5 percent in 1978—as tight a market as the United States has witnessed in the post–World War II years—new construction of unsubsidized rental apartments has remained in the range of 250,000, the lowest level in two decades. Total new construction of multi-family units was close to 600,000 for calendar 1978, but 200,000 of these were federally subsidized units, and an estimated 150,000 to 175,000 were condominium ownership units. With a growing public demand for home ownership on the one hand, and restrictive rent controls or freezes on the other, the apartment-rental field is turning into a federally subsidized industry. The only real exceptions to this trend have been in the rapid-growth Southwestern metropolitan areas, where land costs are not prohibitive and rent controls aren't yet a threat.

• Led on by the popular belief that you can't lose with apartments, the small investor often has suffered the worst. When in August 1978 the Los Angeles City Council imposed a rent freeze on apartments, the owners of small- to moderate-sized buildings who had bought them at inflated prices—twelve to fifteen times gross rental income, rather than the traditional seven to eight times—found themselves awash in red ink. Rent controls in other cities pushed small apartment owners into condominium conversions that dislocated tenants and further aggravated the low-vacancy problem.

In short, it's harder to succeed in multi-family housing than ever before, but it *can* be done. Thousands of investors around the country are still making money—sometimes lots of it—by owning and efficiently operating multi-family buildings. According to the Census Bureau, there are over 500,000 apartment buildings in the United States containing between 5 and 49 units, and the majority of these are owned and operated by individual investors. Most of them are not currently covered by rent controls, and many turn a profit. The key to success is in the bottom-line numbers. More often than not, the numbers work where the possibility of indefinite, steady rent increases exists, and where investors are sharp enough, and the market permits them, to acquire properties below their true economic value. Watch out for situations in which the figures are padded or shaved for sales purposes, or in which there is no real likelihood of a positive cash flow for a number of years.

This chapter will examine some of the essential ingredients to successful rental-property acquisition. Such topics as tenant-landlord relations, leases, negotiations, and taxes have already been covered in Chapter 2, so the treatment here stops at financing options.

ANALYZING MARKETS AND BUILDINGS
FOR RENTAL INVESTMENT

How do you recognize a market where purchase of an apartment building can bring you a healthy net annual operating income? How do you determine whether your particular area is a good one for rental investment? And how do you locate and analyze buildings that can fulfill your objective?

As a prospective investor you research the market to determine effective demand for the type of project(s) you're considering, and you probe the experiences of current building owners. Different geographic areas of the country have traditionally had different ranges of acceptable returns. In California's major urban markets, for example, it was considered acceptable during 1977–78 for purchasers of existing 10- to 40-unit buildings to have little or no cash flow—or even to run sharply negative cash flows—for several years. Richard Wahlgren of Santa Monica's

First Federal Savings and Loan Association, and other southern California lenders, estimated that between 1977 and 1978, 95 *to* 99 *percent* of apartment-financing packages there were on the basis of negative cash flows. In healthier markets in such cities as Phoenix, Dallas-Fort Worth and Houston, annual acceptable cash-on-cash returns for well-managed buildings must be in the 8 to 10 percent range. (In past years in markets like these, the returns were in the 10 to 15 percent range.)

If you contact the metropolitan apartment owners' association and talk with local realtors specializing in commercial, income-producing property, you ought to be able to develop a feel for the market, its prevailing returns, prices and politics. You can obtain specific operating-cost statistics from the local affiliate of the Building Owners and Managers Association (BOMA), the local affiliate of the National Association of Home Builders, or the Institute for Real Estate Management (155 East Superior Street, Chicago, Ill. 60611), which produces average-cost data every year for buildings in representative markets across the country.

Signs of health you should look for locally include:

• An effective vacancy rate at or under 5 percent. Today a number of city markets have rates in the 2 to 3 percent range; outlying suburban areas tend to be higher.

• An expanding economy that shows annual net gains—or at least stability—in employment, retail sales and new housing construction.

• A high proportion of singles, younger married couples, and "empty nesters" in the population, and a strong historical demand for rental units.

Markets you should avoid would be those where:

• Vacancy rates are at 8 percent or higher, indicating weak demand and/or overbuilding of new units, and forcing owners to provide rent breaks or other concessions to attract tenants.

• The local economy is flat, or dependent upon one major employer whose industry is stagnant nationally.

• Rent controls of any type are either in force or in the offing, and condominium conversions are under any type of actual or probable restrictions.

You go into a multi-family acquisition with a range of financial data in mind: you (or your limited partnership or joint venturers) have a rough investment scale that narrows your choices. If, for example, you have $50,000 available for investment, you translate that into a price range of $250,000 to $300,-000, operating on the assumption that you can leverage your money five or six to one, exclusive of transfer costs. Your $50,-000 may be in the form of cash, of notes and stocks, of equity in other real estate suitable for exchange (see Chapter 10), or of something else. Just keep in mind that you have limits, and your analysis from here on in is greatly affected by those limits.

NEIGHBORHOODS AND BUILDINGS: CHECKLIST

The checklist starting on page 202 is a practical "walk-through" device for analyzing rental projects in the small- to mid-size range (10 to 75 units). Although it resembles the checklist in Chapter 2 for one- to four-unit properties, its heavy emphasis on income and expense data underscores the key difference between these two types of investment.

Let's proceed through the main items.

Section I. Location. This section is virtually self-explanatory. Rental projects that you give many excellent ratings to in this category should be your prime investment targets. Buildings inconvenient to transportation, shopping, and employment not only command lower rents but also appreciate less rapidly in capital value. Buildings located in areas that are considered marginal today, but that you believe will turn strongly upward in market attractiveness within a couple of years, are riskier, but probably offer the largest potential capital growth.

Pay special attention to public plans for the immediate area, and to public or private redevelopment possibilities on adjacent lots. A sizable upper-income condominium project planned across the street, in place of the row of rundown duplexes currently there, could be a big plus for your prospective rental building. On the other hand, a new public-housing project on the same site could make it hard to rent apartments in your quiet, five-story, all-adult building.

EVALUATION CHECKLIST FOR MEDIUM-SIZED (10 TO 75 UNITS) APARTMENT BUILDING

Address of Property _____

Owner _____ Phone Number _____

Agent _____ Phone Number _____

Asking Price _____ Age _____ Structural Type _____

Total Units _____

Unit Composition	Number
Efficiencies	
One Bedroom	
Two Bedroom	
Three Bedroom	
Other	

I. LOCATION	Excellent	Average	Poor
A. Is it in a neighborhood or community with a good to excellent economic future?			
1. Property values are increasing or are projected to increase.			
2. Demand for rental housing is strong, and vacancy low.			
3. No rent controls or freezes exist currently or are anticipated in the foreseeable future that would affect this building.			
4. Public plans for the area will foster or permit strong residential market for foreseeable future.			

	Excellent	Average	Poor

B. Does its location offer advantages to tenants?

   1. Is public transportation convenient?

   2. Are there adequate schools in the vicinity?

   3. Are shopping facilities convenient?

   4. Are employment facilities convenient?

   5. Are police and fire services adequate?

   6. Does the area offer special attractions to tenants, such as cultural facilities, recreational facilities, etc.?

C. Is the property adequately situated away from such adverse influences as excessive traffic, noise, pollution, freeways, an airport, flood-hazard areas, etc.?

D. Are any adjacent lots or structures subject to development or redevelopment under present zoning that would have an adverse (or positive) effect on the value or use of your building?

E. Does the property offer inherent locational advantages for its current rental range, such as special views or siting, etc.?

II. CURRENT INCOME

A. Actual rent roll

	Unit No.	Current Rent	Occupancy Status

Efficiencies

One Bedrooms

Two Bedrooms

	Unit No.	Current Rent	Occupancy Status
Three Bedrooms			
Other			

Total Efficiencies	$_____
Total One Bedrooms	$_____
Total Two Bedrooms	$_____
Total Three Bedrooms	$_____
Other	$_____
ANNUAL GROSS RENTS	$_____

B. Other income (annualized net)
   Laundry _____ Vending Machines _____
   Parking _____ Extra Storage _____
   Other _____   _____
   Total $_____

C. Current annual gross income
   (A + B): $_____

D. Vacancy losses $_____
   Credit losses $_____
   Total vacancy and credit losses $_____ Equals what
                                              percentage
                                   _____% of gross
                                              income?

E. Annual gross operating income
   (C − D) $_____

III. CURRENT EXPENSES

	Actual per Month	Actual per Year (19)
A. Utilities (paid by owner)		
Electricity	_____	_____
Water and sewer	_____	_____
Gas	_____	_____
Fuel oil	_____	_____

	Actual per Month	Actual per Year (19)
B. Taxes		
Local property taxes		
Payroll taxes		
Licenses and fees		
Personal property taxes		
C. Management		
Resident manager		
Professional manager/ consulting		
Gardener/janitorial/ maintenance		
Other		
D. Insurance		
Hazard and liability		
E. Repairs/general maintenance		
Special facilities maintenance		
Pool		
Landscaping		
Other		
F. Office/business expenses		
Accounting		
Legal		
Marketing/advertising		
Dues		
Telephone		
Miscellaneous supplies		
G. Reserves for capital expenditures		
H. Gross operating expenses		
I. Net operating income (Section II, item E, minus Section III, item H)		
J. Expenses as percentage of gross income _____ percent		

IV. MORTGAGE FINANCE COSTS

	First Mortgage	Second	Additional
Principal balance			
Held by			
Monthly amortization			
Interest rate			
Remaining term			
Assumable?			
Cost of assumption			
Total current monthly mortgage costs	$_____		

V. CURRENT ANNUAL CASH FLOW

Net operating income $_____
Less mortgage costs $_____
Pretax cash flow $_____   Approximate current
cash-on-cash yield
to owner _____

VI. STRUCTURAL

A. Does the overall condition of the building fit your investment strategy? That is to say, if the apartment structure is in less than adequate condition, are the necessary repairs achievable within your resources? Does the building show signs of a high degree of deferred maintenance?

B. *Structural Checklist and Rating*

	Rating	Costs of Repair/ Improvement
1. *Basement:*		
Walls/foundation		
Floor		
Visible flooding/dampness		
Visible termite damage?		
Structural supports?		
2. *Plumbing:*		
Pipes (condition/type)		
Hot-water heater (capacity/type/age)		

	Rating	Costs of Repair/ Improvement

3. *Electrical system:*
   Service amperage
   Need additional for rental
      usage?
   Separate metering for
      units?
   Condition/type of wiring

4. *Heating/air conditioning:*
   Furnace condition/age/
      type
   Radiators/vents—age/type
   Air conditioners—condi-
      tion/age/type
   Insulation

5. *Individual units:*
   Overall size and layout
   Kitchens—size and layout
   Condition/quality of
      appliances
   Cabinets—condition/
      quality/capacity
   Electrical outlets
   Ventilation
   Special amenities
   Balconies, patios
   Furnishings—condition
      Drapes
      Rugs
      Furniture
      Lighting
      Other
   Units with special problems
      (addendum)

6. *Walls and ceilings:*
   Condition/painted surface

7. *Floors:*
   Type and condition

	Rating	Costs of Repair/ Improvement

8. *Windows:*
   Condition and type
9. *Doors:*
   Condition and type
   Locks and hardware
   Peepholes
10. *Roof:*
    Condition/age
11. *Elevator(s):*
    Condition/age
12. *Gutters/downspouts:*
    Condition and type
13. *Exterior:*
    Condition and type
    Adequacy of current finish
14. *Landscaping:*
    Overall quality and
    condition
15. *Parking:*
    Garage/carport/spaces:
    condition and adequacy
16. *Pool:*
    Condition/age
17. *Other special amenities or
    problems:*

TOTALS $_____

VII. SELLING-PRICE ANALYSIS

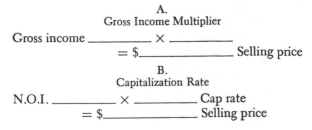

A.
Gross Income Multiplier

Gross income _____ × _____
= $_____ Selling price

B.
Capitalization Rate

N.O.I. _____ × _____ Cap rate
= $_____ Selling price

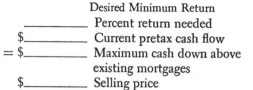

C.
Desired Minimum Return
_____ Percent return needed
$_____ Current pretax cash flow
= $_____ Maximum cash down above
existing mortgages
$_____ Selling price

VIII. PROJECTED ACQUISITION COSTS
(at $_____ sales price)

A. Cash down $_____

B. Financing:
Mortgages
$_____ trust/mortgage
_____ percent rate
_____ term

C. Financing-related fees
(commitment fee, placement fee, etc.) $_____

D. Local and state transfer fees $_____

E. Settlement and miscellaneous expenses $_____

F. Other $_____

TOTAL $_____

IX. ESTIMATED TAX IMPACTS

A. Depreciation (based on esti-   Per Year
mate of _____ years economic   _____
life of building, _____ percent
of property value assigned to
building itself; and _____
depreciation method)

B. Deductible costs:
1. Interest
2. Taxes
3. Insurance
4. Management/maintenance
5. Capitalized improvements
6. Other

C. Estimated tax savings   _____

X. PROJECTED APPRECIATION OF PROPERTY

Market Value	At _____%	At _____%	At _____%
End of year 1	_____	_____	_____
End of year 2	_____	_____	_____
End of year 3	_____	_____	_____
End of year 4	_____	_____	_____
End of year 5	_____	_____	_____

XI. How does this property compare overall with others in terms of price, monthly costs versus projected income, tax benefits and projected appreciation?

Section II. Current Income. Investors in apartment buildings often fail to accurately determine scheduled income and current expenses. Since building owners know that the market value of their property will be a function of the building's capitalized income, they occasionally go to great lengths to puff up their rent rolls immediately prior to offering their property for sale. Be aware of the possibility of such maneuvers.

• Just exactly how many rental units are there? A "22-unit" building, for example, may actually have only 19 rent-producing units. The seller may count some storage areas as units, or a resident manager's extra-large ground-floor unit as two because "all you have to do is add a wall here and there." Just remember that conversion will cost *you* money and that no actual rents have even been collected from these spaces.

• Some sellers pack their projects with tenants, and can show you highly impressive rent rolls and a zero vacancy rate. But when you talk to the tenants after you've bought the place you find out that (a) during the final six months of his ownership, the former landlord refunded $30 worth of the rent in the form of groceries at the end of the month; (b) the landlord rented a number of the units at concessionary rates to family members and friends, but listed the full rent on the rent rolls; (c) the economic vacancy rate of the building—the annual loss for carrying empty units—may in reality be 10 to 15 percent, not 0 to 2 percent as the rent roll suggests.

To protect yourself from rental-income shenanigans, get an actual income statement for a specific period prior to the transaction from the owner or his broker or accountant. The breakdown sheet should show specific unit numbers, their scheduled rents, and the length of time the tenant has occupied the unit (under "occupancy status"). Do not be satisfied with "average" rent figures by type of unit. And spot-check to confirm these facts, in informal discussions with a few tenants. Other income should also be verifiable: the split the building owner takes of the leased coin-laundry equipment and other vending machines on the premises (often half of gross dollars); parking fees (sometimes as much as $25 to $30 per space a month); and money from any other commercial space that produces income for the building.

Current annual gross income—Section II, item C—is a crucial figure in your analysis of the building. From it must come all operating expenses and mortgage service if you're going to obtain your desired cash flow. Here you must take into consideration the dollars lost in potential rents during the year due to vacancies and nonpayments. Where lease records are readily available, you (or your broker) can verify the seller's or broker's vacancy estimates. In buildings where leases are not used, verification may be more difficult, but figures should be obtainable from the project's accountant. Don't simply accept an owner's rough estimate of, say, 5 percent; this happens to be the traditional industry-wide rule of thumb on what vacancies are likely to be in an average year.

If the building has an unusually high vacancy or nonpayment rate, determine why it does before writing it off as an acquisition. By good management and better relations with the tenants, you may be able to turn a bad situation around. But high vacancy rates can also be caused by poor location, chronic structural problems, and other factors that you have less ability to control—in which case you just might do better with another building.

Item E in Section II is your adjusted gross operating income, the number you can multiply by a factor—say, 7 or 8—to arrive at a selling price. In the case of a suburban Ohio apartment building with a gross operating income of $300,000 a year, the owner would multiply by eight to come up with a market price of $2,400,000. In California's more speculative climate, the same building might be valued at ten times gross, or $3,000,000.

Section III. Current Expenses. Just as owners eager to sell their apartment buildings have an understandable tendency to magnify income, so too do they tend to omit or decrease expenses. You and your broker should therefore use a checklist like the one in Section III to make sure that nothing important gets left out. The seller's accountant should be able to provide you with enough information to fill out every item satisfactorily; if the project's records are in such a jumble that essential data isn't available, think hard before continuing negotiations.

While you're examining the figures you do get, ask *how* and *by whom* the expenses were incurred. Many buildings that rack up low operating expenses may be largely self-managed by the owner; he or she may paint vacated units, fix what needs fixing, and handle all the books. That's admirable, but can you afford to do it yourself? If you're a typical apartment investor, you are not going to manage the project yourself. Also bear in mind that some of the expense items may reflect economies of scale: the current owner may be a corporation controlling hundreds of units in the area, and one that can bring in management or service personnel part-time at low cost by simply moving them about as they are needed. Large owners can also spread their legal, accounting and organizational expenses across all their projects, thereby impressively cutting down expenses on a project-by-project basis. Can you, as an individual investor, match that sort of performance?

The expense items on the list are straightforward. *Utilities* are a matter of record; you or your broker should see an entire twelve-month cycle of paid bills for electricity, fuel, water, and gas. Is the usage on an average per-unit basis exceptionally high or low? (The local utility companies can tell you if it is.) And if so, why? How fast are these costs likely to rise in the coming year?

Property taxes are a matter of public record, and there's little you can do about the numbers. Don't neglect to add in license costs and fees (in post–Proposition 13 California these skyrocketed as a source of revenue for local governments); payroll taxes; and where appropriate personal property taxes on furniture and other items.

Management fees will vary according to the size of the building, the current apartment market, and current rent levels. Part-time on-site managers of small buildings may receive only rent reductions as compensation, and that would be reflected in Section II above. Professional management of larger projects can involve fees ranging from 5 to 10 percent of gross rents, depending upon the number of units and the duties specified in the management package. Some top-flight management companies won't touch rental complexes with less than a hundred units; other firms will take on such projects but will charge higher rates.

Insurance expenses deserve scrutiny. The current owner may have nowhere near the minimum adequate hazard coverage on the property, or he may be spreading insurance costs among several projects. His policy may not include the important "loss of rents" clause that protects an investor following a disastrous fire or other such damage. Your insurance costs could be double or triple the figure quoted by the present owner.

Under expenses for *repairs/maintenance,* include all items considered *deductible* by the IRS, such as routine painting, patching walls, fixing broken hardware, and so forth. Do not include such capital items as replacing the roof, repainting the entire façade, converting the basement into a laundry area, or the like. If maintenance costs in a ten- to twenty-year-old project you're considering are low, this can mean that the owner has put off a lot of necessary maintenance which will fall on your shoulders if you buy, or that the project was simply well constructed and managed from the start.

Although sometimes overlooked in cost analyses of rental projects, office and business expenses can add up to a significant amount over the course of a year. Owners of most small- to medium-sized rental buildings usually require accounting assistance, but some owners do their own accounting, thereby cutting thousands of dollars a year off the expense column. Advertising and other marketing expenses can also be a big drain if the building is poorly located or has a high turnover rate.

Does the current owner maintain reserves out of gross rental income to handle replacement or repair of such capital items as the boiler, air conditioning units, kitchen appliances, carpeting, furniture or pool equipment? If not, his operating budget will probably be inflated on the income side, and you'd better watch for large, costly expenditures he's leaving for the new owner. In any case, should you decide to buy a building, you will need to set up a realistic schedule of anticipated capital-item replacements/repairs. List by category all capital items on the premises, and note the probable number of them you'll need to replace or repair over a five- to ten-year period. The estimated costs of these reserves, year by year, should be included in your own balance-sheet calculations *before* you sign a contract.

Your preliminary bottom line, before you deduct mortgage costs, is your net operating income (N.O.I.): gross income less operating expenses. In the case of the average existing building (where tenants pay their own utilities), expenses should total no higher than 45 percent of gross income; where the utilities are all paid by the landlord, the number can stretch to 55 to 60 percent. Go much higher and you're looking at a probable loss after today's mortgage costs are figured in.* In newer buildings, look for current expense ratios no higher than 35 to 40 percent. If your rough calculations suggest you can do significantly better on expenses than the current owner, these percentages can increase a little, but don't overestimate your miracle-working talents in management.

Section IV. Mortgage Finance Costs. These are the current owner's, not yours, but they tell you a lot about the seller and his building. Is the owner leveraged to the hilt, with multiple mortgages and little real equity in the property? If so, he may have relatively little flexibility on his price because he owes so much to others. Is there any advantage to assuming his current first mortgage or deed of trust, and if so, what costs will be exacted by his lender?

Section V. Current Annual Cash Flow. What does the present owner actually get (before taxes) on the money he's sunk

---

* Buildings with financing dating back five or more years may make money, even running operating cost ratios of 65 to 70 percent, thanks to their bargain-basement loan interest costs. But unless you can assume such loans, they'll be of no help to *your* balance sheet.

into the building? Ten percent a year? Two percent? Nothing—
or even less? And what are you likely to be able to produce,
given your own management of operating expenses, different
rent levels if appropriate, and different financing?

At this point, you may already have worked out your decision
on the building you're considering. If the figures look strong,
move on to the next item. If they're deeply in the red, and
management economies don't look promising, your only option
—other than to look at another property—is to move directly to
Section VII and begin cutting the owner's selling price down
to size.

Section VI. Structural. The items here are basically the same
—with such exceptions as elevators, equipment in individual
units, a pool—as those discussed in detail in Chapter 2 (see
pp. 31–33). Review that section with care; keep in mind that
in large buildings, you or your consulting engineer/inspector
will need to consider the value and condition of many pieces of
kitchen equipment, and ideally should examine every unit prior
to sale. The dollar figures you end up with in the right-hand
(costs of repair) column become bargaining chips when you
negotiate with the seller.

Section VII. Selling-Price Analysis. To facilitate calculation
of the price you'll offer for the building, the checklist provides
several alternative valuation methods:

A. *Gross Income Multiplier Approach.* This is a common
rule of thumb you'll encounter in the field, and one you'll often
hear as the seller's basis for his asking price because it produces
large numbers independent of operating costs. It involves adding
up gross rents and other income, subtracting the vacancy loss,
and multiplying the remainder by a factor ranging anywhere
from 6 to 12.*

---

* As noted above, the multiplier varies from area to area and changes
over time. Rental buildings in New York that sold for multiples of nine
times gross income in 1968 fell to three or four times gross in the depths
of the city's 1974–75 financial crisis. Multiples of fifteen times gross income
in Beverly Hills, California, were chalked up in 1978, but these were temporary extremes.

B. *Capitalization Rate Approach.* An analogous technique, this is based on the concept of capitalizing net income to achieve the real worth of a piece of property. Cap rates vary, but the most common is 10.

C. *Desired Return Approach.* If you know that you want to obtain no less than a specific percentage return on your invested dollars, and you know the current pretax cash flow on the building (from Section V above), then you can calculate how large a down payment you can afford to make, above existing assumable financing.

To illustrate each of these, here are the income and expense figures from a hypothetical set-up (broker's statistical presentation on an apartment building) on a 90-unit building.

90-UNIT BUILDING *(all units unfurnished)*

I. Income:

Unit Type	No.	Average Rent per Month	Total Annual Rental Income
Efficiency	15	$200	$ 36,000
One Bedroom	20	275	66,000
Two Bedrooms	45	350	189,000
Three Bedrooms	10	$425	$ 52,000
Total Rent	90		$343,000
Laundry, extra parking spaces, vending machines			12,000
			$355,000
Less 3 percent vacancy and credit losses			−10,650
GROSS OPERATING INCOME			$344,350

II. Expenses: 42 percent of gross
           operating income   144,626

            NET OPERATING INCOME $199,724

III. Debt Service: $1,500,000 25-year loan at
                  9.25 percent (8.57
                  constant) $154,260

IV. Cash Flow Before Taxes: $ 55,464

Let's plug this data into our three alternative valuation approaches and see what value ranges they suggest (see below). Under the gross income multiplier method, we arrive at a valuation of $2,410,450, using a multiplier of 7. Under the cap rate method, we come up with a valuation of $1,999,724. The third option produces the two following possibilities. If we want a 10 percent return on our money, we can afford to put down $555,464 above the existing assumable loan of $1,500,000. That results in a $2,055,464 valuation. If, however, we will take a cash-on-cash return of just 5 percent, we could double our acceptable maximum down payment to $1,110,928, and could go as high as a $2,610,928 price for the building.

These rule-of-thumb techniques virtually always produce contrasting results, and are prone to wide individual variations when you plug in different local multipliers or cap rates. Using a 10:1 multiplier of gross income, for instance, would produce a $3,400,000 possible market value for the building. A 6:1 ratio, on the other hand, would result in a $2,060,000 price. Which figure you go with in a speculative market containing proper ties bought and sold at both ends of the spectrum could involve

A. Gross Income Multiplier

$344,350 × 7 = $2,410,450 possible market value

B. Capitalization Rate

$199,724 × 10 = $1,999,724 possible market value

C. Desired Minimum Return

10 percent return needed
$55,464 current cash flow
$55,464 = 10 percent of $555,464 + $1,500,000
                                               existing loan
                                    _____
                                         $2,055,464

5 percent return needed
$55,464 current cash flow
$55,464 = 5 percent of $1,110,928 + $1,500,000
                                               existing loan
                                    _____
                                         $2,610,928

hundreds of thousands of dollars per project. Normally, you would bring in a professional appraiser with long local experience in income-producing property valuations to give you still another, more definitive figure. Your calculations in A, B, and C are useful for a quick analysis, and for comparison with the appraiser's, but shouldn't be relied on exclusively.

Section VIII. Projected Acquisition Costs. Financing is the key item here, and we'll discuss it separately below. The other factors are listed to enable you to have a clear idea of what's to come out of your pocket at closing. The more you need here, the less you may have for a down payment and the lower the mortgage amount for which you'll be able to qualify.

Section IX. Estimated Tax Impacts. A key part of any multi-family acquisition decision should be the tax impact a particular project will have on you. Does the building qualify for either of the most rapid accelerated depreciation methods (200 percent declining balance or sum-of-the-years'-digits)?* Do you expect to use 125 percent declining balance or straight-line? Does the project have a high ratio of building-to-land value, enabling you to write off a higher depreciation percentage per year? (Elevator structures of four stories and up tend to be the most efficient in this regard; sprawling garden apartment projects are the least efficient.) How low an economic life can you get by with for tax purposes without provoking the IRS into an audit? What annual total tax savings or shelter can you expect from the building for your likely period of ownership? When this is added to cash flow, what sort of real return on your investment will you be receiving? The answers to these questions will ultimately have to come from your accountant, but the questions should be posed as you do your initial analysis or walk-through.

Sections X and XI. Capital Growth. You may be buying a project that has a minimal cash-on-cash return with the expectation of a favorable long-term gain in the property's market value. This long-term growth in capital is essentially speculative, but

---

* Review the tax discussion on pp. 76–87 for fundamentals of depreciation, capital gains, and so forth.

the odds are better in communities and neighborhoods that produce strong ratings on the checklist. One aspect of value of the property may be its potential for conversion to condominium (or co-op in New York). The value of a rental project may appreciate only 3 to 4 percent a year, but the sales value of the same property could jump 30 percent in one year if it is marketed for conversion. (See pages 177–185 for pointers on what sort of rental projects make good condos, at what price and at what risk.) In general, you shouldn't bother with negative cash flow–producing projects that aren't likely to grow in market value by at least 5 to 8 percent a year. Your real return, net of your years of losses, will otherwise be too low to justify your time, risk and capital.

FINANCING

The key ingredient in the positive cash flow in the 90-unit project discussed above was its attractive existing mortgage, whose 9.25 percent interest rate is well below prevailing interest rates in today's market. To get an idea of what financing can do to a bottom line, let's look at the same building, with the same rents, but with a less advantageous, newer loan. Assuming a 10 percent annual constant rate on the $1,500,000 mortgage, the result is debt service of $180,000 a year rather than $154,000, and a pretax cash flow of only $19,000 instead of $55,000. An $1,800,-000 mortgage on the same property with an annual constant rate of 10 percent would produce annual debt service of $216,-000—putting the project over $16,000 in the red per year.

In today's economy, the cost of money is the crusher that turns even well-managed moderate-sized buildings into cash drains for their owners. Securing the most advantageous possible mortgage financing has thus become much more important in the past several years.

Sources. Where you seek money for the purchase of an existing multi-family project depends on your overall investment strategy. Basic approaches and sources don't differ greatly from those outlined for one- to four-unit investment property, but terms and required documentation vary greatly.

Savings and loan associations are your best bet for new loans on existing properties of 5 to 75 units. Loan-to-value ratios can go up to 80 percent, but normally are in the 70 to 75 percent range, and terms tend to be in the 25- to 30--year range. Points and placement fees are likely to be imposed, as are prepayment and assumption fee clauses. S&Ls prefer to make loans for properties in their immediate community and require formal loan request packages detailing your management abilities and the building's operating statements from past years, among other data. Your application package should provide all of the income, expense and market-analysis information covered in the checklist above, plus:

• A legal description of the site, its square footage, a locator map (and/or aerial photo), and whatever marketing-study results you have on the building and its neighborhood.

• Floor-by-floor blueprints showing units, square footage, and service cores.

• Data on all essential equipment (heating plant, elevators, plumbing, etc.) in the project.

• A written summary of your specific investment objectives with respect to acquisition of the project; information on how you plan to improve or otherwise alter the building's current operating cost performance.

• An economic feasibility analysis, if you've had one prepared for you, by an independent consultant.

• Your financial status—assets, income, liabilities, net worth.

With S&Ls you must shop around, submitting three or four applications to start. Some S&Ls specialize in small single-family owner-occupied properties and don't want to put large chunks of capital into apartment houses, despite the attractive yield. Other S&Ls feel they know the economics of apartment lending better, and will provide superior terms.

Commercial banks are another potential local source, but commercial banks tend to prefer larger commercial projects and loan-to-value ratios that are closer to 50 percent. If you have a good relationship with a bank or are a large depositor, you'll have an easier task and access to more generous loan-to-value terms.

Mortgage bankers will attempt to link you up with an institutional lender, such as an out-of-town insurance company, pension fund or real estate investment trust. If your applications to local S&Ls turn up no money, mortgage bankers should be able to help—but at a premium rate for their efforts. Mortgage bankers may be able to locate terms specially suited to your cash flow or tax needs, such as variable-rate mortgages from institutional or private lenders, interest-only payment loans, and so forth.

As was emphasized in Chapter 2, *sellers* may be your single best source. The current owner of the property is often highly motivated to sell, knows the building's track record in the market intimately, and may be willing to provide loans personally tailored to meet your needs. In the case of a project with very favorable existing financing but a larger equity gap for you to fill than you can afford, the seller may be willing to make a *wraparound* secondary loan that cuts your down payment requirement sharply. The wraparound may even qualify as an *installment* transaction under IRS rules, and thereby be even more attractive to the seller.*

Assumption of the seller's existing loan may be advantageous if you can come up with the cash necessary to fill the gap, and can pay the assumption fee his lender demands.

FEDERAL AID FOR RENTAL APARTMENTS

Over two-fifths of the new construction of rental apartments from 1978 to 1980 will be either federally subsidized or insured under programs administered by the Department of Housing and Urban Development (HUD) and the Farmers Home Administration. Although new construction is far beyond the limited scope of this chapter, some of the federal programs do offer opportunities for financial assistance to owners of existing apartment projects.

---

* See Chapter 10 for a discussion of these financing options. See Chapter 2 for a general discussion of other sources of secondary loans.

The largest and most important of these is HUD's Section 8 program, aimed at moderate- and lower-income tenants. As it applies to owners (or prospective purchasers) of buildings, the Section 8 program offers long-term federal contracts under which the government agrees to pay the difference between what an assisted tenant can afford to pay (15 to 25 percent of adjusted gross income) and the fair market rent that the tenant should be paying for accommodations in your building. As the costs of running rental apartments in your area go up, so do the fair market rents permitted by HUD on each unit, thereby protecting you against sudden losses caused by sharp increases in utilities, taxes and the like. The Section 8 program sidesteps local rent controls; in some cities with municipal controls, landlords have found Section 8 a good way to keep their buildings full at *higher* rents than they otherwise could have obtained in the market.

The program is definitely worth a look if your building (or prospective purchase) is aimed at lower- or moderate-income tenants—those with incomes less than 80 percent of your area's median. Information on Section 8 is available through your local public housing authority, your city housing and community development agency, or the Department of Housing and Urban Development, Washington, D.C. 20410.

Section 223(f). Another potentially useful federal tool for existing apartment buildings is HUD's refinancing program known as Section 223(f), which is open to owners or purchasers of any existing apartment building of eight or more units where no more than 20 percent of the total net rentable area (or 25 percent of the total gross income) is attributable to nonresidential usage (such as offices and shops). The program permits refinancing of conventional or FHA-insured mortgages for up to 85 percent of estimated property value at a favorable interest rate. HUD imposes maximum per-unit mortgage limits similar to those in its regular Section 207 multi-family insurance program.

The utility of Section 223(f) to you as owner or purchaser of a project will depend upon the specifics of the building involved and its current mortgage. The acknowledged experts in dealing with HUD and FHA in such programs are your local mortgage bankers. Check with one to determine whether recasting existing financing through Section 223(f)—lengthening the payback term, cutting monthly payments, or lowering the interest rate—just might improve your bottom line.

8

Real Estate Securities

Most of the investment alternatives in this book require some degree of ongoing involvement in property or loan management, a very real deterrent for many high-income professionals with no desire for more complications in their lives. Investors who want the yield and tax advantages of real estate without the customary hassles should consider real estate securities.

All real estate securities are *group*, as opposed to individual, investments in real estate; and they all put the investor in a relatively *passive* position with respect to management or control of his or her assets. Otherwise, the investments that come under this broad heading are remarkably diverse, ranging from Wall Street–brokered building industry stocks no different from other corporate stocks to highly leveraged equity syndications of federally subsidized housing projects. Other such investments include participation in mortgage-backed bond pools, the purchase of shares in real estate investment trusts (REITs), investment in huge, multi-million-dollar nationwide public real estate funds, and purchase of interests in small local residential property partnerships. Purchasing real estate–related securities can involve virtually no risk (as in the example of buying into federally guaranteed mortgage pools) or truly nerve-racking dangers of capital loss and of tax-shelter recaptures (as in the case of some low-income-housing syndications that go belly-up). Potential returns on the dollar span the same wide spectrum: mortgage-backed securities will dependably yield 9 percent or more; successful income-producing commercial-property syndications can dependably yield in the double digits, and will provide tax benefits and significant capital gains over a period of years; and subsidized-housing syndications may shelter from taxes several times more of your income in a given year than you invest in the deal.

First let's take a look at limited partnerships, the category of real estate securities that is most diverse and most likely to provide opportunities for investors. Then we'll move on to some of the other alternatives.

LIMITED PARTNERSHIPS/SYNDICATES

Wherever you turn in American real estate today, you're certain to come into contact, knowingly or otherwise, with limited partnerships or their vast holdings. The shopping center where you buy groceries, the office building in which you work, the apartment house a friend lives in, the hotel complex you visit on vacation, or the newly constructed low-income housing project on the other side of town—all of these are likely to be in one or another of the fast-growing property portfolios of real estate limited partnerships or syndicates.* Well over $4 billion in new real estate limited-partnership offerings were put on the market between 1970 and mid-1978, and the trend is up sharply. Some of the funds marketed in 1978—such as the $54 million American Property Investors VIII, involving six thousand *individual* partners—were truly gargantuan. More typical of the field in terms of size is the $15 million First Capital Income Properties, Ltd.–Series IV, which is designed to acquire and hold prime

---

* In modern real estate parlance, *syndicate* has come to be virtually synonomous with limited partnership. Technically, a syndicate can be any form of association of individuals who are attempting to accomplish a common goal or enterprise. *Syndication* means raising money for real estate limited-partnership investment from among a group of individuals.

commercial properties in Florida and other Sunbelt states. The offering was marketed in $1,000 units, with $5,000 the minimum purchase.

Definitions. A limited partnership is probably best understood by comparing it with full partnerships and with corporations. A full partnership consists of an association, commonly organized for business purposes, in which all the members or parties share fully in any liabilities arising from the enterprise, and share profits or other returns on a pro-rata basis, according to the extent of their holdings. The partnership per se retains no profits, nor does it pay any taxes on "earnings." These are all passed through on a pro-rata basis. Thus a partnership offers organizational efficiency for small, compatible groups, but gets unwieldy when large numbers and diverse assets are involved. Also, from a real estate point of view, the personal-liability aspect—that is to say, putting one's property, even one's residence, at risk—is highly distressing, given the dollar amounts of liability that may arise.

The corporation is an alternative to the partnership that sidesteps the problem of personal liability. Corporations offer a shield to individual stockholders because they themselves function legally as individuals. Organized under state law, corporations have the following essential characteristics: *centralized management,* an internal specialization that tends to be better suited to larger business ventures than a partnership of co-equals; *continuity of life* until dissolved legally (partnerships can end whenever partners so choose); *readily transferable ownership interests* (in some cases, partnership interests may not be transferable at all); and the *limited personal liability* feature mentioned above.

The drawbacks of corporate ownership of real estate arise in part from their shield; returns and profits on investments go to the corporation and are taxed at the corporate level. Without a vote by the board of directors, there is no pass-through of profits to shareholders. Dividends distributed to shareholders are subsequently taxed at the level of the individual taxpayer. (This constitutes double taxation of returns, and cuts effective yields to investors.) Losses are not passed through to shareholders, but instead are kept at the corporate level; in real estate, where depreciation losses are vital to sheltering ordinary income from taxation, this is a serious drawback indeed.

An intermediate investment-ownership vehicle that has developed rapidly in the past twenty years is the *limited partnership*. It offers some of the inherent protections of a corporation, while qualifying for tax treatment by the Internal Revenue Service as a partnership. Limited partnerships are composed of a general partner, who has full liability for the debts and other obligations of the partnership, and a number of limited partners. The general partner or syndicator (who may be an individual, several individuals, a partnership or a corporation) typically is the force behind the creation of the partnership, and has complete responsibility for managing the enterprises engaged in by the organization.

Underneath the general partner are the limited partners— limited both in their liability, which exists only to the extent of their capital contributions to the partnership, and in their right to influence or direct management decisions of the enterprise. They are for all intents and purposes *passive* partners. They also receive direct pass-throughs of all profits and losses on a pro-rata basis, as in a full partnership. Thus when a limited partnership experiences high operating income from a shopping center it owns, or a large gain as the result of a sale of one of its properties, the income and capital gains are directly passed through, according to an allocation plan agreed to by all partners when the partnership plan was created and filed with a state government. So, too, when a limited partnership that invests in housing experiences high losses in its early years attributable to accelerated depreciation, high mortgage interest and property taxes* relative to rental income, these losses are passed through per the allocation agreement. Limited partners can use the losses to shelter ordinary income from taxation, and can expect treatment of distributions of capital as capital gains.

---

* For a discussion of taxes, depreciation, accelerated depreciation and capital gains, see Chapter 2.

The legal structure of a limited partnership is usually complex, especially in comparison to a partnership. Even small private offerings of limited-partnership interests, which involve only a few shares and are open to a small number of people, can entail lengthy prospectuses and disclosures. This is required under state blue-sky laws and federal securities laws aimed at protecting investors from deceptive offerings that may not in fact qualify as limited partnerships, or that involve fraudulent claims by promoters. A prospectus typically provides details about the general partners, their experience in real estate and financial management, and their plans with respect to the funds raised via sale of limited-partnership units; and gives information about the physical and financial characteristics of the properties (if any) the partnership has contracted to acquire or plans to build. A prospectus will also disclose projected cash flows and tax-related losses the limited partners can anticipate during the course of the partnership existence; the various methods of compensation to be enjoyed by the general partners and the extent of the limited-partner funds that will be eaten up by marketing, legal, realty commissions, and other front-end fees and costs; and a variety of other pertinent information.

INVESTMENT PROS AND CONS OF
REAL ESTATE LIMITED PARTNERSHIPS

The Pluses. The advantages of buying into a limited partnership or syndicate as a limited partner can be impressive.

• The prospects of steady double-digit yields, in income-producing funds, or substantial tax shelters, in syndicates designed for that purpose, attract thousands of investors a year. The tax status and size of pay-outs by funds differ according to the nature of their underlying property transactions, but many large real estate funds provide mixed distributions based on tax-deferred return of capital and net operating income.

• Almost no real estate investment can beat the ease of buying shares in a limited partnership. In some funds, the minimum purchase price is as low as $2,500 (although $5,000 is more common), and there is usually no maximum. Contract in hand, you walk out of your stockbroker's office, and sooner or later you begin receiving checks and periodic financial accountings from "the syndicate."

• *Large, pooled funds offer small investors the possibility of acquiring interests in properties that are far above the quality levels otherwise open to them.* They also provide the means to attract top property and financial managers to guide investors' funds. Such prime income-producing properties as commercial office buildings and shopping centers are simply out of the league of all but the largest (usually institutional) investors. Yet for $5,000 to $10,000, small-scale investors can latch on to big-league real estate. When a fund is particularly well managed, investors have the opportunity to capture some of the windfall gains that occur on advantageous sales of prime properties. For example, in 1973 Balcor Realty Investors–73, a Chicago-based limited partnership, bought a Las Vegas shopping mall (the Boulevard Shopping Center) for $4.4 million, mortgaging the roughly $19 million balance of the price. Four years later, Balcor sold its equity interest in the mall to a group of British investors for *$12.8 million*, producing a stunning gain that rippled through the entire partnership.

• *Limited partnerships are often tailored to the needs of certain classes of investors, allowing plenty of choice in the marketplace.* Some funds are designed to extract and distribute maximum net income from commercial properties and distribute it to partners. Others are designed for long-term capital growth; and still others "specialize" in high tax-sheltered write-offs spanning fifteen to twenty years. Consumers can usually find a public or private partnership that meets their investment needs.

• *Real estate limited partnerships add valuable diversity to an investor's portfolio.* Many investors concentrate their discretionary funds in one area, rather than diversifying and thereby further protecting their income against changes in the economy. With a large limited partnership that invests in income properties around the United States, you are less likely to be wiped out or to have poor yields caused by localized economic misfortunes.

The Minuses. Absence of involvement can also be harmful to the interests of investors. As limited partners, investors are essentially prohibited from advising, influencing or restraining management in portfolio strategy, operations, sales, purchase prices and the like, even if they have more real estate savvy than the general partners. Limited partners can displace general partners/managers only under highly unusual circumstances, and to do so involves serious risks in regard to tax status.

Limited partnerships are sophisticated tools to raise money and sell real estate. The promoters or general partners may structure the funds so as to provide themselves with huge front-end fees, cash payments, and commissions, sometimes compensating themselves with as much as 30 to 35 percent of the *total* funds invested. This means that for every $1.00 you as an investor plunk down on the table, only 65 to 70 cents may be actually working for you in real estate. Inevitably, this cuts your real yield per dollar. Wall Street real estate securities experts confirm that the up-front siphoning off of 20 to 25 percent of investors' money is common in limited partnership offerings. Fees that aggregate 8 to 10 percent are far more reasonable. Self-dealing conflicts of interest are also common in limited partnerships. For example, general partners (in the independent real estate businesses) may acquire property at a low price, mark it up substantially in price, and turn around and sell it to the limited partnership, pocketing a windfall profit as well as a realty commission of 5 to 8 percent. A $1,000,000 building acquired by your fund may in reality be an $800,000 building that one of the general partners sold for $1,000,000 ten days after acquiring it himself. Or the general partners may purchase property only from a company they control, or from a parent company that controls them. The possibilities for highly profitable self-dealing by the general partners are rampant. Securities laws may require disclosure of such conflicts of interest, but small-scale investors may not be equipped to recognize a conflict from the bare facts alone.

• Limited partnerships may not achieve anywhere near the income or tax benefits they promise, regardless of their cash-flow projections in the prospectus. Public offerings of large funds, though examined by federal and state securities officials, don't guarantee specific returns—and many such funds do much worse than they led investors to believe. For example, poorly chosen, overpriced property in a stagnant market can eliminate a limited partnership's cash distributions. Limited partnerships may not even *qualify* as limited partnerships in the IRS's eyes if they fall short on a variety of technical grounds, in which case they turn into an undesirable subspecies of financial pumpkin known as an "association taxable as a corporation." That means double taxation and no pass-throughs.

• Limited-partnership interests are normally difficult to trade or dispose of; as many prospectuses point out in the boilerplate, "a market is not likely to develop" for the purchase or sale of your shares in the XYZ Limited Partnership. The fund may buy back some of its units *if* it has reserve funds, but that is a big if. Thus if the partnership has a life of fifteen years, be prepared when you sign away your money not to see it or to count it as a readily liquifiable asset for fifteen years.

• Although amazingly easy to buy into, buying *wisely* in real estate limited partnerships often demands resources beyond those of the average investor. A prospectus may sing the praises of an office building 2,000 miles away and a shopping center 1,500 miles away; it may even reprint rough operating statements. But you as an investor are hardly likely to be able to fly out and inspect the shopping center and office building, or to be sharp enough to plow through page after page of financial disclosures and find the numbers that are off—the inflated lease income, or the operating budget that is 20 percent below the norm for the locale involved. In most cases, you end up handing your money over to the syndication that your stockholder suggests—and he probably doesn't qualify as a real estate expert either.

TYPES OF LIMITED PARTNERSHIPS/SYNDICATES

There are two broad types of limited partnerships in real estate: large *public* offerings and small *private* offerings. They differ in more than size, however; they tend to make sense to different segments of the investment market.

Public Syndicates. The public offerings, discussed above, can involve thousands of buyers in dozens of states, and are often designed to raise millions of dollars at a time. The most frequent and the biggest offerings tend to come from several experienced firms: Robert A. McNeil and Consolidated Capital, both from California; Integrated Resources in New York (which markets the American Property Investor series); Balcor (Balcor Income Properties) and JMB Realty (JMB Income Properties Ltd.) of Chicago; and Fox and Carshadon Financial, San Francisco. Another successful but less active firm in the field has been SB Partners, a real estate offshoot of the Smith Barney Harris Upham stock brokerage firm in New York.

Offerings from all of these funds undergo a lengthy and complex registration process with the federal Securities and Exchange Commission (SEC), and with state securities authorities. Their prospectuses may take a year or more in drafting and review, and can cost $400,000 to prepare. Excerpts from one recent public offering statement are reproduced opposite. Note the analysis of the planned usage of the revenues collected through syndication: up to 12.75 percent will be eaten up by front-end costs and commissions, leaving 87.25 percent to 88.75 percent for actual real estate.

This particular syndication involved a *blind pool* arrangement. Investors contributed their capital to allow the general partners to select properties for acquisition. As a unit purchaser in the fund you had no idea, other than a few general statements of acquisition priorities, of the specific properties you would one day partially own. Along with the prospectus came a series of glossy color photos of properties managed by other syndicates controlled by the general partners, but nothing more specific than that.

ESTIMATED USE OF PROCEEDS OF OFFERING (1)	Minimum Offering		Maximum Offering	
Gross Proceeds	$1,250,000	100.00%	$15,000,000	100.00%
Less Public Offering Expenses:				
Sales Concessions	109,375	8.75%	1,312,500	8.75%
Organizational Expenses (2)	50,000	4.00%	375,000	2.50%
Amount Available for Investment, Net of Expenses	$1,090,625	87.25%	$13,312,500	88.75%
Property Acquisition Expenses (3)	$ 25,000	2.00%	$ 300,000	2.00%
Cash Payments (4)	1,003,125	80.25%	12,262,500	81.75%
Acquisition Fees (5)	*	*	*	*
Working Capital/Reserves	62,500	5.00%	750,000	5.00%
Proceeds Expended	1,090,625	87.25%	13,312,500	88.75%
Public Offering Expenses	159,375	12.75%	1,687,500	11.25%
Total Application of Proceeds	$1,250,000	100.00%	$15,000,000	100.00%

*In connection with the acquisition of real property investments for the Partnership, First Capital Real Estate Corporation, an affiliate of the General Partners, will receive from the sellers of property to the Partnership or from the Partnership itself, real estate brokerage commissions of up to 13% of the gross proceeds of the Offering ($162,500 if the minimum number of Units is sold and $1,950,000 if the maximum is sold) as compensation for finding suitable properties and for analyzing, structuring and negotiating the purchase of such properties. Assuming 75% leverage, such commissions will be approximately equal to 4% of the cost of Partnership properties. These commissions, to the extent paid by the seller, are generally taken into account by sellers in determining the selling prices of properties to the Partnership, so that, in effect, the Partnership, as purchaser, bears such commissions in the purchase price of the properties. The Partnership also expects to pay commissions in connection with the sale of properties, which will reduce the *Net Proceeds* to the Partnership of any such sales. See "Management Compensation."

(1) These figures represent the Partnership's current estimates. The Partnership has not presently acquired, entered into agreements to acquire, or reached agreements in principle to acquire any specific real property investments.
(2) Includes legal, accounting, printing and other direct and indirect expenses of the offering and distribution of Units. Any expenses of the Offering (in addition to sales concessions) which in the aggregate exceed the lesser of 4.0% of the gross proceeds or $375,000 will be assumed by the General Partners and affiliates, without any charge against Partnership assets.
(3) Including fees for legal, accounting, appraising and other real estate acquisition services.
(4) Including down payments (equity), prepaid items, closing costs and other cash items payable at closing. The purchase price of properties may include Acquisition Fees and the portion of the purchase price representing cash down payments (equity) therefore will include a proportionate share of such fees.
(5) Acquisition Fees are defined as the total of all fees and commissions paid by any party to any party including General Partners or affiliates in connection with the purchase of property by the Partnership, whether designated as real estate brokerage commissions, acquisition fees, finder's fees, selection fees, or any fees of similar nature, however designated.

Blind pools give syndicates carte blanche in what they do with your money. The prospectus doesn't even claim to project equity minimums for specific properties to be purchased. It notes that the fund overall will not incur more than $5 worth of debt for every $1 worth of equity. A building it purchases may have only a 10 percent/90 percent equity-to-loan ratio, or as low as a 5 percent equity position. Another property may have a 30 percent equity. Highly leveraged blind pools can of course entail higher risks for the partnership and individual investors. They can also produce spectacular profits by giving the aggressive real estate entrepreneurs who control the funds the flexibility they need to make money for the limited partners and themselves.

Many syndicates are very *specific* in their prospectuses about the properties they have options on or contracts to buy. The prospectuses will detail the location and nature of the real estate, the identity of the tenants, the length and terms of their leases, the existing financing on the properties, balloon-payment due dates, if any, and the like. On pages 235 and 236 are extracts from a supplement to the Balcor Income Properties Ltd.–II (1978), detailing the operating income picture of one of the multiple properties the syndicate contracted to buy. This happens to be one of *three* Texas shopping centers in the portfolio; the same supplement also provided details on a shopping center in North Carolina. As a potential investor in such a syndicate, you have advance knowledge—if you can make use of the information—of the economic characteristics of the property you'll own with hundreds of other investors. You also have the assurances of the promoters, their accountants, and the SEC that the information presented is accurate.

Public offerings can be structured in an almost limitless number of ways to achieve varying investment or yield goals. One recent syndication, known as Krupp Investors I, sought $9.75 million from investors in six states, with the explicit intent of buying Sunbelt apartment properties on all-cash terms. According to the promoters, this unique no-leverage approach was designed to obtain highly favorable acquisition prices in the absence of mortgages. The syndicate said it planned to re-

CALLAGHAN PLAZA SHOPPING CENTER

The contract to acquire the shopping center is subject to various terms and conditions, including receipt of satisfactory closing documentation. There can be no assurance that all of the terms and conditions of the contract will be satisfied and therefore it is possible that the property will not be acquired.

STATEMENT OF OPERATING INCOME

(Defined as Gross Revenues, Less Direct Operating Expenses Exclusive of Mortgage and Other Interest Expense, Depreciation, Amortization, Management Fees, Administrative and Other General Expenses)

	UNAUDITED Five Months Ended May 31,		Years Ended December 31,			UNAUDITED Six Months Ended December 31,
	1978	1977	1977	1976	1975	1974
Revenues:						
Rental income	$106,030	$87,164	$216,724	$179,289	$141,267	$63,560
Real estate tax and utility contributions—Note B	10,210	10,813	11,921	11,134	1,221	318
Maintenance contributions	1,476	1,487	3,481	2,666	2,666	953
Total	117,716	99,464	232,126	193,089	145,154	64,831
Expenses:						
Repairs, maintenance, and utilities	6,366	7,494	16,014	12,000	8,154	761
Real estate taxes	18,000	15,860	38,063	33,739	28,578	8,694
Insurance	1,968	1,968	4,723	4,922	4,895	2,342
Total	26,334	25,322	58,800	50,661	41,627	11,797
Operating income, exclusive of mortgage and other interest expense, depreciation, amortization, management fees, administrative and other general expenses	$ 91,382	$74,142	$173,326	$142,428	$103,527	$53,034

NOTES:

(A) The initial phases of construction of the shopping center were completed during the years 1974 and 1975, with additional spaces finished in 1976 and 1977. The center comprises approximately 107,062 square feet of leasable space.

(B) The center acquired a large tenant in 1976 who under the lease terms is required to pay substantial real estate tax contributions. The tax and utility contributions are usually received in the first half of the year and recognized as income when received.

(C) Certain tenants are required to pay additional rent when gross sales reach a fixed amount. No rents under this agreement have been required in these periods.

(D) Operating income is stated before certain expenses as indicated to exclude expenses incurred by the present owner which may not be comparable to the operation of the property by Balcor Income Properties Ltd.—II.

The following Estimated Pro Forma Statement of Net Operating Income (Loss) represents the amount of income (loss) which would be received by the Partnership during its first twelve months of ownership of the property, based upon the assumptions set forth in the Notes below.

CALLAGHAN PLAZA SHOPPING CENTER
SAN ANTONIO, TEXAS

ESTIMATED PRO FORMA STATEMENT OF
NET OPERATING INCOME (LOSS) (NOTE 7)
(Unaudited)

Historical Operating Income, exclusive of mortgage and other interest expense, depreciation, amortization, management fees, administrative and other general expenses (Note 1)		$173,000
Pro Forma Adjustments:		
Less:		
Interest expense on mortgage (Note 2)	$160,000	
Depreciation of property (Note 3)	113,000	
Management fee (Note 4)	12,000	285,000
Add: Seller's guarantee (Note 5)		34,000
Pro Forma Operating Loss		$(78,000)

ESTIMATED PRO FORMA STATEMENT OF
FUNDS AVAILABLE (REQUIRED) (NOTE 7)
(Unaudited)

Pro Forma Operating Loss, as above	$(78,000)
Add:	
Depreciation of property (Note 3)	113,000
	35,000
Deduct (Note 6):	
Principal payments (not including cash down payments totaling $1,012,733)	17,000
Pro Forma Funds Available	$ 18,000

NOTES:

(1) The historical operating income is based upon the net operating income of the property for the year ended December 31, 1977, as contained in the statement of operating income, submitted herewith.

(2) Interest is based upon a rate of 9% on a mortgage note of approximately $1,679,000 and 9¾% on a mortgage note of approximately $94,000.

(3) Depreciation is calculated (based upon the total purchase price including Purchase Price Adjustments) using the straight-line method and an estimated useful life of 22 years.

(4) The center will be managed by Balcor Property Management, Inc., an affiliate of the General Partner of the Partnership, for an initial annual management fee of 5% of gross rental income. For purposes of this computation 5% of the actual gross rental income for the year ended December 31, 1977 was used.

(5) Represents the Seller's guarantee that the Partnership will receive $2,795 of monthly cash payments with respect to the vacant space in the Center. To the extent that additional space is leased, the rentals from such leases will reduce the Seller's guarantee obligation.

(6) The cash down payments totaling $1,012,733 will be paid from proceeds of the offering. $17,000 of principal for the year will be paid from operations.

(7) These statements do not purport to forecast actual operating results for any period in the future and thus, there can be no assurance that the foregoing assumptions are valid for future years, or that such results will be attained. These statements should be read in conjunction with the statement of operating income, as defined, submitted herewith.

habilitate 100-unit and larger properties, mortgage them and distribute the tax-free proceeds immediately to limited partners.

Another interesting recent example, known as Century Property Fund XII, offered investors both unsecured promissory notes (with 9 percent interest rates) *and* limited-partnership units. As a buyer (minimum purchase $5,000), you could hedge your bets by trying a little of both: taxable interest income from the notes you hold (say, $3,000 worth) and the possibility of sharp capital growth via your limited-partnership units, should the properties the fund buys do well in terms of income and jump in market value.

Private Offerings. Many syndicate promoters prefer to avoid the hassles of SEC registration and the costs of national marketing campaigns. Through a variety of exemptions permissible under the Securities Act of 1933, they are able to structure small private offerings. Some of these exempt limited partnerships are simply local groups of ten to fifteen people who join together to acquire and rehabilitate rental properties. A general partner with special expertise in real estate handles the business of the mini-syndicate. The limited partners merely contribute the bulk of the capital.

A growing number of private offerings—estimated to be worth as much as $1 billion in 1978–79—involve federally subsidized low-income housing. Restricted to no more than thirty-five investors and normally involving relatively large cash contributions spread over several years, these syndications are aimed *exclusively* at high-income professionals—in the 50 percent tax bracket or higher, with net worths in six figures—who need substantial tax write-offs for extended periods. They are never advertised and thus are limited intentionally to sophisticated investors who receive word of them informally through accountants, attorneys, realty brokers or the syndicate promoters themselves.

The offerings typically are designed to raise funds for construction or substantial rehabilitation of Section 8* projects,

---

* Section 8 is the federal government's principal low-income housing construction program. See Chapter 9 for a concise description.

and cover only one project per limited partnership. They are tax-shelter vehicles, not income producers, and rely on the combined incentives Congress retained to promote low-income housing in the 1976 Tax Reform Act. New and rehabilitated subsidized rental housing qualifies for accelerated depreciation (200 percent declining balance or sum-of-the-years'-digits), and investors can deduct more than the amount of capital they have at risk in the project. That means that a limited partner in a subsidized housing syndicate may be able to deduct twice or three times what he put into the fund during the early years, when depreciation and other "loss" items are concentrated.

The sheer size of the potential loss deductions has created a highly specialized subindustry in the housing field: syndicators who for a price—which may be 20 percent or more of the estimated mortgage of the project to be built—sell the rights to share in projected losses. Low-income syndications are extremely complex investments, and are *not* for the average investor. They require not only high income but *long-term* high income, in the $100,000-and-up range. Even sophisticated investors need extensive professional advice before considering any of these syndications. And professional advice in this case means not just one adviser, but preferably an accountant *and* a lawyer.

INVESTMENT DO'S AND DON'TS OF
REAL ESTATE SYNDICATES

Do:

• Examine the identities, length of experience and *quality of performance* by the general partners/syndicators in any partnership you're offered. Earlier syndication offerings by the promoters may be only sketchily spelled out in the prospectus; don't depend on this data alone. Ask your broker or investment adviser to come up with information on precisely how well the prior syndicates have performed relative to their initial projections. Are the properties yielding more income for partnership unit holders than anyone expected, or much less? Have there been any lawsuits against the general partner by disgruntled unit holders? Any delinquencies on mortgages?

• Examine the structuring of risk and *incentives for high performance* in the partnership agreement. What stake does the general partner have in the deal once he's gotten his initial syndication proceeds? Is his compensation tailored to give him progressively better returns as the partnership's investments perform better and better? Is the general partner's compensation based on a percentage of the limited partners' *equity*—i.e., their real asset worth, which moves up and down with market performance—rather than on a percentage of gross invested dollars, which remain the same?

• Study the prospectus of any offering, keeping an eye out for the many (and often creative) ways the promoters have arranged bonuses, premiums and commissions for themselves, both up front and throughout the life of the partnership. Some syndications are incredible bonanzas for the people who put them together; others yield fruit for everyone.

• Take a hard look at the schedule of contributions and your ability to keep up with them. A one-time purchase of a unit in a large public offering may be readily within your resources, but what about a schedule requiring a contribution of $15,000 or $20,000 every year for five years?

• Look for the *guarantees* to you by the promoter/general partner. Who pays in the case of cost overruns? (He should.) What about performance bonds, guarantees against negative cash flows, guaranteed buy-backs of your units if specified events (such as the closing of the project mortgage) don't occur?

• Make an effort to learn something definitive about the quality of the properties underlying the fund. If the shopping center or office building or housing is so far away that you really can't make or obtain an independent appraisal, perhaps you should pass up this particular partnership and wait for one with property closer to home.

Don't:
• Consider going into a limited partnership unless you're clear on your investment goals. If income is what you really need, tell your broker or adviser to screen out offerings that don't provide you with income. If tax shelter is what you're after,

look for syndications in the low-income housing field. If a safe, *guaranteed* cash flow is what you require, you should probably look elsewhere. Limited partnerships are by their nature somewhat speculative and come with no promises of regular checks in the mail every month.

• Take the cash-flow or tax-loss tables in a prospectus as gospel. They are rough approximations at best, and often are based on assumptions that prudent investors wouldn't use. This is especially true of private offerings, where there is a good chance that the financial projections haven't been subjected to any critical review or analysis—as is mandatory in SEC-registered offerings.

• Rush headlong into deals that offer *only* tax shelter. At some point down the road, your real estate ought to be able to stand on its own (perhaps supplemented with some government housing subsidies, in the case of Section 8 projects). The development should at some point turn a net operating profit for its owners.

• Fail to assess the possible *contingent liabilities* you could incur through your investment in a syndication. You may think your liability extends only to the amount of money you sunk into the deal. Legally, that's true to a point. But limited partners can and do find themselves in situations (particularly where excess accelerated depreciation has been taken and a property faces foreclosure) in which they are forced to shell out more cash to save themselves from recapture of their high previous deductions at their ordinary tax rates—a true tax disaster.

REAL ESTATE INVESTMENT TRUSTS

An alternative to limited partnerships is the *real estate investment trust* (REIT). Once the go-go darlings of Wall Street and the subject of a book entitled *America's Newest Billionaires,* REITs have had a rocky decade. From their peak of $2 billion worth of new offerings in 1971, they hit bottom in the midst of 1975's real estate shake-out, with barely $400,000 in new issues. They have since recovered somewhat, but their total assets are only in the $14 billion range, compared with close to $22 billion in 1974.

Real estate investment trusts are financial conduits designed, with the help of tax incentives, to tap money from the capital markets and channel it into income-producing real estate. Like corporations, they issue stocks, bonds and notes. About sixty REIT stocks are traded on the New York Stock Exchange, and a hundred are traded over the counter.

REITs enjoy favorable tax treatment because they pass income through directly to shareholders, avoiding the double taxation problems of most corporate dividends. In order to qualify for this treatment, however, a realty trust must pay out at least 90 percent of all net taxable income to shareholders, keep no less than 75 percent of its assets in real estate, and obtain in excess of 75 percent of its income from real estate investments.

REITs specialize in a wide variety of activities, from owning and running a stadium to making wraparound mortgage loans, but most fall into one of four categories: equity trusts, which buy and operate commercial office buildings, shopping malls and other properties; construction and development (C&D) trusts, which specialize in short-term development loans; mortgage trusts, which make long-term loans on various types of income real estate; and hybrid trusts, which own properties as well as make loans secured by other real estate. The disasters of the mid-1970s for REITs hit the C&D and mortgage trusts the hardest. They had overextended their resources and often made high-risk, high-ratio loans to developers whose projects were fundamentally unsound; these projects were squeezed into default and foreclosure in the tight real estate market that prevailed for two and a half years. Many of the loans the C&D and mortgage trusts made were uncollectable; their stock plummeted, and numerous near-bankruptcies occurred. Equity trusts generally fared better, and still tend to be among the most advantageous REIT stock purchases in the market.

Why Buy REITs? Some trusts have performed well since 1976, yielding 8 to 9 percent dividends, and are underpriced.

A few offer the promise of future significant capital gains, as the values of their well-managed commercial properties rise rapidly and are coveted by other large investors, such as the big public realty syndicates and the invading hordes of foreign investors. Equity-trust payouts tend to be mixtures of depreciation-sheltered income and capital gains. Mortgage trusts' dividends, on the other hand, are derived from the interest charged commercial borrowers, and must be counted as ordinary income.

Any extended discussion of the 190-plus REITs in existence is far beyond the scope of this chapter. Your stockbroker should be able to supply you with the research information you'll need to assess specific trusts. The National Association of REITs, based in Washington, D.C.,* is also a surprisingly good source of basic data about individual trusts and the field generally.

REITs can be excellent investments, but in light of their tumultuous recent past, most should be classified as speculative.

GINNIE MAEs

Interesting (and assuredly nonspeculative) newcomers on the scene are the $1,000 shares you can buy in federally guaranteed mortgage pools. The mortgages are all backed by the Federal Housing Administration (FHA) or the Veterans Administration (VA), and are further guaranteed by the Government National Mortgage Association (Ginnie Mae or GNMA), a corporate entity within the Department of Housing and Urban Development.

Since 1968, Ginnie Mae has been guaranteeing bonds issued by holders of FHA and VA mortgages. The resultant bonds, commonly known as Ginnie Maes, have sold in minimum $25,000 denominations and have done fabulously well in the market. In fact, GNMA has guaranteed over $50 *billion* of these within a span of just ten years. The bonds, though *double-backed* by the federal government, have produced higher yields in the market than many competing investments of similar size

* NAREIT, 1101 17th St., N.W., Washington, D.C. 20036.

and maturity. They have been bought eagerly and sometimes in huge chunks of up to $100 million at a time by pension funds, credit unions, insurance companies and other institutions. Some individual investors have also purchased them, but of course had to come up with $25,000—an impossibly high entry fee for most people.

In early 1978, several Wall Street firms—Bache Halsey Stuart, Merrill Lynch Pierce Fenner and Smith, and Dean Witter Reynolds—began marketing certificates, secured by GNMA-guaranteed pools, in $1,000 denominations. In other words, the $25,000 trusts were broken down into more readily salable $1,000 units and sold. The yields were in the 8.5 to 9 percent range initially, well in excess of many competitive safe investments. The offerings drew an enthusiastic response and have stimulated a steady stream of follow-up issues. They're worth talking to your broker about, if mortgage-related, gilt-edged securities are your cup of tea.

9

Special Investment Opportunities in Urban Revitalization

One of the most exciting trends in real estate today is the nationwide move to revitalize America's cities. Almost no urban area—however economically depressed, however battered by the riots of 1966–68—has gone unaffected by this powerful phenomenon. Bedford-Stuyvesant in New York; the Soulard District of St. Louis; Washington, D.C.'s worst residential slums; inner-city neighborhoods of Cincinnati, Chicago, Philadelphia, Portland, Seattle, Wilmington, Baltimore, New Orleans, Atlanta —all are experiencing heady reinvestment by private and government capital, and widespread rehabilitation of residential and commercial structures.

Sections of cities that were stagnant for decades are coming back, often with adaptive reuse of their old buildings. In New York City, private investors (with the help of local tax abatement) have converted a great many loft buildings once used for commercial purposes into housing units. Federal, state and local financial aid has made it possible for dozens of Boston's historic but empty downtown buildings to be turned into condominiums, shops, offices and markets; these conversions are producing not only important aesthetic and economic changes for the city at large but big profits for the investors behind the projects.

The new economics of urban real estate investment makes sense not only for large investors but for small ones as well— if they know what to look for and are creative. And revitalization is a wide-open field in dozens of cities with populations of 50,000 to 150,000. Consider these facts:

• Renovation of "born-again" buildings—primarily in cities and in the form of smaller one- to four-unit dwellings—is already an $11-billion-per-year business. Many of the investors and owners involved are relatively small-scale local partnerships, joint ventures, and husband-and-wife teams. Renovation not only produces the customary advantages of rental-housing investment but can offer unique tax advantages when it involves structures in one of the rapidly growing number of historic districts.

• Local, federal and state governments are really pushing investment in the central city, and are making it quite inviting. The Carter administration in particular has reoriented dozens of financing programs to aid private urban reinvestment. These include low-interest rehabilitation loans (Section 312); the $4 billion community development block grants program, large chunks of which are going for housing renovation and historic district revival; a new $1.2 billion program known as Urban Development Action Grants; long-term rehabilitation subsidies for buildings with units for moderate- and lower-income families (Section 8); new lending guidelines for federally chartered savings and loan institutions designed to increase central-city rehabilitation and housing investment; large new funding for the Economic Development Administration and Small Business Administration programs to aid entrepreneurs and developers in downtown neighborhoods; and more.

• Speculative investments in inner-city areas that are turning can offer incredible returns if investors buy before the trend sets in. In two to three years, speculators on Washington, D.C.'s Capitol Hill have quadrupled their small initial investments in rehabilitated row houses. Average selling prices shot up from

$10,000 to $12,000 on some streets in 1974–75 to over $100,000 for the area as a whole by late 1978. Reports of large gains also have come from reviving neighborhoods in San Francisco, Cincinnati, Baltimore, Savannah, Louisville, Galveston, and Philadelphia.

In short, the back-to-the-cities movement can mean dollars for you—if you know the fundamentals of the programs and the tax breaks available, and are aware of a city's economic trends. This chapter provides an overview of some of the most important of these opportunities.

HISTORIC PRESERVATION/ADAPTIVE USE

In 1976, when Paul and Amy Piersma paid $25,000 for their three-story, 65-year-old brick row apartment structure on South Ninth Street, it was a vacant shell not unlike many structures in inner-city St. Louis. What made it crucially different from other rundown dwellings was its location within the Soulard Neighborhood Historic District. This qualified it for special tax incentives contained in Section 2124 of the Tax Reform Act of 1976, and also made purchase of the building an excellent tax-sheltered investment for these two high-income professionals.

As outlined in a case study in *Mortgage Banker* magazine, the Piersmas' rehabilitation of the brick apartment building has led to the creation of five *two-story* rental units (with an average 1,600 square feet of dwelling space apiece) on the upper two floors, and five rental efficiency units on the first floor. The bottom-floor units can easily be converted into commercial offices or shops, as the neighborhood bounces back to economic life.

Total expenses for rehabilitating the building over a six-month period were $152,000; under the 1976 law, $30,400 of this *per year* for five consecutive years is deductible from the Piersmas' other income. The Piersmas have borrowed all but $50,000 of the total acquisition cost, principally from a subsidiary of Mercantile Bancorporation of St. Louis, which holds a $127,000 first mortgage on the property. Meanwhile, all ten imaginatively

restored units of the building have been full, producing excellent rental income, since completion of the rehabilitation.

The Piersmas' form of urban investment—which they confirm was made feasible solely by the 1976 tax incentives—is
becoming one of the hottest segments of real estate. Hundreds
of small-scale investors are trying their hand at it. An estimated
700,000 structures—houses, office buildings, garages, factories,
warehouses, and others—either have been individually designated national, state or local historic properties, or are located
within locally or nationally registered historic districts across
the United States. This is a staggering number of buildings,
and the number of designations is growing rapidly. Chances are
somewhere inside or near your community there is an historic
district with a landmark building available for sale and reuse.
The U.S. Supreme Court's 1978 decision in the New York
Grand Central Terminal case gave fresh impetus to landmark
and historic commissions around the country to designate many
more privately owned structures and areas as worthy of public
assistance for their preservation.

THE LAW

Let's take a look at the mechanics of the 1976 law as they apply
to investors who want to get involved in urban real estate
rehabilitation and reuse. Since this discussion will be tax-
oriented, you may want to refer back to Chapter 2, where such
terms as accelerated depreciation, basis, allowable deductions
and capital expenditures are defined.

Incentives. The Tax Reform Act's Section 2124 was inserted
by Congress to stimulate rehabilitation and discourage destruc-
tion of historic buildings and to encourage donation of "partial
interests" in architecturally significant properties (such as their
façades) in exchange for tax deductions. The law permits a five-
year amortization for federal tax purposes of all costs of a
"certified rehabilitation" of a "certified historic structure." In
cases where an investor owns a building that qualifies as a "sub-

stantially rehabilitated historic property,"* he may depreciate the basis (or cost) of the building at an accelerated rate (200 percent declining balance, for example). In effect, the law allows historic property rehabilitations to be treated as favorably for tax-shelter purposes as subsidized low-income housing.

Note that the property has to be "held for production of income"—rental residential or commercial—in order to qualify for federal tax deductions on any expenditures other than mortgage interest and taxes. In other words, if you buy a landmark residential property, rehabilitate it and live in it, you can't take advantage of the rapid write-offs or the accelerated depreciation. If you buy a landmark property, live in one of its three constituent units, and rent out the other two, you can claim deductions on two-thirds of the expenditures attributable to the rehabilitation.

Eligibility. A "certified historic structure" must qualify under one of the following three categories: it must be (1) listed individually in the National Register of Historic Places; or (2) located within and certified by the Secretary of the Interior as being of historic significance to a district listed in the National Register of Historic Places; or (3) located within a historic district designated under a state or local statute that has been certified by the Secretary of the Interior, and be certified as having historical significance to that district. Category 3, the one used by the Piersmas, may well provide the most fertile ground for local investors, since prices often are low in districts that haven't yet turned around. Buildings already listed on the National Register, on the other hand, may be too costly at the outset for profitable long-term rental use. Your local landmarks commission or state historic preservation office will have lists of properties in the three categories. You might also check with

---

* Under the law, a "substantially rehabilitated" structure is defined as any certified historic structure for which the cost of certified rehabilitation during a two-year period exceeds $5,000 or the adjusted tax basis (or net cost to the owner) of the property—a definition that includes just about any such building on the market today.

either of these to find out which local areas or structures may be on the verge of becoming historic districts or properties. Some owners of buildings about to be designated may not *want* the honor or the restrictions on use that go with it. Buildings with such owners are prime candidates for sale to more imaginative, tax-conscious investors.

How to Qualify. If your property or prospective investment is not individually listed on the National Register, you'll need to obtain an historic preservation certificate application from your state historic preservation office. Part 1 of the application concerns certification of historic structures; it asks for such items as the address of the structure, the name of the historic district, a short description of the alterations you plan to make, and a statement of the historic significance of the structure. If you don't get a reply from the state office within forty-five days of submitting the application, the federal Heritage Conservation and Recreation Service (HCRS) of the Interior Department will review the application directly, using the Secretary of the Interior's standards for evaluation of structures within historic districts. Within thirty days, the HCRS must respond to your application with either a certificate of significance or a notice that the structure "is not of historic significance to the district" —which means tough luck if you're serious about the accelerated depreciation or rapid write-off of rehabilitation work. All this can be carried out *before* you agree to buy the structure; you can sign a contract contingent upon a successful application for certification.

Certifying Rehabilitation Work. Part 2 of the historic preservation certificate application concerns the rehabilitation work and can be completed and submitted any time during the alteration. It asks for descriptions of what you're doing to the building and of how you've attempted to retain significant architectural features, and for illustrations or photographs of the work in progress. After the rehabilitation is completed, a representative of the HCRS will come by upon request to determine that the work meets the criteria for a certified rehabilitation. Later, assuming the project is acceptable, a certificate will be issued for the property.

If you own the building, haven't yet been certified, but want to begin deducting expenses on the five-year accelerated schedple, IRS will let you attach a note with your federal tax return, pointing out your pending application for certification.

HOW THE INCENTIVES WORK: TWO CASE STUDIES

For illustration on how the Tax Reform Act incentives can work for you, here are two examples suggested in modified form by the Interior Department and the National Trust for Historic Preservation.

Case 1: Mr. Danford and His Historic Urban Rental House. Mr. Danford is an unmarried accountant who earns $26,000 a year and who decides to buy a rundown house that happens to be on the National Register for use as a rental property. The combined cost of the land and house are $30,000. He spends another $35,000 to rehabilitate the exterior of the house and converts the interior to three rental apartment units, retaining architectural details such as trim in accordance with the Secretary of the Interior's standards for rehabilitation. Mr. Danford fills out Parts 1 and 2 of the HCRS Tax Reform Act application, sends them to his state historic preservation office, and is accepted in time to include the certification with his tax return for the first year.

Mr. Danford's lot is assessed at $10,000; thus for tax purposes the cost of the structure itself is $20,000. The house is estimated to have a 25-year economic life. Mr. Danford can depreciate the $20,000 structural value, plus the entire $35,000 cost of the rehabilitation. He chooses the double declining balance method and in year one is able to deduct $4,400 in depreciation (that is, the $55,000 tax basis $\times$ 1/25 $\times$ 200 percent = $4,400).

Mr. Danford's tax bracket is 40 percent, and thus his actual tax savings ($4,400 × .40) amount to $1,760. Had the property not qualified for special historic preservation tax treatment, the highest depreciation method Mr. Danford could have used would have been the 125 percent declining balance allowed for used rental properties. This would have produced a $2,750 deduction ($55,000 × 1/25 × 125 percent) and a tax savings of only $1,100.

Case 2: Mrs. Conway's Historic Skating Rink. Here is an example of how an investor with larger resources can use the rapid write-off of the Tax Reform Act and make creative use of an old building that would otherwise go to waste and be torn down. Mrs. Conway is a real estate broker/developer whose joint annual income with her husband averages $150,000. She pays $130,000 for a decrepit old warehouse in a historic district in her area. She hires an architect to convert the building into a skating rink, in full conformity with the Interior Department's standards for rehabilitation. The total cost of restoration and conversion is calculated at $250,000. Mrs. Conway's architect submits Part 1 and 2 of the certificate application, and they are approved. Taking immediate advantage of the five-year write-off, Mrs. Conway can deduct one-fifth of her $250,000 rehabilitation cost, or $50,000. Since the tax bracket of her joint return is 66 percent, she is actually able to save $33,000 out of pocket the first year.

The land component value of the original building is assessed at $30,000 (making the adjusted basis of the warehouse itself $100,000). Its economic life is projected at 25 years. Mrs. Conway chooses to depreciate the structure on a straight-line basis, producing $4,000 a year in deductions ($100,000 × 1/25) and $2,640 in tax savings for a taxpayer in the 66 percent bracket ($4,000 × .66).

Mrs. Conway's combined deductions equal $35,640 a year ($33,000 in rapid amortization of rehabilitation expenses, $2,640 in depreciation on the structure). If four years later Mrs. Conway sold the skating rink for $500,000, she would end up

with an *after-tax profit* of $163,000 ($336,000 minus an estimated $172,800 in capital gains taxes plus recapture of acceler-
ated depreciation).

For more detailed information on opportunities through central city historic preservation, contact your local landmarks
commission or real estate brokers who specialize in this type of
investment property. The Heritage Conservation and Recreation
Service (Department of the Interior, Washington, D.C. 20240)
and the Office of Real Estate and Legal Services, National Trust
for Historic Preservation (740 Jackson Place, Washington, D.C.
20006), are also good sources for additional information.

FEDERAL URBAN PROPERTY REHABILITATION AND FINANCING AIDS

The panoply of types of federally funded aid for urban property
conservation and redevelopment is now so extensive that many
investors have no idea of all the opportunities open to them.
Here is a rundown of the most important.

Section 8 Leased Housing. This is the federal government's
largest subsidy program and one that holds tremendous possibilities for rental-property owners or purchasers in central-city
areas. Under the Section 8 program, the government pays private landlords the difference between 15 to 25 percent of the
adjusted family incomes of eligible tenants and a government-set
fair market rental figure for the type of dwelling unit the tenants
are occupying. Section 8 can be used to ensure 100 percent
occupancy of a building after its rehabilitation, and in some
cities the program has turned buildings on the verge of aban-
donment into net income producers for their owners. A subsidized tenant may pay you as landlord only $120 a month for
a unit that formerly drew $180 a month on the open market.
But HUD, under its often generous fair market rents, may contract to pay you an additional $150 a month for the unit, bring-
ing the new total well beyond the former rent level. Fair market
rents vary widely, however, and in some cities may be lower

than you require. You've got to check the figures on local properties to determine whether it makes sense for your specific situation and area.*

Urban Development Action Grants (UDAG). The Carter administration's major federal initiative for urban redevelopment, the $400-million-per-year Action Grant program, is oriented almost *exclusively* toward attracting private investors into central-city areas. As a result, it can offer the most flexible, low-cost financing for urban real estate activities available anywhere. Administered by HUD through its area offices, the program provides grants, low-interest loans, construction loans, rehabilitation grants and loans, and funds for clearance and planning for projects aimed at creating new employment and strengthening the local economic base. HUD judges applications partially on their "leveraging" effects—the amount of private money attracted per federal grant dollar—so investors should be prepared to demonstrate ratios of 4:1 or better in most cases. HUD also gives preference to redevelopments that offer direct benefits of employment or increased services to local lower- and moderate-income individuals and/or minorities. Examples of real estate projects funded thus far include a $270,000 grant in downtown Trenton, New Jersey, to rehabilitate five rundown historic structures and convert them into office and residential space; $9 million to develop ninety acres of Portland, Oregon, into an in-town residential community of middle-income housing; $2.3 million to package land for a private housing development in El Paso, Texas; $4 million to provide a construction loan to rehabilitate a privately owned hotel in downtown Louisville, Kentucky.†

---

* For information on fair market rent levels and other aspects of Section 8, contact your local Department of Housing and Urban Development (HUD) area office; your city's or county's housing department; or HUD, Office of Housing, Washington, D.C. 20410.

† More information on the highly competitive Action Grant program can be obtained from HUD, Office of Action Grants, Washington, D.C. 20410.

Community Development (CD) Block Grants. Under this $4-billion-plus-per-year program, several thousand cities and small communities receive outright grants from the Department of Housing and Urban Development. The cities may use the money for the following activities, among others:
- Financial assistance, via loans or grants, to owners of commercial or residential property, for rehabilitation.
- Assistance for planning real estate redevelopment or relocating displaced persons.
- Clearance and demolition.
- Historic preservation.

Generally, these activities should be undertaken with an eye to benefiting lower- and moderate-income residents of the locality. Many cities, for example, use their CD grants to make low-interest loans on outright grants for housing rehabilitation in selected neighborhood conservation areas. Such loans may not be available *directly* to investors in those areas, but they can facilitate the sale of properties in the area to families who can qualify for some kind of financial assistance.

Investors or property owners with proposals for redevelopment should contact their local housing or community development department. Use of the federal CD funds, within broadly worded congressional guidelines, are *entirely* up to the local city council. Persuade your local government to solve some of its problems by helping you to profit on some of your existing or prospective properties.*

Section 312 Rehabilitation Loans. Administered by HUD, this program offers 3 percent 30-year loans of up to $50,000 for investor-owned nonresidential rehabilitations, and up to $27,000 for single-family residential rehabilitations. The property must be located within a locally designated renewal area, and the loan application should be made through your local housing or urban redevelopment agency. Section 312 loans can be excellent vehicles for financing central-city housing or commercial structures for subsequent rental.

* Additional information on the CD block grant program is available from HUD, Office of Community Planning and Development, Washington, D.C. 20410.

EDA and SBA Programs. Both the U.S. Department of Commerce's Economic Development Administration and the Small Business Administration have expanded their financial assistance to private real estate enterprises in central cities in the past year. The agencies offer a wide variety of loan guarantees, second mortgages, direct grants, and low-interest loans to redevelopment projects that increase local employment opportunities. For information on programs active in your area, contact your local economic development agency, your state department of community affairs, or the U.S. Department of Commerce, Washington, D.C. 20230.

Creative Real Estate Strategies

What you do with your real estate depends on your resources and objectives as an investor—and on the breadth of your imagination. For some people, one rental property, one piece of land, or one purchase of interests in a real estate limited partnership is enough. But many small-scale investors have hidden resources, wellsprings they've never tapped. They buy a property and then sit on it passively rather than using it actively—not only to expand their holdings but also to cut their taxes. This chapter is a quick overview of the ideas and techniques open to such investors.

PYRAMIDS

The term "pyramid" in the investment context refers to a progression of equity-expanding property acquisitions that build and rest upon one another sequentially. Pyramiding is one of the oldest and fastest routes to real wealth in real estate. The key to the technique is its maximum use of *what you've already got* to move you into much, much more.

Conceptually, you might picture pyramiding as something like this:

256

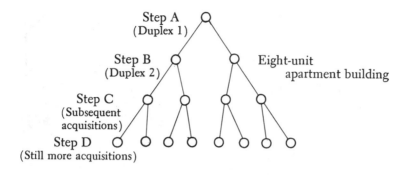

Put yourself in the position of a purchaser of a rental duplex. A couple of years ago you paid $50,000 for it, putting a $40,000 mortgage on it (which is now down to $38,000). Thanks to the rapid appreciation occurring in your area, the property would sell for $75,000 today. You can sell it at a $25,000 profit, which is subject to capital gains taxation, or you can use the inflated equity in the property to begin building a real estate pyramid.

You decide to pyramid, and that puts you at Step A in the diagram. How do you make the $37,000 you've got in the duplex ($75,000 minus the $38,000 loan) work for you actively? There are several alternatives, but the thread that runs through all of them is the requirement that you view your property as a bank account: you can withdraw some or most of that $37,000, or you can leave it in and use it as security for new loans or new mortgages.

Step B involves using your stored-up equity to acquire two more properties. A good way to begin the process would be to *refinance* your duplex. A lender might be willing to provide a 90 percent loan on the property at its new $75,000 appraised value. That would enable you to take upwards of $28,500 completely tax-free from the property:

> $75,000 New loan
> 38,000 Pay-off of original first trust
> ———
> $37,000
>
> −7,500 Your 10 percent equity to qualify
>   for your new 90 percent loan

$29,500

1,000 Less costs of refinancing*
———
$28,500 Net cash

Now you're ready for new acquisitions, taking you from A to B. Perhaps the owner of a duplex in poor physical condition down the street would be willing to sell his property as-is for $60,000. You approach him and discover that he owns it outright—it's been in the family for many years—and that keeping it filled with tenants has been a time-consuming pain in the neck. He's willing to sell, but he really doesn't want to add any more large capital gains into his tax picture this year. You propose instead an installment-sale arrangement whereby the seller will receive only $6,000 in the first year and $6,000 a year for nine more years, plus 9 percent interest each year. As we'll discuss later, this will spread out his tax liability over the period of repayment and will sharply cut the cash you need to take over the property. (Your objective, once you take title to the second duplex, will be to renovate it cleverly, rent it out at significantly higher monthly levels, and boost the property's value much closer to that of your first property.)

You succeed in convincing the seller, and suddenly, for an outlay of perhaps $10,000 of your refinancing proceeds—including all rehabilitation expenses and closing costs—you are the owner of a second duplex, with an enhanced market value of $70,000. Your position looks like this:

Property 1

$75,000 Market value
  67,000 First trust/mortgage
———
$ 7,500 Equity

Property 2

$70,000 Market value
  54,000 Balance on first trust
            held by seller
———
$16,000 Equity

Cash on Hand
$28,500 Initial proceeds of refinancing
−10,000 Acquisition and rehabilitation costs
———
$18,500

* Take a look back at the refinancing example in Chapter 1 for an idea of items comprising these costs.

At this point you're ready for your next acquisition; you are again looking for opportunities where you can make maximum use of the principle of leverage and can move into successively larger properties. You put the word out through brokers and others that you're in the market, and you begin hearing of potential acquisitions. A tantalizing one comes your way in the form of an eight-unit, $150,000 apartment building in the same neighborhood as your two duplexes. The owners or a lending institution will accept $25,000 down (a $125,000 first trust or mortgage), and agree to take $10,000 of your down payment in the form of a high-yielding second-trust note on your second duplex, following an appraisal. Your ultimate objective in buying the small apartment building is to convert it into eight stunning condominium units, thus tapping what you foresee will be a booming interest in the neighborhood by young, two-worker professional couples—but you keep your foresight to yourself.

The appraisal backs up your estimate of the second duplex's new value, and the deal goes through. Your holdings now look like this:

Property 1		*Property 2*	
$75,000	Market value	$70,000	Market value
67,000	First trust	54,000	First trust
		10,000	Second trust
$ 7,500	Equity	$ 6,000	Equity

Property 3		*Total Equity*	
$150,000	Market value	$ 7,500	Duplex 1
125,000	First trust	6,000	Duplex 2
		25,000	Apartment building
$ 25,000	Equity	$38,500	Total

Your total equities haven't grown much at this point—$38,500 versus the $37,000 you had a few months ago in your little duplex—but look at your portfolio! You now control a substantial amount of real estate: twelve housing units with a combined market value of $295,000, in an area you believe has strong potential for yearly appreciation. You have laid out no cash, handling it all from the proceeds of the refinancing, but you have vastly altered your federal income tax picture. With three buildings' worth of depreciation, mortgage interest and other tax write-offs, you are now able to shelter far larger amounts of your ordinary income than ever before. And through your purchase of the eight-unit project, you have opened up the possibility of a quantum leap in your real estate profits through conversion to condominiums. The building's net value, after it is fully converted into units retailing for an average $50,000 apiece, could be upwards of $300,000 to $325,000—a far cry from the $150,000 you paid and your $25,000 equity position. This incremental value exists even if you *personally* do not undertake a condo conversion. The market price you can get for the building depends on its ultimate highest use. If you can demonstrate convincingly to a developer that the property and the area have the future you know they have, your building could become far more valuable within an astonishingly short time.

That takes us through Step B. You're in the swing of things and well on your way to a large net worth. Steps C, D, and so on are really continuations of the same pyramidal theme: you let nothing (or as little as feasible) sit unused; every bit of equity can leverage new pieces of real estate. By artfully using each of the three properties you control at Step B, you can make them produce several additional buildings (or land, warehouses, commercial properties, etc.) by Step C, ten or twelve total properties by Step D, twenty properties or more by Step E, and so forth. Moving from $37,000 worth of equity to $500,000 worth of equities within four or five years is readily achievable in the example we've been discussing, provided you as an investor remain as aggressive and sharp as you were during the first two steps. There is no limit to one's ability to build real estate pyramids.

Pyramiding can involve serious risks and challenges, however. It can be disastrous where a market goes stagnant, where property values decline, or when credit sources dry up. In such situations you can end up with more mortgage debt than equity and with far more in monthly expenses than in income—and that's just one step from bankruptcy. Pyramiding can also be risky if an investor allows himself to be spread so thinly that the slightest cash flow problem—a failure, for example, to make payments on a second mortgage against just one property—can trigger a foreclosure that by chain reaction brings down the entire far-flung real estate pyramid. As several major real estate developers demonstrated during the 1973–75 credit crunch, highly leveraged empires crumble if *anything* goes wrong, causing terrible losses to the people who create and invest in them.

Given these inherent risks, not everyone is likely to possess the moxie necessary for rapid large build-ups of properties using the pyramid approach. But that doesn't rule out the technique for the average investor. Slower-rising pyramids, with larger equity positions in each property and longer periods between acquisitions, can be impressive capital gain producers (albeit over more extended periods) with far less danger. The methods are identical; the steps are simply more widely spaced.

Cashless Assumptions. Refinancing is one common method of constructing pyramids. Another approach involves searching for properties where the current owners might be willing to accept trust notes secured by your existing holdings, rather than cash, as the entry fee for taking over their mortgages. For example, at Step A above, the owner of the second duplex might have agreed to take a $6,000 second trust on the first duplex in lieu of a cash down payment. Or had the owner of the second duplex had a large assumable first deed of trust or mortgage— say, $45,000—he might have accepted a $15,000 high-yielding trust note secured by your property and simply let you step into his shoes. He would gain some tax advantages by taking this route, and would also get a well-secured note to hold for income. Part of your $37,000 equity would then be tied up, but you would have acquired the second duplex at a somewhat lower net cost than the $1,000 you had to pay in refinancing; you also might have ended up with a first mortgage on the property that carries an interest rate well below prevailing market levels.

Buy and Rollover Approaches. Many pyramid builders don't hold on to every property they acquire indefinitely; instead, they buy speculative properties, rehabilitate them, raise the rents and sell them (roll them over) to other investors at a profit. The proceeds of these sales are then used to acquire additional run-down units at low prices and with low (or no) down payments, which in turn generate profits for more property acquisitions. In the course of such buy-and-sell sequences, the initial investors retain only those buildings they believe have the highest potential for income or appreciation as solid bases for junior financing or refinancing later. The rest they sell for immediate profit and reinvestment. The pyramids they create aren't as neat as the one in the diagram on page 000, but the net result is the same: equity is kept hard at work and leads eventually to substantial highly leveraged real estate holdings.

TAX-DEFERRED EXCHANGES

A major drawback of any real estate growth strategy that involves sales of successive properties is the tax impact on the seller. The owner of a piece of land purchased for a song ten years ago and now worth twenty times its original cost faces a potentially staggering tax bite—even under favorable capital gains treatment—if he or she sells outright. So does the owner of any rental property that has risen significantly in market value beyond his or her tax basis or cost. A shrewd technique to defer taxation and facilitate pyramid build-ups of real estate is the *exchange*. Section 1031 of the Internal Revenue Code permits taxpayers to defer recognition of gains and losses on properties that are held for productive business, trade or investment use and are exchanged solely for properties of "like kind." In plain terms, Section 1031 of the code permits you to trade the equity in your real property for someone else's, postponing full taxation until some later date when you finally dispose of the property (or it goes into your estate). The legal theory is simple: since an exchange of identical equities or holdings produces no recognizable gain per se, there should be no taxation until a gain *is* produced. If, as we'll see, there are incidental gains in the course of an exchange of properties, then the tax is only to the extent of the incidental gains.

The law permits you to carry over your tax position or basis into an unlimited succession of new properties, provided each meets certain tests. You can, under 1031, exchange your apartment in Chicago or your duplex in Miami (or both together) for an impressively wide range of properties—for a ranch in Arizona or a shopping center near Atlanta; even for water or mineral rights in unimproved desert land held in fee simple in Wyoming. "Like-kind" property is judged by its function to the taxpayer: it *must* be held for trade, business or investment. It can't be a residence or be held primarily for sale in the inventory of a dealer. The property's specific form, location or quality is of no consequence, provided the owner's fee interests in them are the same.

The value of tax-deferred exchanging can be illustrated by the following case history. Jim Randolph owned a twenty-acre parcel of land used by his family for years for horse breeding and farming. The tract was located on the fringe of a large, economically vigorous metropolitan area, and was squarely in the path of residential development. A national building firm approached Randolph and offered him $1 million for the land— $50,000 an acre—with the intent of turning it into a subdivision of single-family houses. Randolph declined the offer, explaining that his tax liability on the sale would be intolerable. He owned the tract outright, all debts on it having been retired years ago; at initial sale, the tract had cost $100,000. Randolph's taxable gain would thus amount to $900,000. Were he to sell the land in a conventional transaction, his tax position would look like this:

$1,000,000 Sales price
100,000 Basis
—————————
$ 900,000 Gain

Capital Gains Tax on 40 percent of gain =
$360,000 × .70 = $252,000

Randolph would have walked away with nearly $650,000 in net after-tax profit, true, but he also would have irretrievably lost $252,000 to the IRS that could have been working for him.

Ultimately Randolph decided that what he'd really like to do would be to purchase a high-quality, income-producing shopping center. He discussed his objective with the national building firm, which happened to be associated with a commercial real estate brokerage company. After several months of searching for and analyzing alternative properties, the brokers located a shopping center with a strong annual cash flow in the suburbs of a neighboring metropolitan area. The property had a market value of $2.1 million and a $1.1 million mortgage. Randolph agreed to exchange his farm for it if the builders would first buy it as an integral part of the overall exchange. The building firm did and then exchanged the shopping center with Randolph, subject to the existing mortgage, thereby deferring all taxation on the gain for him. The transaction amounted to this:

Randolph		*Building Firm*	
$1,000,000	Farm's sales value	$2,100,000	Shopping-center
0	Mortgages		sales value
		1,100,000	Mortgage
$1,000,000	Equity	$1,000,000	Equity

The advantages to Randolph went well beyond preserving his $1 million equity intact. He actually improved his position significantly because (a) he now owns *depreciable* real property that throws off large annual income-sheltering tax deductions for mortgage interest, property taxes and depreciation (unlike his land); and (b) he owns a piece of prime commercial property with excellent prospects for market-value growth in the coming years.

Exchanges can take manifold shapes and can involve anywhere from two exchangers on up. The simplest and undoubtedly the rarest is the transfer of equal equity interests in different properties by two owners, with no involvement of a third (cash) party. More common is the three-party exchange, illustrated above, where the initial two parties don't have mutually acceptable properties to trade. One of the parties must either slip into something different (as did the building firm) or locate someone who will take the property standing in the way of the initial exchange, and pay cash. (Three-party exchanges involving one cash customer go by various designations in the field, including the "Missouri waltz, 1–2 cashout.")

Professional real estate exchange brokers, who exist in loosely knit clubs and associations throughout the country, often set up exchanges involving four, five, six or more individual owners or properties. These realty brokers earn part or all of their commission incomes by matching equities, tax situations and investment goals. The exchange agreements they structure, which entail carefully scheduled sequences of closings to meet the IRS's and the courts' criteria of true exchanges, can be byzantine in their complexities. Typically, they involve not only "like-kind" property but various types of boot, nonqualifying property that is paid to balance out equities. Boot may be cash, notes, personal property or net mortgage relief via assumptions. For example, if in the case above Randolph's $1 million equity had exceeded the shopping-center owners' equity by $100,000, the shopping center owners would have had to add $100,000 in cash or securities to balance the deal.

Exchanging may prove a superb answer to your reinvestment problems as you move up the real estate ladder, but you should approach it with care. The technique only *postpones* taxes; it doesn't eliminate them. If your present tax bracket is likely to get substantially higher in the coming years, you may lose relatively less through capital gains tax this year than three years hence, when, for example, you could be forced to liquidate your real estate holdings to pay some large debt incurred by losses in another field.

Exchanging, as opposed to refinancing, obviously forces you out of one productive asset into someone else's, which in the long run may not be as suitable or profitable. You may not really want to give up that three-unit building you own in a neighborhood with high future growth potential, just to avoid taxes. Refinancing now—and again later if the building's growth in value allows it—could make more sense.

On the other hand, you may indeed want to get out of that property because:

• The depreciation losses it's now producing for you are declining rapidly every year, and you really need to start up with a higher depreciable basis and higher mortgage and property tax costs, in another, perhaps newer investment property.

• You're no longer interested in the *type* of property you've got. You're sick and tired of managing your ten-unit rental project, and really would like to own some nice, peaceful farmland somewhere far away from the city.

• You've got too many little, scattered properties to handle efficiently, and you'd prefer to consolidate your investments through ownership of one large property. Here you could exchange your individual properties in combination as one negotiable package to another investor, or could undertake the exchange piecemeal.

Before considering an exchange, discuss the concept thoroughly with your accountant or tax attorney. Then contact an experienced broker known to specialize in the exchange field. Most of these are realtors who advertise their experience in this area, and who take part regularly in regional and national exchange seminars with other brokers.

INSTALLMENT SALES

Deferral of capital gains taxes can also be achieved with the installment sale. Rather than selling your property in the conventional way—that is to say, receiving your selling price via the buyer's down payment plus a check for the adjusted balance from his lender—you can spread out receipt of payments over a number of years. As long as you don't receive more than 30 percent of the total payment due on your property in the year of sale, IRS will tax you only on the percentage of the total gain you actually receive year by year, rather than on the full, taxable profit. You will have to receive at least one subsequent payment after the first year's, and will have to receive a sufficient interest rate on the loan you are extending to the purchaser, but otherwise you are free to structure the sale in any way you please. You can take 29 percent in one year and 71 percent the following; or 20 percent for each of five years; or 30 percent in year one, nothing for four years, and a 70 percent balloon payment in the fifth. Before using this technique, however, get professional advice. Installments can get amazingly sticky if not structured to satisfy the IRS.

WRAPAROUND MORTGAGES

A creative way of achieving an installment sale on your property, particularly when you've got a large amount of equity in it and low-interest-rate financing, is the so-called wraparound mortgage. As the name suggests, this is a secondary form of financing that literally wraps around or encompasses existing financing, without disturbing the existing loan(s). The principal amount of the wraparound is equal to the principal amount of the unpaid first loan, *plus* the additional amount necessary for the purchase. The interest rate is virtually always higher on the wraparound, and it applies to the combined principal amounts.

You can appreciate the concept by studying this example. Say you own a $90,000 property with a 7 percent loan and a $20,000 mortgage on it. You bought the property years ago at $60,000, depreciated it substantially, and face a large capital gains tax. You would like to dispose of it, and through business contacts, you find an investor who's interested. She does not, however, have the $70,000 necessary to step into your assumable mortgage or the $20,000 she may need for a conventional S&L loan. All the investor will agree to, in fact, is $10,000 cash down on an $85,000 selling price.

Your solution is the wraparound. In exchange for meeting your full price of $90,000, you agree to (1) accept $10,000 in cash, and (2) provide a junior loan in the amount of $80,000 for ten years at 9.5 percent. The purchaser takes title to your property and begins paying your amortization on the $80,000, 9.5 percent loan, and you continue to make payments on your existing loan. Not only does the spreading out of payments on the sale qualify as an installment transaction under IRS guidelines, but you have actually improved your profits on your investment in two other ways. You've gotten your full $90,000 price and you're making money on the 2.5 interest rate spread on $20,000. You're paying the first-trust lender 7 percent interest on $20,000; every month, though, your purchaser is paying you 9.5 percent interest on *$80,000*. You're getting 9.5 percent on $60,000 and a 2.5 percent spread on $20,000—not bad at all.

Wraparounds are most commonly used in commercial real estate transactions and can get complex, but there's no reason why you can't use them when you want to solve a tax or down payment problem. "Wraps" are perhaps the most flexible financing tool around in the real estate market, so keep them in mind when you're *buying* as well as selling. And don't fail to get competent legal or accounting help in structuring your transaction.

OTHER TOOLS

Land Leases. As you move up into larger properties, a cash-raising technique you may want to keep in mind is the land sale and lease-back. In this technique, you sell the land underneath your building, shopping center or other improved property, and enter into an immediate lease-back agreement with the investor who purchases the land. You continue to own the building(s), receive cash for what may be the true market value of the land, and continue operating your property as before. Often the lease provides for a repurchase agreement that allows you to regain the land under specified terms. The lease is structured to return an attractive profit for the investor-purchaser, may be "net, net" (where you pay all taxes and utilities), and usually is subordinated to your existing financing. Your real property holdings are of course decreased in value, but your depreciation write-offs now need take no account of the land-value component of the property. The lease expenses are all deductible. You have full use of your property and cash on hand for other investments.

Blanket Mortgages. Your expanding portfolio of properties can sometimes be used in whole or in part to obtain financing for additional properties when you don't have the cash. Rather than individual secondary mortgages on individual properties, you may be able to convince an institutional or private lender (or seller) to take a *blanket* second mortgage secured by the equity in a number of properties. This is commonly done and can involve any type of real property that qualifies in the lender's view. The seller of an apartment complex you've invested in, for example, may be willing to take a blanket loan for all or part of your equity requirement if it's secured by prime properties. The security could be four developable lots in a suburban subdivision you own, or three townhouses you own in different parts of the city. The one drawback to this technique, of course, is that a blanket mortgage runs the risk of spreading you too thinly in your properties. It can increase your leverage, but may increase your out-of-pocket monthly costs beyond your means. Keep the technique in mind, but talk it over with your attorney or investment counsel before using it.

Glossary

abstract of title: A summary of the history of the title transfers as
well as any liens and encumbrances on the property from the
original source of the title to the present. The abstract reports
on all the legal documents—contracts, deeds or wills—that affect
the parcel of real estate and its present status. It also includes
a list of the sources consulted in preparation of the report.
accelerated depreciation: A method of calculating the depreciation
of commercial or residential properties at a faster rate than
straight-line depreciation. Developed under the Internal Revenue
Code, options for taking accelerated depreciation include:
- five-year useful-life straight-line depreciation available for rehabilitation expenditures on low- and moderate-income and
certified historic properties.
- 125 percent declining balance for residential properties with
an estimated useful life of twenty years or more.
- 150 percent declining balance for all new commercial real
estate.
- double declining balance (200 percent) for new residential
rental properties.
- sum-of-the-years'-digits.
acceleration clause: A common provision in a mortgage or promis-

sory note allowing the lender to call all sums due (the entire principal) in the event of a default.

adjusted basis: The cost of a property to an owner plus the value of any capital expenditures for improvements to that property, minus any depreciation taken or allowable by IRS regulations.

adverse possession: The legal right by which someone occupying a piece of land could acquire title against the real owner if the occupant's possession of the land has been actual, continuous, hostile, visible and distinct for a statutory period. To avoid this problem, individuals holding raw land often post no-trespassing signs and periodically inspect their property.

alienation: To transfer title to real property from one person to another. Involuntary alienation takes place when a property is sold against the owner's will.

alienation clause: An optional clause in a mortgage or promissory note to allow the mortgagee to demand payment of the entire loan balance upon the sale or other transfer of the title.

amortization: The gradual repayment of a debt through systematic payments of principal and/or interest over a prescribed period until there is a zero balance.

appreciation: The increase in value of a property.

asset depreciation range system (adr): Internal Revenue Service regulations providing standards for determining the period over which to depreciate an asset.

assignment: The transfer of a right or a contract from one individual to another.

assumption of mortgage: The acquisition of title to a property with an existing mortgage. The individual "assuming" the mortgage agrees to be personally liable for its terms and conditions. The seller of such a mortgage becomes secondarily liable unless specifically released by the lender.

balloon payment: The final lump-sum payment of a note or mortgage (usually larger than previous installments) which repays the debt in full.

basis: The amount of financial interest an owner has in an asset for purposes of determining annual depreciation for tax purposes and gain or loss on the sale of that asset. See also *adjusted basis*.

blanket mortgage: A mortgage on more than one parcel or unit, either of land or of improved property. In developing large tracts of land, builders release segments or subdivisions from the blanket mortgage piece by piece.

boot: In an exchange of property, money or other property given to make up any difference in value or equity.

bridge loan or bridge mortgage: Financing (usually short-term) to make up the difference between an initial loan and the total amount required—used until permanent financing is obtained. Also known as gap financing.

capital expenditure: The cost of an improvement made to extend the useful life of a property or to add to its value (for example, a new roof).

capital gain: The taxable profit derived from the sale of a capital asset. The gain is the difference between the property's basis and the adjusted sales price.

capital improvement: Any structure erected as a permanent improvement to real property which adds to its value and useful life.

capital loss: A loss derived from the sale of a capital asset.

capitalization: A method of appraisal that converts net income into an indication of value.

capitalization rate (cap rate): The rate or percentage used to reflect the relationship between real property and the net income it produces. The rate is designed to reflect the recapture of an acceptable rate of return on an investment while providing for the return on borrowed capital.

cash flow: The spendable income from an investment remaining after all expenses are deducted.

closing costs: Expenses incurred in purchasing real estate above the purchase price (in the case of a buyer) and those which must be deducted from the proceeds of the sale (in the case of a seller). A buyer's expenses might include loan fees and/or points, appraisal fees, deed and mortgage recording fees, transfer of real property taxes.

cloud on title: Any conditions (for example, a prior claim, unreleased lien or other encumbrance) adversely affecting title to the property. Usually a cloud on a title is revealed in a title search. It can be removed by a quitclaim deed, release or court action.

comparables: Properties sold recently that are similar in size and location to a property under consideration for purchase. A comparable property is used to gauge the fair market value of the property under consideration. Comparables should be of similar size, location, physical condition, and type of construction.

component depreciation: A way of depreciating components of a building separately for tax purposes. It allows an owner to depreciate elements within a structure over differing time spans or "useful lives."

condominium ownership: A piece of real property consisting of individual interest in a specific apartment, townhouse, or commercial unit and an undivided interest in such common areas as land, parking areas, elevators, or stairways.

constant: A factor that, when multiplied by the total principal amount of a loan, indicates the annual debt service payment (interest and principal) required to amortize a loan during its stated term.

contingency: A provision in a contract that prevents it from binding either the buyer or seller until certain specified activities have taken place. Many contracts are made contingent on a buyer's ability to obtain financing at a particular rate (with a cut-off date) or contingent upon a satisfactory inspection.

cooperative ownership: A form of multiple ownership of real estate in which a corporation or business trust holds title to a property and grants occupancy rights to particular units to shareholders through proprietary leases.

conventional loan: A mortgage loan not insured by FHA or guaranteed by VA.

covenant: Any deed restriction affecting title or use of a property.

deed of trust: A security instrument conveying title in trust to a third party for a particular piece of real estate. In some states a deed of trust is used instead of a mortgage. Also known as a trust deed.

default: A breach of contract or nonperformance of an obligation that is part of a contract. Often it is a failure to make required payments on a mortgage or note.

depreciation: The loss of value in real property through physical deterioration, function or economic obsolescence. For tax purposes, see *accelerated depreciation* and *component depreciation*.

development rights: Rights a landowner sells to improve a property. Sometimes only the development rights are sold, and the owner retains title to the land. Once improvements are made, the purchasers of those improvements then lease the land from the owners.

discount: The sale of a note for less than its face value.

easement: A right to the limited use or enjoyment of land held by another. An easement is an interest in land—to enable sewer or other utility lines to be laid, or to allow for access to a property.

eminent domain: The right of government bodies, public utilities and public service corporations to take private property for public use (roads, schools, landfills, etc.) on payment of its fair market value.

encroachment: An improvement that legally violates someone else's property.

equity: An owner's interest in a property after payment of all liens or other charges on the property.

escalator clause: A contractual device to allow for the adjustment of payments upward or downward to cover certain contingencies. Often long-term commercial leases will include such a clause to take into account future increases in taxes, insurance and operating costs that might not be covered by the rent. In some mortgages, this clause allows the lender to adjust the interest rate to the prevailing rate (see *flexible-payment mortgage*).

exchange: A transaction in which part of the payment for the purchaser of property is the transfer of a property of a like kind.

Federal Home Loan Mortgage Corporation (FHLMC) (Freddie Mac): A federal agency that purchases mortgages in the secondary mortgage market from commercial banks with insured deposits or from federally insured savings and loan association members of the Federal Home Loan Bank System. It has become a key source of condominium mortgage funds.

Federal Housing Administration (FHA): A federal agency designed to provide home financing through the insurance of housing mortgages and credit and to act as a stabilizing force in the mortgage market.

Federal National Mortgage Association (Fannie Mae): A federally chartered private corporation that buys mortgages originated by primary lending institutions, thus allowing a degree of liquidity in the mortgage market through the establishment of this secondary market for existing mortgages.

flexible-payment mortgage: A mortgage designed to meet a borrower's financial position—in which payments may be smaller in the early years and larger in subsequent years.

foreclosure: A legal procedure, under the terms of a mortgage or deed of trust, in which the title of the property is passed to the holder of the note or to a third party who purchases the property at a foreclosure sale—usually applied in a case of default.

Government National Mortgage Association (GNMA) (Ginnie Mae): A federal agency that guarantees payments on mortgage-backed securities issued by lending institutions.

ground lease: A lease of land alone, as distinguished from a lease of land with the improvements on it, usually on a long-term basis.

installment sale: A method of deferring taxation on gain received from a real estate transaction. In order to qualify as an installment sale, the seller cannot receive more than 30 percent of the sale price in the year of the sale and must be paid in two or more installments over two or more years.

joint tenancy: A unit or interest in real estate held by two or more individuals equally. In the event of the death of one tenant, the property is divided equally among the surviving owners.

joint venture: The joining of two or more individuals for the purposes of investing in a business enterprise. A form of partnership.

junior mortgage: See *second mortgage.*

land leaseback: A device whereby a developer sells raw land to an investor who then leases it back to the developer on a long-term basis, often with the option to repurchase the property at the end of the lease. This arrangement provides the developer with much needed liquidity for obtaining development financing.

lease: An agreement transferring the right to exclusive possession and use of a particular property to an individual or individuals for a distinct period of time and a specified fee. A lease usually states the conditions under which the lessee is granted the right to occupy the property.

leverage: In investment terms, the use of borrowed funds to magnify returns.

lien: A claim on the property of another as security for a debt or obligation.

limited partnership: A partnership agreement in which one person serves as a general partner—charged with the organization and operation of the partnership—while the other limited partners are passive investors. This arrangement limits the liability of the limited partners to the amount which they invest, whereas the general partner is totally responsible for any losses incurred by the investment.

liquidity: The ability to convert an asset into cash at a level close to its true value.

loan-to-value ratio: The relationship of a mortgage loan to the appraised value of a security. This ratio is expressed to a potential purchaser of property in terms of the percentage a lending institution is willing to finance—for example, many investors qualify for 80 percent financing and sometimes higher ratios.

market value: The highest price a property might command if offered for sale.

mortgage: A legal document used to convey an interest in real property as security for payment of a debt. A valid mortgage requires both a debt and a pledge to repay that debt under specified conditions.

multiple listing: An agreement which allows a real estate broker to distribute information on a property for sale to other members of a multiple listing organization, thereby increasing the numbers of individuals aware of the availability of a particular property.

negative cash flow: A situation in which expenditures required to maintain an investment exceed income received on the property.

net lease: Usually a commercial lease in which the lessee pays rent, maintenance and operating expenses.

open-end mortgage: A mortgage with a provision that the outstanding loan amount can be increased on mutual agreement of the lender and the borrower, not to exceed the original borrowing limit.

option: An agreement to keep open, over a set period, an offer to sell or purchase property. An option, like a bid, must contain all the terms pertaining to the ultimate contractual agreement.

origination fee: The fee charged by a lender to prepare loan documents, make credit checks, inspect and sometimes appraise a property. The fee is usually computed as a percentage of the face value of the loan.

partnership: An association of two or more persons who carry on a business for profit as co-owners.

planned unit development (PUD): A method of increasing the density allowed under zoning restrictions by clustering housing around limited-access streets and thus providing maximum utilization of open spaces.

point: A percentage of the principal loan amount, assessed by the lender and generally payable at closing. The intent of the assessment is to increase the overall yield of the loan.

prepayment penalty: An amount set by a lender as a penalty to the debtor for paying off the debt prior to its maturity. It is charged to recoup a portion of the interest that would have been earned if the loan had been carried to maturity. Ofter the prepayment penalty is specified in the mortgage.

private mortgage insurance (PMI): A form of insurance protecting the mortgage lender against loss in the event of a default on that mortgage.

proprietary lease: The type of lease used in cooperative buildings that defines the rights of a tenant or shareholder to occupy a particular apartment.

quitclaim deed: A legal instrument stating that the grantors do not warrant title or possession to whatever right, title or interest the grantor may have had when a deed to that land was executed. A quitclaim deed is required to remove a cloud from a title.

real estate investment trust (REIT): A trust offering the tax advantages of a partnership/syndication while retaining many of the attributes and advantages of a corporate operation. Investors purchase certificates of ownership in the trust.

real property: Legally, the earth's surface, the air above and the earth below, as well as any improvements to the land (excluding growing crops).

recapture of depreciation: The IRS code requires that depreciation taken on real property in excess of the amount allowed under the straight-line method is subject to recapture provisions of the code on the taxable disposition of the property.

refinance: To pay off one loan with the proceeds from another.

rent control: Regulation by governmental agencies restricting the amount of rent landlords can charge their tenants.

savings and loan association: Associations founded to promote thrift and homeownership. Deposits with these associations customarily earn higher interest than that given by commercial banks. Those deposits are invested in residential mortgage loans.

second mortgage: A junior or second mortgage that is subordinate to a first mortgage. Usually the term of a second mortgage is shorter and the interest rate higher than on a first mortgage. Also known as a junior mortgage. In states where deeds of trust are the predominant instrument, second trusts are the junior loans.

secondary mortgage market: A system whereby lenders and investors buy existing mortgages as long-term investments, and in so doing provide greater availability of funds for mortgage loans by banks and savings and loan associations. Active purchasers of existing mortgages include: Federal National Mortgage Association, Government National Mortgage Association, and the Federal Home Loan Mortgage Corporation.

security deposit: Money deposited with a landlord by a tenant to be held for the duration of a lease to cover failure to pay rent or necessary repairs to bring a property back to the condition it was in when rented, or to compensate for damages caused by a tenant who wrongfully quit the unit prior to the expiration of a lease.

spot loan: A loan on a property made by a lender who was not involved in the original financing of the subdivision or project.

subchapter S corporation: A corporation that elects to be treated as a partnership. It is an entity that exists in corporate form which does not pay corporate taxes. The company must meet certain requirements of the IRS to qualify as a subchapter S corporation.

syndicate: An entity, usually a limited partnership, established for the purposes of making an investment. It is a device in which a real estate investor can attain high depreciation deductions while avoiding corporate problems of double taxation.

tandem plan: A government program to encourage the purchase in the secondary mortgage market of high-risk, low-yield mortgages at current market rates. The mortgages are purchased by the Government National Mortgage Association (Ginnie Mae), which absorbs the difference between the current market rate for these mortgages and their regulated yield. The Federal National Mortgage Association normally purchases these from GNMA.

tax shelter: A device used to counterbalance an individual investor's income and thereby reduce his overall tax liability.

title: The right to or ownership of land.

title insurance: Insurance providing the policyholder with protection against losses that might occur due to any defect or cloud on the title.

title search: See *abstract of title*.

transfer tax: Taxes on the conveyance of real estate imposed by state and local bodies of government. Such taxes are often paid by the seller.

trust: An arrangement in which a third party (trustee) holds and manages legal title to a property for a beneficiary.

VA mortgage: A mortgage loan or trust made by a private lender and guaranteed by the Veterans Administration (VA). These

GI loans are designed to assist veterans in financing the purchase of homes with small or no down payments at a comparatively low rate of interest.

variable interest rate: A means whereby a lender is permitted to shift the interest rate to reflect changes in the prime rate—usually within a prescribed range and with advance notice.

warranty deed: A deed in which the seller of property guarantees that he is providing good and marketable title.

wraparound mortgage: A refinancing technique involving the creation of a subordinate mortgage that includes the balance due on the existing mortgage(s) plus a new amount.

yield: The profit gained on an investment and expressed as a percentage of the amount invested.

Index

About the Author

KENNETH R. HARNEY is editor and a co-founder of the *Housing and Development Reporter,* a weekly information service on housing and community development, and a columnist on the *Washington Post,* where he covers housing and real estate finance. His articles have appeared in a number of magazines and newspapers, and he is both a regular consultant on housing and mortgage finance to Drexel Burnham Lambert's Washington Forum and himself an active and successful investor in Washington real estate, including central-city and suburban properties. He is a graduate of Princeton and attended the University of Pennsylvania Graduate School. He lives in Bethesda, Maryland.